Expert AWS Development

Efficiently develop, deploy, and manage your enterprise apps on the Amazon Web Services platform

Atul V. Mistry

BIRMINGHAM - MUMBAI

Expert AWS Development

Commissioning Editor: Vijin Boricha
Acquisition Editor: Meeta Rajani
Content Development Editor: Devika Battike
Technical Editor: Prachi Sawant
Copy Editor: Safis Editing
Project Coordinator: Judie Jose
Proofreader: Safis Editing
Indexer: Pratik Shirodkar
Graphics: Tom Scaria
Production Coordinator: Arvindkumar Gupta

First published: March 2018

Production reference: 1280318

Published by Packt Publishing Ltd.
Livery Place
35 Livery Street
Birmingham
B3 2PB, UK.

ISBN 978-1-78847-758-1

www.packtpub.com

`mapt.io`

Mapt is an online digital library that gives you full access to over 5,000 books and videos, as well as industry leading tools to help you plan your personal development and advance your career. For more information, please visit our website.

Why subscribe?

- Spend less time learning and more time coding with practical eBooks and Videos from over 4,000 industry professionals

- Improve your learning with Skill Plans built especially for you

- Get a free eBook or video every month

- Mapt is fully searchable

- Copy and paste, print, and bookmark content

PacktPub.com

Did you know that Packt offers eBook versions of every book published, with PDF and ePub files available? You can upgrade to the eBook version at `www.PacktPub.com` and as a print book customer, you are entitled to a discount on the eBook copy. Get in touch with us at `service@packtpub.com` for more details.

At `www.PacktPub.com`, you can also read a collection of free technical articles, sign up for a range of free newsletters, and receive exclusive discounts and offers on Packt books and eBooks.

Contributors

About the author

Atul V. Mistry holds all three AWS Associate certifications and has been a winner at AWS IoT HackDay, 2017 event in Singapore. He has worked consistently with AWS and on software design and development with JEE technology. He has diverse work experience, having worked around the globe, and participated extensively in cross-functional project delivery in the finance industry.

Writing this book would have been very difficult without the support of my parents, C.V. Mistry and V. L. Mistry, family, and friends. Above all I am very thankful to the entire Packt team as they supported me as per their progressive symbol. Finally, I would like to thank Rashmi, my wife, and two kids (Mahi and Shivansh) for their cooperation.

About the reviewer

Miguel Angel Sanchez Marti has 4 years' experience of architecting solutions in AWS, having worked for many clients. Currently, he's a business consultant at Datadec, which has migrated most of its clients from on-premise to cloud solutions. They're involved in delivering the latest technology and he is in charge of developing AI and machine learning solutions for their clients.

He has been an AWS Certified Solutions Architect since June 2016. He was involved in many software projects working for Binn.es as a software project manager.

Thanks to my family for being patient with me right from the time I took up this book, as it decreased the amount of time I could spend with them—especially my wife, Julie, and my 6-year-old son, Alexander.

Packt is searching for authors like you

If you're interested in becoming an author for Packt, please visit `authors.packtpub.com` and apply today. We have worked with thousands of developers and tech professionals, just like you, to help them share their insight with the global tech community. You can make a general application, apply for a specific hot topic that we are recruiting an author for, or submit your own idea.

Table of Contents

Preface

Continuous Integration/Continuous Deployment and the Agile methodology have enabled huge advances in modern applications. This book will enable the reader to make use of these rapidly evolving technologies to build highly scalable applications within AWS using different architectures.

You will begin by installing the AWS SDK and will then get hands-on experience of creating an application using the AWS Management Console and the AWS Command Line Interface (CLI). Next, you will be integrating Applications with AWS services such as DynamoDB, Amazon Kinesis, AWS Lambda, Amazon SQS, and Amazon SWF.

Following this, you will get well versed with CI/CD workflow and work with four major phases in the release processes—Source, Build, Test, and Production. Next, you will learn to apply AWS Developer tools in your Continuous Integration (CI) and Continuous Deployment (CD) workflow. Later, you will learn about user authentication using Amazon Cognito and also how you can evaluate the best architecture as per your infrastructure costs. You will learn about Amazon EC2 and deploy an app using it. You will also get well versed with container service, which is Amazon EC2 Container Service (Amazon ECS), and you will learn how to deploy an app using it. Along with EC2 and ECS, you will also deploy a practical real-world example of a CI/CD application with the Serverless Application Framework, which is known as AWS Lambda. Finally, you will learn how to build, develop, and deploy an application using AWS Developer tools such as AWS CodeCommit, AWS CodeBuild, AWS CodeDeploy, and AWS CodePipeline as per your project needs. You will also be able to develop and deploy applications within minutes using AWS CodeStar from the wizard.

By the end of this book, you will be able to effectively build, deploy, and manage applications on AWS along with scaling and securing applications with best practices and troubleshooting tips.

Who this book is for

This book targets developers who would like to build and manage web and mobile applications and services on the AWS platform. If you are an architect, you will be able to deep dive and use examples that can be readily applied to real-world scenarios. Some prior programming experience is assumed, along with familiarity with cloud computing.

What this book covers

Chapter 1, *AWS Tools and SDKs*, introduces the AWS SDK and covers installation and the programming languages that are supported. The reader will get hands-on experience of creating an application. This chapter also covers SDKs for IoT devices and mobiles.

Chapter 2, *Integrating Applications with AWS Services*, covers how to integrate applications with AWS services such as DynamoDB, Amazon Kinesis, AWS Lambda, Amazon SQS, and Amazon SWF.

Chapter 3, *Continuous Integration and Continuous Deployment Workflow*, introduces the four major phases in the release processes—Source, Build, Test, and Production.

Chapter 4, *CI/CD in AWS Part 1 – CodeCommit, CodeBuild, and Testing*, explains how to apply AWS developer tools in your Continuous Integration (CI) and Continous Deployment (CD) workflow.

Chapter 5, *CI/CD in AWS Part 2 – CodeDeploy, CodePipeline, and CodeStar*, discusses other AWS Code family tools such as AWS CodeDeploy, AWS CodePipeline, AWS CodeStar, and AWS X-Ray.

Chapter 6, *User Authentication with AWS Cognito*, explains how to manage user authentication with AWS Cognito and also covers AWS Cognito service, which is a simple and secure user authentication for mobile and web applications.

Chapter 7, *Evaluating the Best Architecture*, covers traditional web hosting and web hosting on the cloud using AWS discussing, the best architecture for applications.

Chapter 8, *Traditional Web Hosting – Amazon EC2 and Elastic Load Balancing*, discusses Amazon EC2 best practices and troubleshooting. The chapter also covers about Elastic Load Balancing, auto-scaling, and fault-tolerant advanced topics. Finally, we will deploy an example of a CI/CD application using Amazon EC2 instances.

Chapter 9, *Amazon EC2 Container Service*, covers Docker, container instances, clusters, scheduling Ttsks, and Windows containers. Then, we will deploy an example of a CI/CD application with Amazon EC2 container services.

Chapter 10, *Amazon Lambda – AWS Serverless Architecture*, goes into more detail more about Microservices, Serverless Framework, how you can achieve serverless on the AWS platform using AWS Lambda, and you will learn how to deploy applications with the AWS Serverless Application Model (SAM).

To get the most out of this book

This book assumes that readers are already familiar with the basics of Amazon Web Services (AWS) and have some development background. It explains readers about Continuous Integration (CI) and Continuous Deployment (CD) and how they are achieved on AWS using Developer tools. Readers will also learn about different architectures and implement CI/CD on these architectures. Some of the troubleshooting and cost optimization tips are really helpful to the users while using different AWS services. Users can use free-tier cloud providers wherever possible; certain services might cost a small amount of money.

From a hardware point of view, you can work on any modern computer running for any operating system supported by AWS.

Download the example code files

You can download the example code files for this book from your account at `www.packtpub.com`. If you purchased this book elsewhere, you can visit `www.packtpub.com/support` and register to have the files emailed directly to you.

You can download the code files by following these steps:

1. Log in or register at `www.packtpub.com`.
2. Select the **SUPPORT** tab.
3. Click on **Code Downloads & Errata**.
4. Enter the name of the book in the **Search** box and follow the onscreen instructions.

Once the file is downloaded, please make sure that you unzip or extract the folder using the latest version of:

- WinRAR/7-Zip for Windows
- Zipeg/iZip/UnRarX for Mac
- 7-Zip/PeaZip for Linux

The code bundle for the book is also hosted on GitHub at `https://github.com/PacktPublishing/Expert-AWS-Development`. In case there's an update to the code, it will be updated on the existing GitHub repository.

We also have other code bundles from our rich catalog of books and videos available at `https://github.com/PacktPublishing/`. Check them out!

Download the color images

We also provide a PDF file that has color images of the screenshots/diagrams used in this book. You can download it here: `https://www.packtpub.com/sites/default/files/downloads/ExpertAWSDevelopment_ColorImages.pdf`.

Conventions used

There are a number of text conventions used throughout this book.

`CodeInText`: Indicates code words in text, database table names, folder names, filenames, file extensions, pathnames, dummy URLs, user input, and Twitter handles. Here is an example: "You will see `pom.xml` file will be generated under `..\AWS SDK Example\javamaven-demo` folder."

A block of code is set as follows:

```
<dependency>
  <groupId>com.amazonaws</groupId>
  <artifactId>aws-java-sdk</artifactId>
  <version>1.11.106</version>
</dependency>
```

Any command-line input or output is written as follows:

```
mvn clean compile exec:java
```

Bold: Indicates a new term, an important word, or words that you see onscreen. For example, words in menus or dialog boxes appear in the text like this. Here is an example: "Once you click on **Install New Software** it will open **Available Software** dialog box."

 Warnings or important notes appear like this.

 Tips and tricks appear like this.

Get in touch

Feedback from our readers is always welcome.

General feedback: Email `feedback@packtpub.com` and mention the book title in the subject of your message. If you have questions about any aspect of this book, please email us at `questions@packtpub.com`.

Errata: Although we have taken every care to ensure the accuracy of our content, mistakes do happen. If you have found a mistake in this book, we would be grateful if you would report this to us. Please visit `www.packtpub.com/submit-errata`, selecting your book, clicking on the Errata Submission Form link, and entering the details.

Piracy: If you come across any illegal copies of our works in any form on the Internet, we would be grateful if you would provide us with the location address or website name. Please contact us at `copyright@packtpub.com` with a link to the material.

If you are interested in becoming an author: If there is a topic that you have expertise in and you are interested in either writing or contributing to a book, please visit `authors.packtpub.com`.

Reviews

Please leave a review. Once you have read and used this book, why not leave a review on the site that you purchased it from? Potential readers can then see and use your unbiased opinion to make purchase decisions, we at Packt can understand what you think about our products, and our authors can see your feedback on their book. Thank you!

For more information about Packt, please visit `packtpub.com`.

AWS Tools and SDKs

Most probably, if you are reading this book, you are a code-drink lover who is trying to explore or probably using **Amazon Web Services (AWS)**. AWS contains around 20 different kinds of category/product, which have 110+ services. In this chapter, we will explore AWS tools and SDKs, which are under the Developer tools category of AWS products.

In the software world, a software development kit is known as SDK. It includes software development tools that allow you to create applications, software packages, frameworks, computer systems, gaming consoles, hardware platforms, operating systems, or similar kinds of software/hardware development platforms. Some SDKs are useful for developing platform-specific applications; for example, for Android applications on Java, you need the **Java Development Kit (JDK)** and for iOS applications, you need the iOS SDK. This is the basic idea of SDKs.

AWS also provides primary developer tools, command-line tools, toolkits, and SDKs to develop and manage AWS applications. It provides a variety of tools and SDKs as per the programming knowledge and project needs. With the help of these tools and SDKs, you can quickly and easily build and manage great applications on the AWS Cloud. This chapter will show you how to install and use these SDKs for different programming languages.

By the end of this chapter, you will understand how to install AWS SDKs and use them for development in different programming languages.

This chapter will cover the following topics:

- Brief introduction to AWS tools and SDKs
- AWS SDK for Java
- AWS SDK for Java using Apache Maven
- Configuring an SDK as a Maven dependency
- AWS SDK for Java using Gradle
- AWS SDK for Java using Eclipse IDE
- AWS SDK for Node.js

Brief introduction to AWS tools and SDKs

As we discussed in the introduction, AWS provides developer and command-line tools, toolkits, and SDKs to develop and manage AWS applications. Currently, AWS provides nine SDKs for different programming languages, six SDKs for IoT devices, and five SDKs for mobile devices. Let's take a brief look at this:

- **Developer tools**: Developer tools are used to store source code securely and version-control it. They also help with build automation and testing and deploying applications to AWS or on-premise. They include the AWS CodeCommit, AWS CodePipeline, AWS CodeBuild, and AWS CodeDeploy services. We will cover these in `Chapter 4`, *CI/CD in AWS Part 1 – CodeCommit, CodeBuild, and Testing* and `Chapter 5`, *CI/CD in AWS Part 2 – CodeDeploy, CodePipeline, and CodeStar*.
- **SDKs**: They provide APIs for programming languages, IoT, and mobile devices.
- **IDE toolkits**: Cloud tools which can integrate to your integrated development environment to speed up your AWS development.
- **Command line**: This is used to control AWS services from the command line and create scripts for automated service management.
- **Serverless development**: Serverless applications built on AWS Lambda can test and deploy using AWS **Serverless Application Model** (**SAM**) and SAM Local. We will cover Amazon Lambda in `Chapter 10`, *Amazon Lambda – AWS Serverless Architecture*.

AWS provides SDKs for the different languages and hardware devices to connect AWS IoT and mobile devices.

The following are the different kinds of SDK. In this chapter, we will cover two programming language SDKs, Java and Node.js:

	Java	Node.js	Python
Programming Language SDKs	Go	.Net	C++
	JavaScript	Ruby	PHP
IoT Devices SDKs	Embedded C	JavaScript	Arduino Yún
	Java	Python	C++
Mobile Devices SDKs	Android	iOS	Xamarin
	Unity	React Native	

AWS SDK for Java

Let's start with the Java SDK. This SDK helps to minimize the complexity and provision to coding using Java APIs for AWS Services such as Amazon EC2, Amazon DynamoDB, Amazon S3, and many more. You can download a single package from the AWS website which includes the AWS Java library and code samples with documentation.

Currently, you can download the AWS SDK for Java v1.11.x code base and AWS has recently launched an AWS SDK for Java v2.0, which is major code change. This version is built on Java 8. It has added features such as non-blocking I/O and a pluggable API layer (by default, it will use Apache but you can change this as per your project needs). In this version, you can see some API changes:

- Client builders are the only way to create the client services, which means the clients are immutable after creation
- All **Plain Old Java Objects** (**POJOs**) are immutable and must be created from the builder
- Many region classes such as `Region`, `Regions`, and `RegionUtils` are merged into a single `Region` class

This AWS SDK for Java v2.0 is a developer preview version and not recommended for production use.

Let's explore how to install, set up, and use AWS SDK for Java.

You need to set up AWS SDK for Java on your machine to use in your project. Please perform the following steps to set up the environment and run the sample code in Java using the AWS SDK:

1. **AWS account setup and IAM user creation**: You have to set up an AWS account and credentials to use AWS SDK. To increase the level of security for your AWS account, it is always preferable to create an IAM user. Use the created IAM user instead of the root user. Once you create an IAM user, you have to create an access key. You can download or view the access key ID and secret access key in the resulting dialog box. It's always best practice to download and store them in your local environment.

2. **AWS credentials and region setup**: For your local application development, you need to set up credentials and regions.

   The AWS credentials profile file is located in your filesystem. It should be at the following path:

   - For Linux, macOS, or Unix: `~/.aws/credentials`
   - For Windows: `C:\Users\USERNAME\.aws\credentials`

   The file format should be as follows:

   ```
   [default]
   aws_access_key_id = downloaded_access_key_id
   aws_secret_access_key = downloaded_secret_access_key
   ```

Another alternative is to set up `AWS_ACCESS_KEY_ID` and `AWS_SECRET_ACCESS_KEY` environment variables. Now, replace your AWS access key ID and secret access key for the values of `downloaded_access_key_id` and `downloaded_secret_access_key`.

The AWS region configuration file is located in your filesystem. It should be at the following path:

- For Linux, macOS, or Unix: `~/.aws/config`
- For Windows: `C:\Users\USERNAME\.aws\config`

This file format should be as follows:

```
[default]
region = your_region_name
```

Now, replace your AWS region for the value or region. Another alternative is you can set up `AWS_REGION` as an environment variable.

- **Java Development Environment**: JDK 6.0 or later versions are required for the AWS SDK. The latest JDK versions are available for download from the Oracle website. J2SE 6.0 does not support SHA 256-signed SSL certificates, which are required for all HTTP connections with AWS after September 2015. You can use J2SE7.0 or newer versions, which are not affected by the certificate issue.

You can use different methods to include the AWS SDK for your Java project. We will explore all methods in this chapter:

- **Apache Maven**: You can use specific SDK components or the full SDK with the help of Apache Maven.
- **Gradle**: Maven **Bill of Materials (BOM)** in a Gradle project can be used to automatically manage the dependency for your project.
- **Eclipse IDE**: The AWS toolkit can be integrated into an existing Eclipse IDE. It will automatically download, install, and update the Java SDK with a few settings.

AWS SDK for Java using Apache Maven

Please perform the following steps to include AWS SDK for Java using Apache Maven.

1. Assuming that you have already installed Maven in your machine, create a new folder called AWS SDK Example or any name. Go to this folder and execute the following command to set up the environment:

```
mvn archetype:generate -
DarchetypeGroupId=org.apache.maven.archetypes -
DarchetypeArtifactId=maven-archetype-quickstart
```

```
D:\AWS SDK Example>mvn archetype:generate -DarchetypeGroupId=org.apache.maven.archetypes -DarchetypeArtifactId=maven-archetype-quickstart
[INFO] Scanning for projects...
[INFO]
[INFO] ------------------------------------------------------------------------
[INFO] Building Maven Stub Project (No POM) 1
[INFO] ------------------------------------------------------------------------
[INFO]
[INFO] >>> maven-archetype-plugin:3.0.1:generate (default-cli) > generate-sources @ standalone-pom >>>
[INFO]
[INFO] <<< maven-archetype-plugin:3.0.1:generate (default-cli) < generate-sources @ standalone-pom <<<
[INFO]
[INFO]
[INFO] --- maven-archetype-plugin:3.0.1:generate (default-cli) @ standalone-pom ---
[INFO] Generating project in Interactive mode
[INFO] Archetype [org.apache.maven.archetypes:maven-archetype-quickstart:1.1] found in catalog remote
Define value for property 'groupId': com.packt
Define value for property 'artifactId': java-maven-demo
Define value for property 'version' 1.0-SNAPSHOT : : 1.0-SNAPSHOT
Define value for property 'package' com.packt: : com.packt.example
Confirm properties configuration:
groupId: com.packt
artifactId: java-maven-demo
version: 1.0-SNAPSHOT
package: com.packt.example
 Y: : Y
[INFO] ------------------------------------------------------------------------
[INFO] Using following parameters for creating project from Old (1.x) Archetype: maven-archetype-quickstart:1.1
[INFO] ------------------------------------------------------------------------
[INFO] Parameter: basedir, Value: D:\AWS SDK Example
[INFO] Parameter: package, Value: com.packt.example
[INFO] Parameter: groupId, Value: com.packt
[INFO] Parameter: artifactId, Value: java-maven-demo
[INFO] Parameter: packageName, Value: com.packt.example
[INFO] Parameter: version, Value: 1.0-SNAPSHOT
[INFO] project created from Old (1.x) Archetype in dir: D:\AWS SDK Example\java-maven-demo
[INFO] ------------------------------------------------------------------------
[INFO] BUILD SUCCESS
[INFO] ------------------------------------------------------------------------
[INFO] Total time: 01:28 min
[INFO] Finished at: 2017-10-24T02:18:15+08:00
[INFO] Final Memory: 14M/121M
[INFO] ------------------------------------------------------------------------
```

2. After it has successfully executed, you will see the following folder structure under the AWS SDK Example folder:

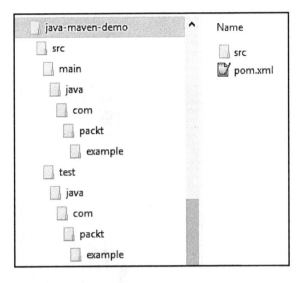

You will see the `pom.xml` file generated under the `..\AWS SDK Example\java-maven-demo` folder.

Configuring an SDK as a Maven dependency

Please perform the following steps to configure AWS SDK as Maven dependency.

1. To add AWS SDK for Java in your project, you need to add the dependency to the `pom.xml` file. From SDK version 1.9.*, you can import single or individual components. If you want to add the entire SDK as a dependency, add the following code in the `<dependency>` tag in the `pom.xml` file:

```
<dependency>
    <groupId>com.amazonaws</groupId>
    <artifactId>aws-java-sdk</artifactId>
    <version>1.11.106</version>
</dependency>
```

2. If you are using SDK Version 1.9.* or above, you can import many individual components, such as EC2, S3, CodeCommit, or CodeDeploy:

```
<dependency>
    <groupId>com.amazonaws</groupId>
    <artifactId>aws-java-sdk-s3</artifactId>
</dependency>
```

3. After setting up the `pom.xml` file, you can build your project with the `mvn package` command. It will generate a **Java Archive (JAR)** file in the target directory after successful execution:

```
D:\AWS SDK Example\java-maven-demo>mvn package
[INFO] Scanning for projects...
[INFO]
[INFO] ------------------------------------------------------------------------
[INFO] Building java-maven-demo 1.0-SNAPSHOT
[INFO] ------------------------------------------------------------------------
[INFO]
[INFO] --- maven-resources-plugin:2.6:resources (default-resources) @ java-maven-demo ---
[INFO] Using 'UTF-8' encoding to copy filtered resources.
[INFO] skip non existing resourceDirectory D:\AWS SDK Example\java-maven-demo\${env.HOME}\.aws
[INFO] --- maven-compiler-plugin:3.1:compile (default-compile) @ java-maven-demo ---
[INFO] Changes detected - recompiling the module!
[INFO] Compiling 2 source files to D:\AWS SDK Example\java-maven-demo\target\classes
[WARNING] /D:/AWS SDK Example/java-maven-demo/src/main/java/com/packt/example/S3MavenExample.java: Some input files use or override a deprecated API.
[WARNING] /D:/AWS SDK Example/java-maven-demo/src/main/java/com/packt/example/S3MavenExample.java: Recompile with -Xlint:deprecation for details.
[INFO]
[INFO] --- maven-resources-plugin:2.6:testResources (default-testResources) @ java-maven-demo ---
[INFO] Using 'UTF-8' encoding to copy filtered resources.
[INFO] skip non existing resourceDirectory D:\AWS SDK Example\java-maven-demo\src\test\resources
[INFO]
[INFO] --- maven-compiler-plugin:3.1:testCompile (default-testCompile) @ java-maven-demo ---
[INFO] Changes detected - recompiling the module!
[INFO] Compiling 1 source file to D:\AWS SDK Example\java-maven-demo\target\test-classes
[INFO]
[INFO] --- maven-surefire-plugin:2.12.4:test (default-test) @ java-maven-demo ---
[INFO] Surefire report directory: D:\AWS SDK Example\java-maven-demo\target\surefire-reports

-------------------------------------------------------
 T E S T S
-------------------------------------------------------
Running com.packt.example.AppTest
Tests run: 1, Failures: 0, Errors: 0, Skipped: 0, Time elapsed: 0.021 sec

Results :

Tests run: 1, Failures: 0, Errors: 0, Skipped: 0

[INFO]
[INFO] --- maven-jar-plugin:2.4:jar (default-jar) @ java-maven-demo ---
[INFO] Building jar: D:\AWS SDK Example\java-maven-demo\target\java-maven-demo-1.0-SNAPSHOT.jar
[INFO] ------------------------------------------------------------------------
[INFO] BUILD SUCCESS
[INFO] ------------------------------------------------------------------------
[INFO] Total time: 55.707 s
[INFO] Finished at: 2017-10-24T02:22:49+08:00
[INFO] Final Memory: 21M/115M
[INFO] ------------------------------------------------------------------------
```

4. Now you need to add the following code in the `pom.xml` file to connect with the AWS SDK. You have to mention your main Java class under the `Configuration | mainClass` tag. We will create the `S3MavenExample.java` file in the next step:

```xml
<build>
    <resources>
        <resource>
            <directory>${env.HOME}/.aws/</directory>
        </resource>
    </resources>
    <plugins>
        <plugin>
            <groupId>org.codehaus.mojo</groupId>
```

```
            <artifactId>exec-maven-plugin</artifactId>
            <version>1.2.1</version>
            <executions>
                <execution>
                    <goals>
                        <goal>java</goal>
                    </goals>
                </execution>
            </executions>
            <configuration>
  <mainClass>com.packt.example.S3MavenExample</mainClass>
            </configuration>
        </plugin>
    </plugins>
</build>
```

5. Let's create the `S3MavenExample.java` file in the `com/packt/example` package. We are going to create an S3 bucket as per the specific region with a random number generator, prefix it with `s3-maven-bucket-`, and then delete the bucket:

```
import java.util.UUID;
import com.amazonaws.regions.Region;
import com.amazonaws.regions.Regions;
import com.amazonaws.services.s3.AmazonS3;
import com.amazonaws.services.s3.AmazonS3Client;
```

6. You have imported `UUID` to generate the pseudo random number. You are importing `Region` and `Regions` to create the bucket in a specific region, and `AmazonS3` and `AmazonS3Client` to access the AWS S3 services:

```
AmazonS3 s3 = new AmazonS3Client();
Region s3Region = Region.getRegion(Regions.AP_SOUTHEAST_1);
s3.setRegion(s3Region);
```

7. Here you are creating an S3 client and specifying the specific region where it will create the bucket:

If you do not specify any region, it will create it at **US East (N. Virginia)**. This means the default region is **US East (N. Virginia)**.

```
String bucketName = "s3-maven-bucket-" + UUID.randomUUID();
```

8. Here you are creating the `s3-maven-bucket-` prefix with some random UUID:

    ```
    s3.createBucket(bucketName);
    ```

9. To create the bucket, you can use `createBucket()` method. You have to pass the bucket name as a parameter in this method:

    ```
    s3.deleteBucket(bucketName);
    ```

10. To delete the bucket, you can use the `deleteBucket()` method. You have to pass the bucket name as a parameter in this method. After creating the Java file, execute the following command:

    mvn clean compile exec:java

    It will create and delete the bucket as per the specified regions:

```
Command Prompt

D:\AWS SDK Example\java-maven-demo>mvn clean compile exec:java
[INFO] Scanning for projects...
[INFO]
[INFO] ------------------------------------------------------------------------
[INFO] Building java-maven-demo 1.0-SNAPSHOT
[INFO] ------------------------------------------------------------------------
[INFO]
[INFO] --- maven-clean-plugin:2.5:clean (default-clean) @ java-maven-demo ---
[INFO] Deleting D:\AWS SDK Example\java-maven-demo\target
[INFO]
[INFO] --- maven-resources-plugin:2.6:resources (default-resources) @ java-maven-demo ---
[INFO] Using 'UTF-8' encoding to copy filtered resources.
[INFO] skip non existing resourceDirectory D:\AWS SDK Example\java-maven-demo\${env.HOME}\.aws
[INFO]
[INFO] --- maven-compiler-plugin:3.1:compile (default-compile) @ java-maven-demo ---
[INFO] Changes detected - recompiling the module!
[INFO] Compiling 2 source files to D:\AWS SDK Example\java-maven-demo\target\classes
[WARNING] /D:/AWS SDK Example/java-maven-demo/src/main/java/com/packt/example/S3MavenExample.java: Some input files use or override a deprecated API.
[WARNING] /D:/AWS SDK Example/java-maven-demo/src/main/java/com/packt/example/S3MavenExample.java: Recompile with -Xlint:deprecation for details.
[INFO]
[INFO] >>> exec-maven-plugin:1.2.1:java (default-cli) > validate @ java-maven-demo >>>
[INFO]
[INFO] <<< exec-maven-plugin:1.2.1:java (default-cli) < validate @ java-maven-demo <<<
[INFO]
[INFO]
[INFO] --- exec-maven-plugin:1.2.1:java (default-cli) @ java-maven-demo ---
Amazon S3 will create and delete bucket
Creating bucket s3-maven-bucket-b8c8e9d6-4c97-40bd-a68f-d013872b8b43

Deleting bucket s3-maven-bucket-b8c8e9d6-4c97-40bd-a68f-d013872b8b43

[INFO] ------------------------------------------------------------------------
[INFO] BUILD SUCCESS
[INFO] ------------------------------------------------------------------------
[INFO] Total time: 18.592 s
[INFO] Finished at: 2017-10-24T02:26:12+08:00
[INFO] Final Memory: 26M/256M
[INFO] ------------------------------------------------------------------------

D:\AWS SDK Example\java-maven-demo>
```

If you have completed this step and you can see the creation and deletion of the bucket, it means you have successfully completed AWS SDK for Java using Maven in your project.

AWS SDK for Java using Gradle

Please perform the following steps to include AWS SDK for Java using Gradle:

1. Assuming that you have already installed Gradle in your machine, create a new folder called `java-gradle-demo` or any other name. Go to this folder and copy the following files:
   - The `gradle` folder: Contains necessary files for the wrapper
   - `build.gradle`: Gradle build file
   - `gradlew`: Gradle startup script for Unix
   - `gradlew.bat`: Gradle startup script for Windows:

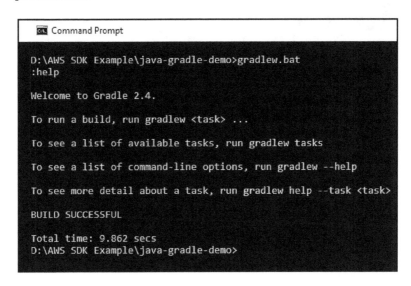

2. Now execute the following command:

   gradlew.bat

```
D:\AWS SDK Example\java-gradle-demo>gradlew.bat
:help

Welcome to Gradle 2.4.

To run a build, run gradlew <task> ...

To see a list of available tasks, run gradlew tasks

To see a list of command-line options, run gradlew --help

To see more detail about a task, run gradlew help --task <task>

BUILD SUCCESSFUL

Total time: 9.862 secs
D:\AWS SDK Example\java-gradle-demo>
```

After completing this execution, you can see the `.gradle` folder.

3. Now you need to update your `build.gradlew` file to connect with AWS:

```
apply plugin: 'java'
apply plugin: 'application'

mainClassName="com.packt.example.S3GradleExample"
repositories {
    mavenCentral()
}
dependencies {
    compile 'com.amazonaws:aws-java-sdk:1.9.6'
}
```

4. Let's create a `S3GradleExample.java` file under the `com.packt.example` folder. This is the same file as `S3MavenExample.java`:

```
package com.packt.example;
import java.util.UUID;
import com.amazonaws.regions.Region;
import com.amazonaws.regions.Regions;
import com.amazonaws.services.s3.AmazonS3;
import com.amazonaws.services.s3.AmazonS3Client;
public class S3GradleExample {
    public static void main(String[] args) {
        AmazonS3 s3 = new AmazonS3Client();
        Region s3Region = Region.getRegion(Regions.AP_SOUTHEAST_1);
        s3.setRegion(s3Region);
        String bucketName = "s3-gradle-bucket-" + UUID.randomUUID();
        System.out.println("Amazon S3 will create/delete bucket");
        // Create a new bucket
        System.out.println("Creating bucket " + bucketName + "\n");
        s3.createBucket(bucketName);
        // Delete a bucket.
        System.out.println("Deleting bucket " + bucketName + "\n");
        s3.deleteBucket(bucketName);
    }
}
```

5. After creating the Java file, execute the following command:

```
gradlew clean build run
```

It will create and delete the bucket as per the specified regions:

```
Command Prompt

D:\AWS SDK Example\java-gradle-demo>gradlew clean build run
:clean
:compileJava
:processResources UP-TO-DATE
:classes
:jar
:startScripts
:distTar
:distZip
:assemble
:compileTestJava UP-TO-DATE
:processTestResources UP-TO-DATE
:testClasses UP-TO-DATE
:test UP-TO-DATE
:check UP-TO-DATE
:build
:run
Amazon S3 will create/delete bucket
Creating bucket s3-gradle-bucket-1bb7fc84-c1fb-45de-8447-e96b360b749c

Deleting bucket s3-gradle-bucket-1bb7fc84-c1fb-45de-8447-e96b360b749c


BUILD SUCCESSFUL

Total time: 1 mins 27.593 secs
D:\AWS SDK Example\java-gradle-demo>
```

AWS SDK for Java using Eclipse IDE

I am assuming that you have already installed Eclipse 4.4 (Luna) or a higher version on your machine as the AWS toolkit supports that.

There are two ways to install an AWS toolkit in your IDE:

- Click on **Help** | **Install New Software...** and install
- Click on **Help** | **Eclipse Marketplace**, search for AWS, and install

We will install using the first method. Now please perform the following steps and refer to the following screenshot:

1. Once you click on **Install New Software**, it will open the **Available Software** dialog box.
2. In this dialog box, you have to click on **Add** to add the AWS toolkit.
3. It will open the **Add Repository** dialog box.
4. In this dialog box, add the **Name** and **Location** as `https://aws.amazon.com/eclipse`.
5. Click on **OK**.

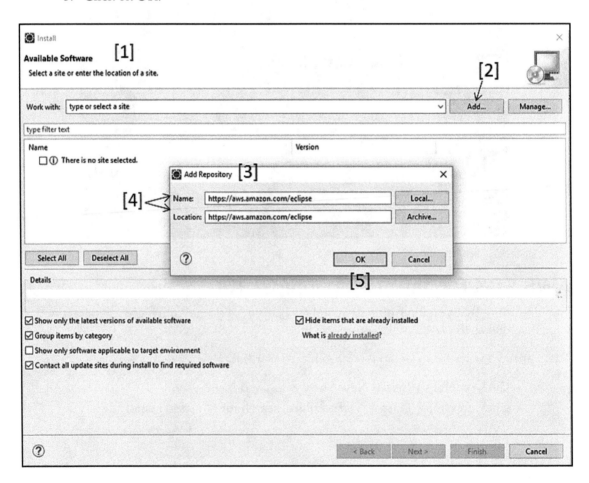

6. On the next page, you will see all available AWS tools. You can select **AWS Core Management Tools** and other tools as per your project requirements:

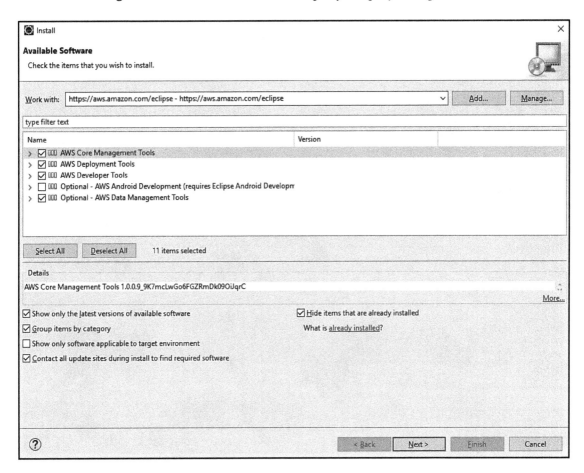

7. A preview page will display to confirm the installation details. Click on **Next** and you will see the **Review License** page, where you click **Accept** and **Finish** to complete the AWS installation:

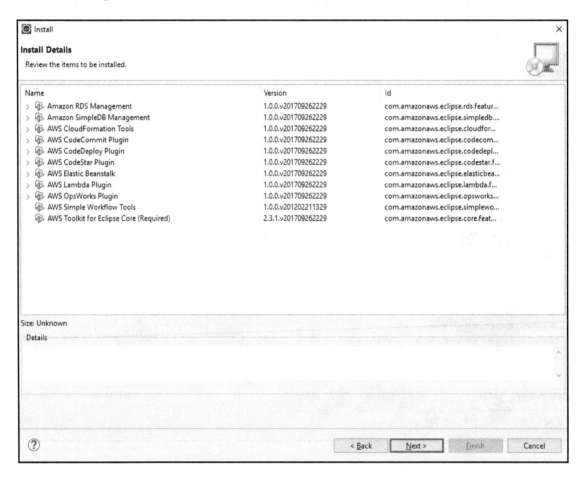

8. After successful installation, your IDE will restart. After restarting, you will see the AWS toolkit icon in the toolbar:

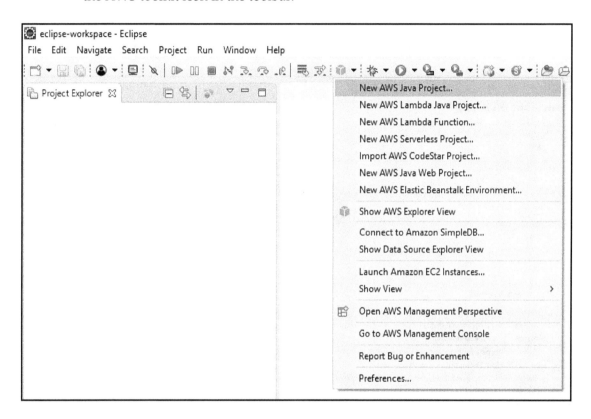

9. Now let's create a sample AWS Java project. When you click **New AWS Java Project....**, you will see the following screen. You need to add the necessary details for the project. Here I have used S3Demo as my **Project name**, com.packt as my **Group ID**, and examples as my **Artifact ID**. I have selected **Amazon S3 Sample** from the Java samples:

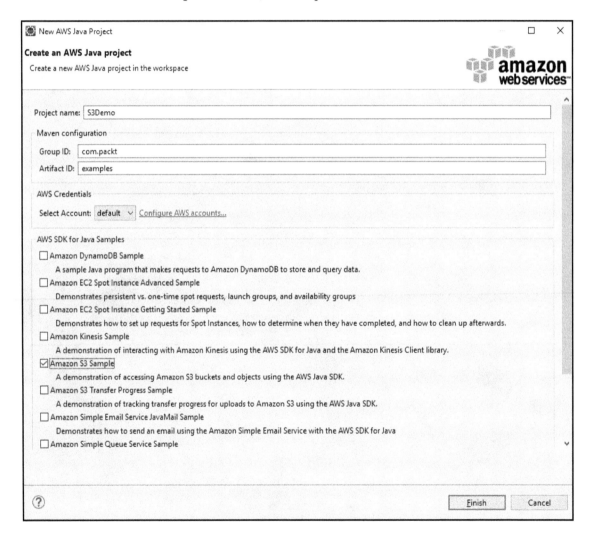

10. If you want to add new AWS accounts, click on the **Configure AWS accounts...** link. You can add the credentials in two ways:
    - Add **Profile Name**, **Access Key ID**, and **Secret Access Key** under the **Profile Details** screen.
    - You can specify your credentials file path or browse to your credentials file. Once you have added that, you can select **Apply and Close**:

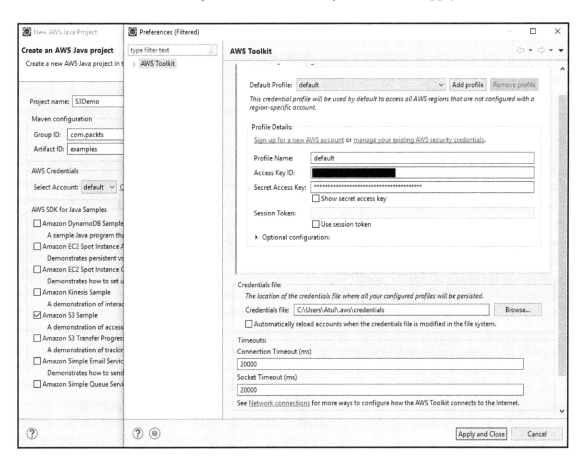

11. Now it will generate the projects and create the necessary files. You can see the following screen with generated files. It will generate a S3Sample.java file. You can right-click on this file and select **Run As | Java Application**. It will create the bucket, list the bucket, upload a new object to S3, download an object, list an object, delete an object, and delete the bucket:

```
<terminated> S3Sample [Java Application] C:\Program Files\Java\jre1.8.0_121\bin\javaw.exe (O
================================================

Creating bucket my-first-s3-bucket-b4f4af50-6a7f-4620-a8d4-1e3034a5f228

Listing buckets




 - my-first-s3-bucket-b4f4af50-6a7f-4620-a8d4-1e3034a5f228



Uploading a new object to S3 from a file

Downloading an object
Content-Type: text/plain
    abcdefghijklmnopqrstuvwxyz
    01234567890112345678901234
    !@#$%^&*()-=[]{};':',.<>/?
    01234567890112345678901234
    abcdefghijklmnopqrstuvwxyz

Listing objects
 - MyObjectKey  (size = 135)

Deleting an object

Deleting bucket my-first-s3-bucket-b4f4af50-6a7f-4620-a8d4-1e3034a5f228
```

So far, you have learned how to add the AWS Java toolkit into your project using Maven, Gradle, and Eclipse IDE. Now we will see how to add the AWS SDK for Node.js into your project.

AWS SDK for Node.js

Node.js is a free, open source, cross-platform framework. It is used to execute JavaScript code on the server side. In Node.js, you can use AWS SDK for JavaScript. This SDK will help to remove the complexity of coding by providing JavaScript objects to use the AWS services. A single downloaded package includes the AWS JavaScript library as well documentation.

You can install AWS SDK for Node.js in two ways:

- **From GitHub**: You can get the source code from `https://github.com/aws/aws-sdk-js`
- **From Node.js Package Manager (npm)**: You can install AWS SDK from the Node.js package manager

Let's install the AWS SDK package and create a sample application to create and delete a bucket on S3 using the following steps:

1. You can download (`https://nodejs.org/en/download/`) and install Node.js If you haven't already installed it. Once you have installed Node.js, you can open the Node.js command prompt from (**Run** | **Node.js command prompt** in Windows.

2. You need to create a `package.json` file to mention the required dependency to install AWS SDK and UUID. We need `aws-sdk` to install the required Node modules for AWS services and a UUID to create a pseudo random number:

   ```
   package.json
   {
       "dependencies": {
           "aws-sdk": ">= 2.0.9",
           "uuid": ">= 1.4.1"
       }
   }
   ```

3. Now open the command prompt and execute the following command:

```
npm install aws-sdk
```

```
Node.js command prompt

D:\AWS SDK Example\node js example>npm install aws-sdk
D:\AWS SDK Example\node js example
`-- aws-sdk@2.138.0
  +-- buffer@4.9.1
  | +-- base64-js@1.2.1
  | +-- ieee754@1.1.8
  | `-- isarray@1.0.0
  +-- crypto-browserify@1.0.9
  +-- events@1.1.1
  +-- jmespath@0.15.0
  +-- querystring@0.2.0
  +-- sax@1.2.1
  +-- url@0.10.3
  | `-- punycode@1.3.2
  +-- uuid@3.1.0
  +-- xml2js@0.4.17
  `-- xmlbuilder@4.2.1
    `-- lodash@4.17.4

npm WARN node js example No description
npm WARN node js example No repository field.
npm WARN node js example No license field.

D:\AWS SDK Example\node js example>
```

4. It will create a `node_modules` folder and install AWS SDK for Node.js. Now you need to set the credentials in the AWS credentials profile file on your local system, located at the following:
    - For Linux, macOS, or Unix: `~/.aws/credentials`
    - For Windows: `C:\Users\USERNAME\.aws\credentials`

5. The file format should be as follows:

```
[default]
aws_access_key_id = downloaded_access_key_id
aws_secret_access_key = downloaded_secret_access_key
```

6. Now, replace your AWS credentials values with the values `downloaded_access_key_id` and `downloaded_secret_access_key`.

7. Now let's create a `S3Example.js` file which will connect to AWS and create and delete the bucket on S3:

```
var AWS = require('aws-sdk');
var uuid = require('uuid');
```

8. First, you have to create variable such as `AWS` and `UUID` to load SDK for JavaScript:

```
var s3 = new AWS.S3();
var bucketName = 'node-sdk-sample-' + uuid.v4();
var params={Bucket: bucketName}
```

Here you are creating s3 as an S3 service object, `bucketname` with `node-sdk-sample` as the prefix with a random number, and `params` as the parameters to call the bucket:

```
s3.createBucket(params, function(err, data) {
    if (err) console.log(err, err.stack); // an error occurred
    else console.log("Successfully Created Bucket: "+bucketName);
    // successful response
});
```

The preceding method is used to create the bucket with parameters and callback functions:

```
s3.waitFor('bucketExists', params, function(err, data) {
  if (err) console.log(err, err.stack); // an error occurred
    else {
        s3.deleteBucket(params, function(err, data) {
            if (err) console.log(err, err.stack); // an error occurred
            else console.log("Successfully Deleted
Bucket:"+bucketName);
            // successful response
        });
    }
});
```

Here it will check whether the bucket is exists or not. If it exists then it will delete the bucket. If it is not exist than it is trying to delete the bucket which is not created yet. In that case, you will get an error.

9. You can execute the file with `node S3Example.js` and you can see that it will create and delete the bucket:

```
Node.js command prompt

D:\AWS SDK Example\node js example>node S3Example.js
Successfully Created Bucket: node-sdk-sample-d58a93f5-8f68-4139-82cb-81dde00e9677
Successfully Deleted Bucket: node-sdk-sample-d58a93f5-8f68-4139-82cb-81dde00e9677

D:\AWS SDK Example\node js example>_
```

Previously, we discussed AWS SDKs for different programming languages and we have covered Java and Node.js with setup and examples. Now we will see how you can set up SDKs on IoT devices.

AWS SDKs for IoT devices

IoT is the Internet of Things, where the internet is connected with things such as software, hardware, physical devices, home appliances, vehicles, or any kind of sensor, actuator, or network, and exchanges data between them. In simple terms, your thing or device will collect, sense, and act on data and send it to an other device from the internet. These connected devices are communicating with each other from various technologies and flow data autonomously. IoT devices can be useful for consumer applications, enterprise applications, smart homes, agriculture, and many industries.

AWS provides different kinds of SDK for the IoT to connect securely and seamlessly to your hardware devices.

The following are the different kinds of AWS SDK:

IoT Devices SDKs	Java	JavaScript	Arduino Yún
	Embedded C	Python	C++

AWS SDKs for mobile devices

AWS provides different kinds of SDKs to connect securely and seamlessly to your mobile devices.

The following are the different kinds of AWS SDKs. In this chapter, we will cover AWS SDK for Android:

Mobile Devices SDKs	Android	iOS	Xamarin
	Unity	React Native	

AWS Mobile SDK for Android

For Android, AWS provides an open source SDK that is distributed under an Apache license. This will provide libraries, code examples, and documentation to develop mobile applications using AWS.

Currently, AWS supports the following services for AWS Mobile SDK for Android:

- **Amazon Cognito Identity**:
    - Controls authentication and provides temporary credentials to connect devices and/or other untrusted environments
    - Saves user data and synchronizes it
    - Manages identity throughout the lifetime of an application
    - We will discuss this topic in more detail in `Chapter 6`, *User Authentication with AWS Cognito*
- **Amazon Cognito Sync**:
    - Enables application-specific data to sync on cross-devices
    - Syncs user data across the web and devices
    - Caches data locally so the device can access data offline; it can sync when the device is online
    - Notifies other devices if sync push is set up
- **Mobile Analytics**:
    - Collects, analyzes, visualizes, and understand the apps
    - Generates reports for users, sessions, in-app revenues, and events
    - Filters reports by data range and platform

- **Amazon S3**:
  - Mobile apps can directly access Amazon S3 to store data
  - Provides Transfer Utility/Transfer Manager (Older Version) to consume S3 services

- **DynamoDB**:
  - SDK contains a high-level library to access and work with DynamoDB Object Mapper
  - Can perform CRUD operations such as Create, Read, Update, and Delete for client-class

- **Amazon Kinesis**:
  - Provides simple, high-level design
  - Stores real-time data on disk and sends it all together to save battery life

- **Lambda**:
  - Lambda function receives app and device data to create a personalized and rich app experience

- **Amazon Lex**:
  - You can integrate a chat box on mobile devices

- **Amazon Polly**:
  - Mobile SDK provides add text to speech integration for Amazon Polly

- **Amazon Pinpoint**:
  - Integrates Amazon Pinpoint to send push notification campaigns from Android apps

 Currently, Android 2.3.3 (API level 10) or higher can use AWS Mobile SDKs.

Now let's understand how to set up the AWS Mobile SDK and then we will see an example with Amazon S3.

The AWS Mobile SDK is available at the following two resources for download:

- http://sdk-for-android.amazonwebservices.com/latest/aws-android-sdk.zip
- https://github.com/aws/aws-sdk-android

This SDK includes class libraries, code example, and documentation:

- Class libraries will include the Java Archive Files (.jar) files for the AWS services. You can include the class for the service which you are using in your applications.
- The code example provides you with an example of using the service in your application using class libraries.
- Documentation is reference material for the use of AWS Mobile SDK for Android.

 AWS **Secure Token Service** (**STS**) and Amazon Cognito Identity are bundled with the AWS Mobile SDK core library. You will get a compile-time error if you include it as a separate JAR file.

In the next section, you will see how to set up AWS Mobile SDK for Android.

AWS Mobile SDK setup for Android

With the help of the AWS Mobile SDK, you can create a new project or update an existing project.

The following are prerequisites:

- AWS account
- Android 2.3.3 (API level 10 or higher)
- Android Studio (https://developer.android.com/studio/index.html)

You need to do the following configuration:

- Configure AWS Mobile SDK for Android
- Set permissions in the Android manifest file
- Use Amazon Cognito to set the AWS credentials

Now let's explore the entire configuration step by step and make changes accordingly.

Configuring AWS Mobile SDK for Android

Let's start configuring AWS Mobile SDK for Android in the following three ways:

- **Using Maven**: Apache Maven is a build automation and dependency management tool, which contains a `pom.xml` file for configurations. It is used to mention the specific Amazon web service which you will use in the project instead of the entire SDK.

 Amazon Mobile SDK for Android v 2.1.3 or above supports Maven.

In the `pom.xml` file, you have to add a `<dependency>` element in which you have to add three subelements such as `groupid`, `artifactid`, and `version`.

`groupid` will be the same as `com.amazonaws` for all AWS services.

In `artifactid`, you have to mention the appropriate service which you are using in your applications.

In `version`, you have to mention the acceptable AWS Mobile SDK version for Android for the given dependency:

```xml
<dependencies>
    <dependency>
        <groupid>com.amazonaws</groupid>
        <artifactid>aws-android-sdk-core</artifactid>
        <version>[2.2.0, 2.3)</version>
    </dependency>
    <dependency>
        <groupid>com.amazonaws</groupid>
        <artifactid>aws-android-sdk-s3</artifactid>
        <version>[2.2.0, 2.3)</version>
    </dependency>
    <dependency>
        <groupid>com.amazonaws</groupid>
        <artifactid>aws-android-sdk-ec2</artifactid>
        <version>[2.2.0, 2.3)</version>
    </dependency>
</dependencies>
```

- **Using Gradle**: When using Android Studio, you can add additional individual services with `aws-android-sdk-core` services as a dependency in your `build.gradle` file:

```
dependencies {
    compile 'com.amazonaws:aws-android-sdk-core:2.6.6'
    compile 'com.amazonaws:aws-android-sdk-s3:2.6.6'
    compile 'com.amazonaws:aws-android-sdk-ec2:2.6.6'
}
```

Avoid + in version numbers. Use `com.amazonaws:aws-android-sdk-core:#.#.#` instead of `com.amazonaws:aws-android-sdk-core:#.#.+`.

- **Import JAR files**: As mentioned previously, you can download the AWS Mobile SDK from the AWS website or GitHub and use it into your project.

In Android Studio, you can add the AWS Mobile SDK JAR file in your application by dragging it into the **Project View**. You can also add the individual JAR file for your services. It will add it to the build path automatically. Then use the Gradle file to sync your project.

Set a permission in the Android manifest file. In your `AndroidManifest.xml` file, you need to set the following permission:
`<uses-permission android:name="android.permission.INTERNET" />`.

Using Amazon Cognito to set AWS credentials

You have to use Amazon Cognito Identity Provider to obtain AWS credentials. Those credentials you can use in your mobile application to access AWS services. You can also set user-specific permissions to access particular AWS services. You don't have to embed personal credentials. Amazon Cognito will be covered in more detail in `Chapter 6`, *User Authentication with AWS Cognito*.

So far, we have covered AWS SDK for IoT and AWS Mobile SDK for Android. Let's explore an example for the Transfer Utility to consume Amazon S3 services. Here we will upload a file from a mobile device and download a file to a mobile device. We will use Android Studio, Amazon Cognito, Amazon S3, and Amazon IAM. Please perform the following steps:

1. Start Android Studio and create a new project. Add the required information and click **Next**:

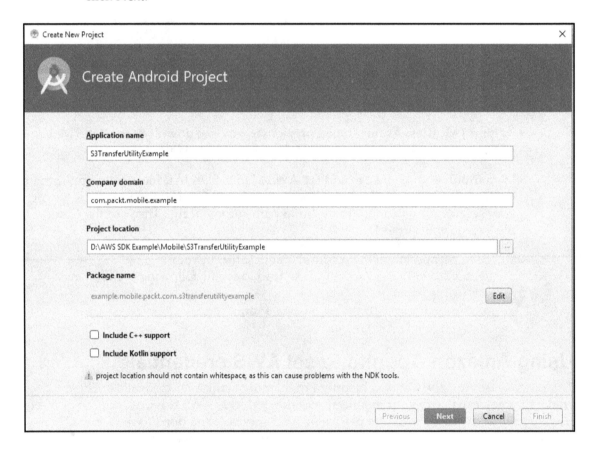

2. Select the **Target Android Devices**. Here I have selected **Phone and Tablet** and the API version is 15, which supports 100% of devices:

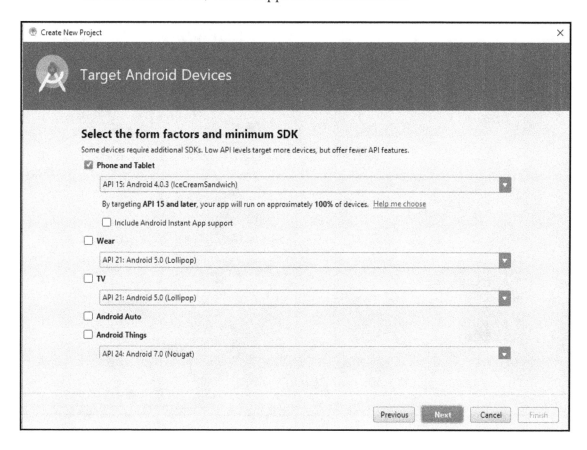

3. Select the activity as per your project needs:

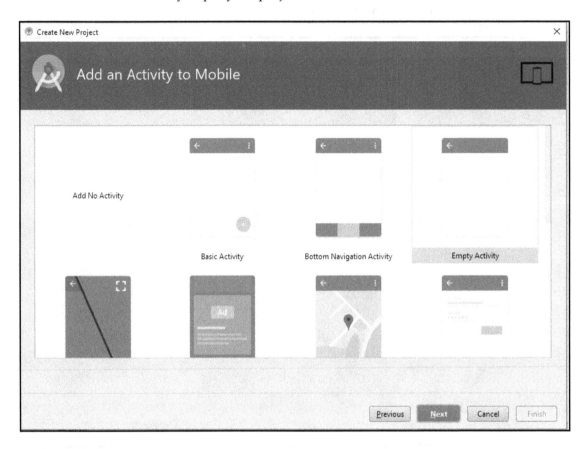

4. In the **Configure Activity** screen, you can change the **Activity Name** and **Layout Name** or you can keep them as they are:

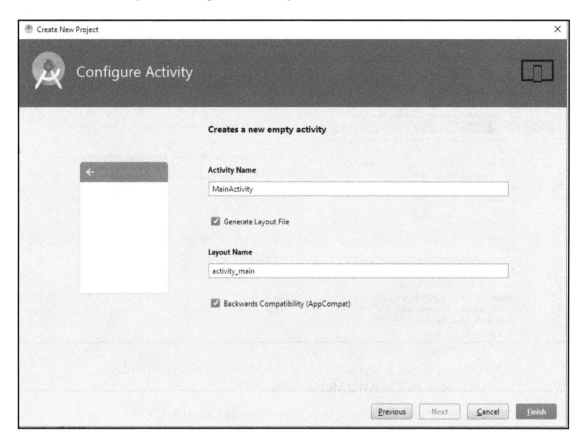

5. You can see the following screen after successfully creating the project:

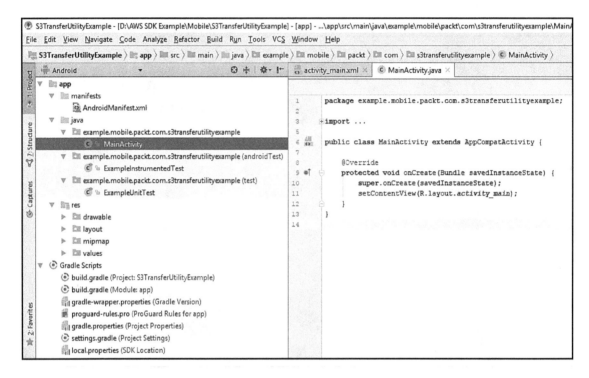

6. Open the `app/build.gradle` file and add the following modules as dependencies for the AWS Mobile SDK:

```
compile 'com.amazonaws:aws-android-sdk-core:2.6.6'
compile 'com.amazonaws:aws-android-sdk-cognito:2.6.6'
compile 'com.amazonaws:aws-android-sdk-s3:2.6.6'
```

7. Amazon S3 will transfer files using the `TranferUtility` service. For that, open the `app/manifests/AndroidManifest.xml` file and add the `TransferUtility` service in the application:

```
<service
android:name="com.amazonaws.mobileconnectors.s3.transferutility.Tra
nsferService"
android:enabled="true" />
```

8. Add the following permissions under the `manifest` tag, which will give you permission to upload and download files from the internet through Android devices:

```
<uses-permission android:name="android.permission.INTERNET"/>
<uses-permission
android:name="android.permission.ACCESS_NETWORK_STATE" />
<uses-permission
android:name="android.permission.WRITE_EXTERNAL_STORAGE"/>
<uses-permission
android:name="android.permission.READ_EXTERNAL_STORAGE" />
<uses-permission android:name="android.permission.ACTION_DOWN"/>
<uses-permission
android:name="android.permission.SMARTBONDING_FEATURE_ENABLED" />
```

9. To access Amazon services from your mobile applications, you have to configure the AWS credentials. Amazon Cognito is used as the credential provider. You have to create the identity pool under the **Federated Identities** in Amazon Cognito and provide the IAM role. You have to create two roles, one for authenticated users and another for unauthenticated users, and provide the following policy. We will cover user authentication with Amazon Cognito in more detail in `Chapter 6`, User *Authentication with AWS Cognito*:

```
{
    "Version": "2012-10-17",
    "Statement": [{
        "Sid": "Stmt1510936216000",
        "Effect": "Allow",
        "Action": ["s3:*"],
        "Resource": ["arn:aws:s3:::<Bucket_Name>/*"]
    }]
}
```

10. To enable file upload and download to and from S3, we need to create a button and add an `onClick` event. You have to add the following code into your `acitvity_main.xml` file:

```
<Button
    android:id="@+id/upload_file"
    android:layout_width="wrap_content"
    android:layout_height="wrap_content"
    android:text="File Upload to S3"
    android:onClick="uploadFile"/>

<Button
    android:id="@+id/downaload_file"
```

```
android:layout_width="wrap_content"
android:layout_height="wrap_content"
android:text="File Download from S3"
app:layout_constraintLeft_toRightOf="@id/upload_file"
android:onClick="downloadFile"/>
```

11. You need to add following imports in the `MainActivity.java` file to use the Amazon Cognito, Amazon S3, and `TransferUtility` services:

```
import com.amazonaws.auth.CognitoCachingCredentialsProvider;
import
com.amazonaws.mobileconnectors.s3.transferutility.TransferObserver;
import
com.amazonaws.mobileconnectors.s3.transferutility.TransferUtility;
import com.amazonaws.regions.Region;
import com.amazonaws.regions.Regions;
import com.amazonaws.services.s3.AmazonS3;
import com.amazonaws.services.s3.AmazonS3Client;
```

12. You need to create an instance of `S3` and `TransferUtility`. You need to specify the file path for upload and download:

```
AmazonS3 s3Client;
TransferUtility transferUtility;
File uploadFilePath = new File(<FILE_UPLOAD_PATH>);
File downloadFilePath = new File(<FILE_DOWNLOAD_PATH);
```

13. The `onCreate` method will initialize the activity. Add the following method for Cognito credentials and Transfer Utility:

```
getCognitoCredentials();
createTransferUtility();
```

14. The following method will create Cognito credential providers. You can pass the Android context, Identity Pool, and region to create the instance:

```
Public void getCognitoCredentials(){
    CognitoCachingCredentialsProvider credentials

  = new CognitoCachingCredentialsProvider(
            getApplicationContext(),
            <Identity_Pool_ID>,
            Regions.<Your_Cognito_IdentityPool_Region>
    );
    createS3Client(credentials);
}
```

15. The following method will create the Amazon S3 client where you have to pass Cognito credentials and set your bucket region:

```
public void createS3Client(CognitoCachingCredentialsProvider
credentials){
    s3 = new AmazonS3Client(credentials);
    s3.setRegion(Region.getRegion(Regions.US_EAST_1));
}
```

16. The following method will create a Transfer Utility instance. Note that `TransferUtility` is used to upload a single file in multiple parts using multiple threads. It is useful for uploading large files mentioning the file path than stream:

```
public void createTransferUtility(){
    transferUtility = new TransferUtility(s3,
getApplicationContext());
}
```

17. The following method will be used to upload files from `transferUtility`'s upload. You have to specify the bucket name, filename, and upload file path:

```
public void uploadFile(View view){

    TransferObserver transferObserver = transferUtility.upload(
            "<S3_Bucket_Name>",
            "<Upload_File_Key_Name>",
            uploadFilePath

    );
}
```

18. The following method will be used to download files from `transferUtility`'s download. You have to specify the bucket name, filename, and download file path:

```
public void downloadFile(View view){

    TransferObserver transferObserver = transferUtility.download(
            "<S3_Bucket_Name>",

            "<Download_File_Key_Name>",
            downloadFilePath
    );
}
```

19. You will see the following screen on your mobile device after successfully running the application:

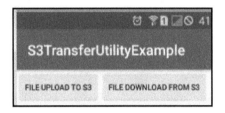

When you tab on **FILE UPLOAD TO S3**, if the file is uploaded successfully, you can see it in your S3 bucket from the console:

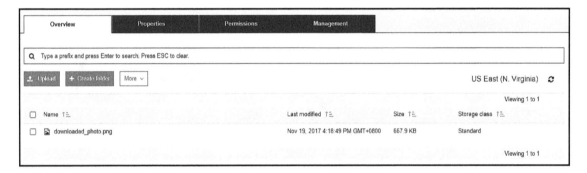

When you click on **FILE DOWNLOAD FROM S3**, if the file is downloaded successfully, you can see it in your folder or path:

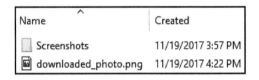

Summary

So far, we have completed the setup of AWS SDK on Java and Node.js with examples. This is a good starting point for developers who have a limited knowledge of AWS SDKs.

In the next chapter, you will see how to integrate applications with relevant AWS services such as DynamoDB, Amazon Kinesis, AWS Lambda, Amazon SQS, and Amazon SWF.

Integrating Applications with AWS Services

2

Sometimes you have to integrate your existing on-premise resources with cloud services. This is known as the hybrid cloud. It will help you achieve business goals without investing more in on-premises hardware and software. AWS provides hybrid capabilities for networking, storage, database, application development, and management tools for secure and seamless integration.

In this chapter, we will integrate applications with various AWS services such as Amazon DynamoDB, Amazon Kinesis, Amazon Lambda, Amazon SQS, and Amazon SWF, which are highly available and fully managed by AWS.

Amazon DynamoDB is a fast, fully managed, highly available, and scalable NoSQL database service from AWS. DynamoDB uses key-value and document store data models. Amazon Kinesis is used to collect real-time data to process and analyze it. Amazon Kinesis comes with different capabilities such as Amazon Kinesis Firehose to load the streaming data to AWS, Amazon Kinesis Stream to process and analyze the real-time streaming data, and Amazon Kinesis Analytics to analyze the real-time streaming of data with the help of standard SQLs.

Amazon **Simple Queue Service** (**SQS**) is a fully managed, highly scalable hosted queue service. It is used to store messages in transit between systems. Amazon **Simple Workflow Service** (**SWF**) is a workflow service to coordinate work across different distributed components. It will help developers to do asynchronous programming for application development.

By the end of this chapter, you will know how to integrate applications with relative AWS services and best practices.

In this chapter, we will cover the following topics:

- **Amazon DynamoDB**
- **Amazon Kinesis**
- **Amazon SQS**
- **Amazon SWF**

Amazon DynamoDB

The Amazon DynamoDB service falls under the Database category. It is a fast NoSQL database service from Amazon. It is highly durable as it will replicate data across three distinct geographical facilities in AWS regions. It is used for applications which need consistent, single-digit millisecond latency. Its reliable performance and flexible data models make it suitable for web, mobile, gaming, and IoT applications. DynamoDB will remove the burden of administrating operating and scaling databases. It will take care of software patching, hardware provisioning, cluster scaling, setup, configuration, and replication. You can create a database table and store and retrieve any amount and variety of data. It will delete expired data automatically from the table. It will help to reduce the usage storage and cost of storing data which is no longer needed.

Amazon DynamoDB Accelerator (**DAX**) is a highly available, fully managed, and in-memory cache. For millions of requests per second, it reduces the response time from milliseconds to microseconds.

DynamoDB is allowed to store up to 400 KB of large text and binary objects. It uses SSD storage to provide high I/O performance.

We will cover the following topics with regard to DynamoDB:

- Integrating DynamoDB into an application
- Low-level interface
- Document interface
- Object persistence (high-level) interface
- DynamoDB low-level API
- Troubleshooting in Amazon DynamoDB

Integrating DynamoDB into an application

The following diagram provides a high-level overview of integration between your application and DynamoDB:

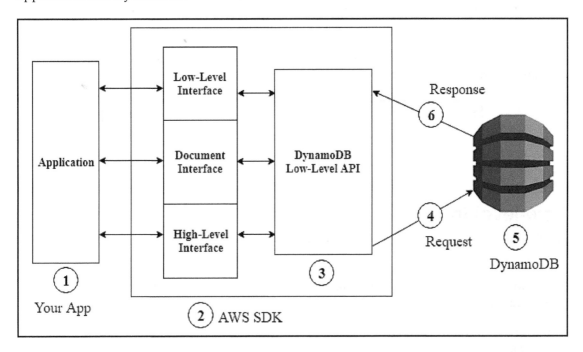

Please perform the following steps to understand this integration:

1. Your application in your programming language which is using an AWS SDK.
2. DynamoDB can work with one or more programmatic interfaces provided by AWS SDK.
3. From your programming language, AWS SDK will constructs an HTTP or HTTPS request with a DynamoDB low-level API.
4. The AWS SDK will send a request to the DynamoDB endpoint.
5. DynamoDB will process the request and send the response back to the AWS SDK. If the request is executed successfully, it will return HTTP 200 (OK) response code. If the request is not successful, it will return HTTP error code and error message.
6. The AWS SDK will process the response and send the result back to the application.

The AWS SDK provides three kinds of interfaces to connect with DynamoDB. These interfaces are as follows:

- Low-level interface
- Document interface
- Object persistence (high-level) interface

Let's explore all three interfaces. The following diagram is the Movies table, which is created in DynamoDB and used in all our examples:

name	fans	rating	year
Airplane	James	*****	1980
Bill & Ted's Excellent Adventure	Sara	****	1989

Low-level interface

AWS SDK programming languages provide low-level interfaces for DynamoDB. These SDKs provide methods that are similar to low-level DynamoDB API requests.

The following example uses the Java language for the low-level interface of AWS SDKs. Here you can use Eclipse IDE for the example.

In this Java program, we request getItem from the Movies table, pass the movie name as an attribute, and print the movie release year:

1. Let's create the MovieLowLevelExample file. We have to import a few classes to work with the DynamoDB.

   AmazonDynamoDBClient is used to create the DynamoDB client instance. AttributeValue is used to construct the data. In AttributeValue, *name* is datatype and *value* is data:

   - GetItemRequest is the input of GetItem
   - GetItemResult is the output of GetItem

2. The following code will create the dynamoDB client instance. You have to assign the credentials and region to this instance:

   ```
   Static AmazonDynamoDBClient dynamoDB;
   ```

3. In the code, we have created `HashMap`, passing the value parameter as `AttributeValue().withS()`. It contains actual data and `withS` is the attribute of `String`:

```
String tableName = "Movies";

HashMap<String, AttributeValue> key = new HashMap<String,
AttributeValue>();
key.put("name", new AttributeValue().withS("Airplane"));
```

4. `GetItemRequest` will create a request object, passing the table name and key as a parameter. It is the input of `GetItem`:

```
GetItemRequest request = new GetItemRequest()
        .withTableName(tableName).withKey(key);
```

5. `GetItemResult` will create the `result` object. It is the output of `getItem` where we are passing request as an input:

```
GetItemResult result = dynamoDB.getItem(request);
```

6. It will check the `getItem` null condition. If `getItem` is not null then create the object for `AttributeValue`. It will get the year from the result object and create an instance for `yearObj`. It will print the year value from `yearObj`:

```
if (result.getItem() != null) {
    AttributeValue yearObj = result.getItem().get("year");
    System.out.println("The movie Released in " + yearObj.getN());
} else {
System.out.println("No matching movie was found");
}
```

```
Example for Low-level Interface
The movie was released in 1980
```

Document interface

This interface enables you to do **Create, Read, Update, and Delete** (CRUD) operations on tables and indexes. The datatype will be implied with data from this interface and you do not need to specify it.

The AWS SDKs for Java, Node.js, JavaScript, and .NET provides support for document interfaces.

The following example uses the Java language for the document interface in AWS SDKs. Here you can use the Eclipse IDE for the example.

In this Java program, we will create a table object from the `Movies` table, pass the movie name as attribute, and print the movie release year.

We have to import a few classes. DynamoDB is the entry point to use this library in your class. `GetItemOutcomeis` is used to get items from the DynamoDB table. `Table` is used to get table details:

```
static AmazonDynamoDB client;
```

The preceding code will create the client instance. You have to assign the credentials and region to this instance:

```
String tableName = "Movies";
DynamoDB docClient = new DynamoDB(client);
Table movieTable = docClient.getTable(tableName);
```

DynamoDB will create the instance of `docClient` by passing the client instance. It is the entry point for the document interface library. This `docClient` instance will get the table details by passing the `tableName` and assign it to the `movieTable` instance:

```
GetItemOutcome outcome = movieTable.getItemOutcome("name","Airplane");
int yearObj = outcome.getItem().getInt("year");
System.out.println("The movie was released in " + yearObj);
```

`GetItemOutcome` will create an outcome instance from `movieTable` by passing the name as key and movie name as parameter. It will retrieve the item `year` from the outcome object and store it into the `yearObj` object and print it:

```
Example for Low-level Interface
The movie was released in 1980
```

Object persistence (high-level) interface

In the object persistence interface, you will not perform any CRUD operations directly on the data; instead, you have to create objects which represent DynamoDB tables and indexes and perform operations on those objects. It will allow you to write object-centric code and not database-centric code.

 The AWS SDKs for Java and .NET provide support for the object persistence interface.

Let's create a `DynamoDBMapper` object in AWS SDK for Java. It will represent data in the Movies table. This is the `MovieObjectMapper.java` class. Here you can use the Eclipse IDE for the example.

You need to import a few classes for annotations. `DynamoDBAttribute` is applied to the `getter` method. If it will apply to the class field then its `getter` and `setter` method must be declared in the same class. The `DynamoDBHashKey` annotation marks property as the hash key for the modeled class. The `DynamoDBTable` annotation marks `DynamoDB` as the table name:

```
@DynamoDBTable(tableName="Movies")
```

It specifies the table name:

```
@DynamoDBHashKey(attributeName="name")
public String getName() { return name;}
public void setName(String name) {this.name = name;}

@DynamoDBAttribute(attributeName = "year")
public int getYear() { return year; }
public void setYear(int year) { this.year = year; }
```

In the preceding code, `DynamoDBHashKey` has been defined as the hash key for the `name` attribute and its `getter` and `setter` methods. `DynamoDBAttribute` specifies the column name and its getter and setter methods.

Now create `MovieObjectPersistenceExample.java` to retrieve the movie year:

```
static AmazonDynamoDB client;
```

The preceding code will create the client instance. You have to assign the credentials and region to this instance. You need to import `DynamoDBMapper`, which will be used to fetch the `year` from the `Movies` table:

```
DynamoDBMapper mapper = new DynamoDBMapper(client);
MovieObjectMapper movieObjectMapper = new MovieObjectMapper();
movieObjectMapper.setName("Airplane");
```

The `mapper` object will be created from `DynamoDBMapper` by passing the client.

The `movieObjectMapper` object will be created from the POJO class, which we created earlier. In this object, set the movie name as the parameter:

```
MovieObjectMapper result = mapper.load(movieObjectMapper);
if (result != null) {
System.out.println("The song was released in "+ result.getYear());
}
```

Create the result object by calling `DynamoDBMapper` object's load method. If the result is not null then it will print the year from the result's `getYear()` method.

DynamoDB low-level API

This API is a protocol-level interface which will convert every HTTP or HTTPS request into the correct format with a valid digital signature. It uses **JavaScript Object Notation (JSON)** as a transfer protocol. AWS SDK will construct requests on your behalf and it will help you concentrate on the application/business logic.

The AWS SDK will send a request in JSON format to DynamoDB and DynamoDB will respond in JSON format back to the AWS SDK API. DynamoDB will not persist data in JSON format.

Troubleshooting in Amazon DynamoDB

The following are common problems and their solutions:

- If error logging is not enabled then enable it and check error log messages.
- Verify whether the DynamoDB table exists or not.
- Verify the IAM role specified for DynamoDB and its access permissions.

- AWS SDKs take care of propagating errors to your application for appropriate actions. Like Java programs, you should write a try-catch block to handle the error or exception.
- If you are not using an AWS SDK then you need to parse the content of low-level responses from DynamoDB.
- A few exceptions are as follows:
    - `AmazonServiceException`: Client request sent to DynamoDB but DynamoDB was unable to process it and returned an error response
    - `AmazonClientException`: Client is unable to get a response or parse the response from service
    - `ResourceNotFoundException`: Requested table doesn't exist or is in CREATING state

Now let's move on to Amazon Kinesis, which will help to collect and process real-time streaming data.

Amazon Kinesis

The Amazon Kinesis service is under the Analytics product category. This is a fully managed, real-time, highly scalable service. This service is used to collect, load, process, and analyze real-time massive-scale data. It can collect and process massive-scale data from multiple sources in real time. You can easily send data to other AWS services such as Amazon DynamoDB, AmazaonS3, and Amazon Redshift. You can ingest real-time data such as application logs, website clickstream data, IoT data, and social stream data into Amazon Kinesis. You can process and analyze data when it comes and respond immediately instead of waiting to collect all data before the process begins.

We will cover the following topics:

- Amazon Kinesis streams
- Troubleshooting tips for Kinesis streams
- Amazon Kinesis Firehose
- Troubleshooting tips for Kinesis Firehose

Now let's explore an example of using Kinesis streams and Kinesis Firehose using AWS SDK API for Java.

Amazon Kinesis streams

In this example, we will create the stream if it does not exist and then we will put the records into the stream. Here you can use Eclipse IDE for the example.

You need to import a few classes. AmazonKinesis and AmazonKinesisClientBuilder are used to create the Kinesis clients. CreateStreamRequest will help to create the stream. DescribeStreamRequest will describe the stream request. PutRecordRequest will put the request into the stream and PutRecordResult will print the resulting record. ResourceNotFoundException will throw an exception when the stream does not exist. StreamDescription will provide the stream description:

```
Static AmazonKinesis kinesisClient;
```

kinesisClient is the instance of AmazonKinesis. You have to assign the credentials and region to this instance:

```
final String streamName = "MyExampleStream";
final Integer streamSize = 1;
DescribeStreamRequest describeStreamRequest = new
DescribeStreamRequest().withStreamName(streamName);
```

Here you are creating an instance of describeStreamRequest. For that, you will pass the streamNameas parameter to the withStreamName() method:

```
StreamDescription streamDescription =
kinesisClient.describeStream(describeStreamRequest).getStreamDescription();
```

It will create an instance of streamDescription. You can get information such as the stream name, stream status, and shards from this instance:

```
CreateStreamRequest createStreamRequest = new CreateStreamRequest();
createStreamRequest.setStreamName(streamName);
createStreamRequest.setShardCount(streamSize);
kinesisClient.createStream(createStreamRequest);
```

The createStreamRequest instance will help to create a stream request. You can set the stream name, shard count, and SDK request timeout. In the createStream method, you will pass the createStreamRequest:

```
long createTime = System.currentTimeMillis();
PutRecordRequest putRecordRequest = new PutRecordRequest();
putRecordRequest.setStreamName(streamName);
putRecordRequest.setData(ByteBuffer.wrap(String.format("testData-%d",
createTime).getBytes()));
```

```
putRecordRequest.setPartitionKey(String.format("partitionKey-%d",
createTime));
```

Here we are creating a record request and putting it into the stream. We are setting the data and `PartitionKey` for the instance. It will create the records:

```
PutRecordResult putRecordResult =
kinesisClient.putRecord(putRecordRequest);
```

It will create the record from the `putRecord` method and pass `putRecordRequest` as a parameter:

```
System.out.printf("Success : Partition key \"%s\", ShardID \"%s\" and
SequenceNumber \"%s\".\n",
putRecordRequest.getPartitionKey(), putRecordResult.getShardId(),
putRecordResult.getSequenceNumber());
```

It will print the output on the console as follows:

```
Kinesis Stream "MyExampleStream" has a status of "ACTIVE".
Putting records in stream : "MyExampleStream" until this application is stopped...
Success : Partition key "partitionKey-1510596635446", ShardID "shardId-000000000000" and SequenceNumber "49578856183557438877423927844079469532024951432017870850".
Success : Partition key "partitionKey-1510596635739", ShardID "shardId-000000000000" and SequenceNumber "49578856183557438877423927844080678457844566129912053762".
Success : Partition key "partitionKey-1510596636009", ShardID "shardId-000000000000" and SequenceNumber "49578856183557438877423927844081887383664180759086759938".
Success : Partition key "partitionKey-1510596636279", ShardID "shardId-000000000000" and SequenceNumber "49578856183557438877423927844083096309483795388261466114".
Success : Partition key "partitionKey-1510596636550", ShardID "shardId-000000000000" and SequenceNumber "49578856183557438877423927844084305235303410017436172290".
Success : Partition key "partitionKey-1510596636818", ShardID "shardId-000000000000" and SequenceNumber "49578856183557438877423927844085514161123024715330355202".
Success : Partition key "partitionKey-1510596637090", ShardID "shardId-000000000000" and SequenceNumber "49578856183557438877423927844086723086942639344505061378".
```

Troubleshooting tips for Kinesis streams

The following are common problems and their solutions:

- **Unauthorized KMS master key permission error**:
  - Without authorized permission on the master key, when a producer or consumer application tries to writes or reads an encrypted stream
  - Provide access permission to an application using Key policies in AWS KMS or IAM policies with AWS KMS
- **Sometimes producer becomes writing slower.**
  - **Service limits exceeded**:

    Check whether the producer is throwing throughput exceptions from the service, and validate what API operations are being throttled.

You can also check Amazon Kinesis Streams limits because of different limits based on the call. If calls are not an issue, check you have selected a partition key that allows distributing put operations evenly across all shards, and that you don't have a particular partition key that's bumping into the service limits when the rest are not. This requires you to measure peak throughput and the number of shards in your stream.

- **Producer optimization**:

It has either a large producer or small producer. A large producer is running from an EC2 instance or on-premises while a small producer is running from web client, mobile app, or IoT device. Customers can use different strategies for latency. Kinesis Produce Library or multiple threads are useful while write for buffer/micro-batch records, PutRecords for multi-record operation, PutRecord for single-record operation.

- **Shard iterator expires unexpectedly**:

The shard iterator expires because its `GetRecord` methods have not been called for more than 5 minutes, or you have performed a restart of your consumer application.

The shard iterator expires immediately, before you use it. This might indicate that the DynamoDB table used by Kinesis does not have enough capacity to store the data. It might happen if you have a large number of shards. Increase the write capacity assigned to the shard table to solve this.

- **Consumer application is reading at a slower rate**:

The following are common reasons for read throughput being slower than expected:

- Total reads for multiple consumer applications exceed per-shard limits. In the Kinesis stream, increase the number of shards.
- Maximum number of `GetRecords` per call may have been configured with a low limit value.
- The logic inside the `processRecords` call may be taking longer for a number of possible reasons; the logic may be CPU-intensive, bottlenecked on synchronization, or I/O blocking.

We have covered Amazon Kinesis streams. In the next section, we will cover Kinesis Firehose.

Amazon Kinesis Firehose

Amazon Kinesis Firehose is a fully managed, highly available and durable service to load real-time streaming data easily into AWS services such as Amazon S3, Amazon Redshift, or Amazon Elasticsearch. It replicates your data synchronously at three different facilities. It will automatically scale as per throughput data. You can compress your data into different formats and also encrypt it before loading.

AWS SDK for Java, Node.js, Python, .NET, and Ruby can be used to send data to a Kinesis Firehose stream using the Kinesis Firehose API.

The Kinesis Firehose API provides two operations to send data to the Kinesis Firehose delivery stream:

- `PutRecord`: In one call, it will send one record
- `PutRecordBatch`: In one call, it will send multiple data records

Let's explore an example using `PutRecord`. In this example, the `MyFirehoseStream` stream has been created. Here you can use Eclipse IDE for the example.

You need to import a few classes such as `AmazonKinesisFirehoseClient`, which will help to create the client for accessing Firehose. `PutRecordRequest` and `PutRecordResult` will help to put the stream record request and its result:

```
private static AmazonKinesisFirehoseClient client;
```

`AmazonKinesisFirehoseClient` will create the instance `firehoseClient`. You have to assign the credentials and region to this instance:

```
String data = "My Kinesis Firehose data";
String myFirehoseStream = "MyFirehoseStream";
Record record = new Record();
record.setData(ByteBuffer.wrap(data.getBytes(StandardCharsets.UTF_8)));
```

As mentioned earlier, `myFirehoseStream` has already been created.

A record in the delivery stream is a unit of data. In the `setData` method, we are passing a data blob. It is base-64 encoded. Before sending a request to the AWS service, Java will perform base-64 encoding on this field.

 A returned `ByteBuffer` is mutable. If you change the content of this byte buffer then it will reflect to all objects that have a reference to it. It's always best practice to call `ByteBuffer.duplicate()` or `ByteBuffer.asReadOnlyBuffer()` before reading from the buffer or using it.

Now you have to mention the name of the delivery stream and the data records you want to create the `PutRecordRequest` instance:

```
PutRecordRequest putRecordRequest = new PutRecordRequest()
            .withDeliveryStreamName(myFirehoseStream)
            .withRecord(record);
putRecordRequest.setRecord(record);
PutRecordResult putRecordResult = client.putRecord(putRecordRequest);
System.out.println("Put Request Record ID: " +
putRecordResult.getRecordId());
```

`putRecordResult` will write a single record into the delivery stream by passing the `putRecordRequest` and get the result and print the `RecordID`:

```
PutRecordBatchRequest putRecordBatchRequest = new
PutRecordBatchRequest().withDeliveryStreamName("MyFirehoseStream")
                .withRecords(getBatchRecords());
```

You have to mention the name of the delivery stream and the data records you want to create the `PutRecordBatchRequest` instance. The `getBatchRecord` method has been created to pass multiple records as mentioned in the next step:

```
JSONObject jsonObject = new JSONObject();
jsonObject.put("userid", "userid_1");
jsonObject.put("password", "password1");
Record record = new
Record().withData(ByteBuffer.wrap(jsonObject.toString().getBytes()));
records.add(record);
```

In the `getBatchRecord` method, you will create the `jsonObject` and put data into this `jsonObject`. You will pass `jsonObject` to create the record. These records add to a list of records and return it:

```
PutRecordBatchResult putRecordBatchResult =
client.putRecordBatch(putRecordBatchRequest);
for(int i=0;i<putRecordBatchResult.getRequestResponses().size();i++){
    System.out.println("Put Batch Request Record ID :"+i+": " +
putRecordBatchResult.getRequestResponses().get(i).getRecordId());
}
```

`putRecordBatchResult` will write multiple records into the delivery stream by passing the `putRecordBatchRequest`, get the result, and print the `RecordID`. You will see the output like the following screen:

Troubleshooting tips for Kinesis Firehose

Sometimes data is not delivered at specified destinations. The following are steps to solve common issues while working with Kinesis Firehose:

- **Data not delivered to Amazon S3**:
    - If error logging is not enabled then enable it and check error log messages for delivery failure.
    - Verify that the S3 bucket mentioned in the Kinesis Firehose delivery stream exists.
    - Verify whether data transformation with Lambda is enabled, the Lambda function mentioned in your delivery stream exists, and Kinesis Firehose has attempted to invoke the Lambda function.
    - Verify whether the IAM role specified in the delivery stream has given proper access to the S3 bucket and Lambda function or not.
    - Verify your Kinesis Firehose metrics to check whether the data was sent to the Kinesis Firehose delivery stream successfully.
- **Data not delivered to Amazon Redshift/Elasticsearch**:
    - For Amazon Redshift and Elasticsearch, verify the points mentioned in *Data not delivered to Amazon S3*, including the IAM role, configuration, and public access.

- **For CloudWatch and IoT, delivery stream not available as target**:
  - Some AWS services can only send messages and events to a Kinesis Firehose delivery stream which is in the same region. Verify that your Kinesis Firehose delivery stream is located in the same region as your other services.

We will discuss Amazon **SQS** in the next section, which will help you to manage message queuing when messages are waiting to be processed.

Amazon SQS

Amazon SQS is a fully distributed, highly scalable, reliable, and managed message queuing service. Amazon SQS is easy to scale and decouples microservices, serverless applications, and distributed systems.

This service will help to create message queuing applications and store messages in transit between distributed systems. This application can run on any computer.

With Amazon SQS, you will not lose any messages when you move data between application components, without requiring that each and every component will be available.

Amazon SQS will help you focus on creating and building robust and sophisticated applications without concentrating on how to store, manage, and retrieve messages from any volumes.

Amazon SQS has two types of queues:

- **Standard queue**: This queue is available for all regions:
  - **At-Least-Once Delivery**: Message will be delivered a minimum of once and sometimes more than once
  - **High Throughput**: It supports unlimited number of transactions per second per API action
  - **Best-Effort Ordering**: Sometimes messages will be delivered but not the same order in which you sent them

You can use this method when the throughput is important.

- **FIFO queue**: This queue is available in limited regions:
    - **Exactly-Once Processing**: Messages will be delivered only once and will be available until the customer deletes them. Duplicates will not come into the queue.
    - **Limited Throughput**: It supports a limited number of transactions. Without batching, it supports 300 messages per second per operation. With maximum batching of 10 messages per operation, it can support up to 3,000 messages per second.
    - **First-In-First-Out Delivery**: Messages will be delivered in the same order in which you sent them.

You can use this method when the order of events is important.

Benefits and features of Amazon SQS

Let's explore a few benefits of Amazon SQS:

- **Operational efficiency**: Amazon SQS will help to eliminate the administrative overhead and complexity associated with infrastructure and dedicated **message-oriented middleware** (**MoM**).

    There isn't any upfront cost. No need to install, acquire, or configure any messaging software.

    With Amazon SQS, message queues are created dynamically and scale automatically to build applications quickly.

- **Reliability**: Amazon SQS helps to transmit any amount of data, at any throughput, without losing messages. To increase the overall fault tolerance of the system, SQS can help to decouple application components to run and fail independently. SQS queues can store messages of any components in distributed applications.

    Messages are stored in multiple availability zones so that they will be available whenever the application needs them.

    Messages will be delivered once with the FIFO queue and at least once with the standard queue.

- **Security:** In Amazon SQS, applications use **server-side encryption** (**SSE**) to encrypt the message body while exchanging sensitive data. AWS **Key Management Service** (**KMS**) with Amazon SQS SSE integration allows you to manage the keys centrally. Authentication mechanisms help to secure the messages stored in SQS message queues.
- **Integration:** AWS services can easily integrate with Amazon SQS to build scalable and flexible applications. You can integrate Amazon EC2, **Amazon Simple Storage Service** (**Amazon S3**), Amazon DynamoDB, Amazon RDS, Amazon EC2 Container Service (Amazon ECS), and AWS Lambda.

  Amazon SQS works very well with Amazon **Simple Notification Service** (**SNS**) for a powerful messaging solution.

- **Productivity**: You can start Amazon SQS message queuing using a console or SDK. SQS has four APIs which you can easily add: `CreateQueue`, `SendMessage`, `ReceiveMessage`, and `DeleteMessage`. You can use the same APIs in standard queues or FIFO queues.
- **Scalability**: It scales elastically and manages pre-provisioning and capacity planning with the application. Costs to use Amazon SQS are based on use and not on an **always-on** model.

Amazon SQS provides the following major features:

- **Redundant infrastructure**: It provides high availability to produce and consume messages and highly-concurrent to access the messages.
- **Multiple producers and consumers**: Multiple consumers or producers are available in your system at the same time.
- **Configurable settings per queue**: All of your queues may have different configuration settings for example, if one queue requires more time for processing than others.
- **Variable message size**: Message size is 256 KB. Large messages can be split into smaller ones. Large message content can be stored in Amazon S3 or Amazon DynamoDB.
- **Access control**: Sender and receiver can be controlled.
- **Delay queues**: Default delay can be set on a queue so that it will delay enqueued messages for a specified time.

To use the AWS SDK for Amazon SQS, it has the same setup and configuration which we have discussed in `Chapter 1`, *AWS Tools and SDKs*. Here I will use Eclipse IDE for the example.

Let's explore an example of Amazon SQS:

1. Open Eclipse IDE and create a new AWS Java project. Add information such as **Project name**, **Group ID**, **Artifact ID**, **Version**, and **Package Name**.

2. Crate a new Java class under this project and import a few classes to use the Amazon SQS.

3. `AmazonSQS` and `AmazonSQSClientBuilder` are used to create an instance of `sqsclient`. Other imports are used to create and delete queues, and to send, receive, and delete messages:

```
AmazonSQS sqsClient = AmazonSQSClientBuilder.standard()
                        .withCredentials(credentials)
                        .withRegion(Regions.US_WEST_2).build();
```

An `sqsClient` object will be created from `AmazonSQSClientBuilder`. It needs to set the credentials and region where you want to create the SQS.

4. `MyDemoQueue` will be created from the `CreateQueueRequest` class. You will get the queue URL from the `sqsClient` by calling the `getQueueUrl` method of `createQueue`:

```
CreateQueueRequest createQueue = new
CreateQueueRequest("MyDemoQueue");
String myDemoQueueUrl =
sqsClient.createQueue(createQueue).getQueueUrl();
```

5. New messages will be sent from `sqsClient`by calling the `SendMessageRequest` class:

```
sqsClient.sendMessage(new SendMessageRequest(myDemoQueueUrl, "This
is SQS Demo Example Test Message."));
```

6. `receiveMessageRequestTest` will receive messages from `MyDemoQueue`:

```
ReceiveMessageRequest receiveMessageRequest = new
ReceiveMessageRequest(myDemoQueueUrl);
```

7. It will create the instance of `messageList` and get information such as message ID, body, and so on:

```
List<Message> messageList =
sqsClient.receiveMessage(receiveMessageRequest).getMessages();
for (Message msgInfo : messageList) {
 System.out.println("MessageId:" + msgInfo.getMessageId());
 System.out.println("ReceiptHandle:"+ msgInfo.getReceiptHandle());
```

```
System.out.println("MD5 Of Body:" + msgInfo.getMD5OfBody());
System.out.println("Body: " + msgInfo.getBody());
}
```

8. You can delete the message by calling the deleteMessage method of sqsClient:

```
String messageReceiptHandle =
messageList.get(0).getReceiptHandle();
sqsClient.deleteMessage(new DeleteMessageRequest(myDemoQueueUrl,
messageReceiptHandle));
```

9. You can delete the queue by calling the deleteQueue method of sqsClient:

```
sqsClient.deleteQueue(new DeleteQueueRequest(myDemoQueueUrl));
```

Troubleshooting in Amazon SQS

Sometimes Amazon SQS Dead-Letter Queues do not behave as expected. The following are common problems or issues and their solutions:

- **Message moved to Dead-Letter Queue**:

  Viewing messages from the AWS console might cause problems with a message and move it to a Dead-Letter Queue. You can adjust this behavior in the following way:

  - For the corresponding queue's redrive policy, increase the Maximum Receives setting
  - From AWS Management Console, avoid viewing the corresponding queue messages

- **Send and receive messages doesn't match**:

  When a message is sent to a Dead-Letter Queue manually, it will be captured by the NumberOfMessagesSent metric. If, however, a message is sent to a Dead-Letter Queue as a result of a failed processing attempt, it isn't captured by this metric. Thus the values of NumberOfMessagesSent and NumberOfMessagesReceived don't match.

In the next section, we will discuss Amazon **Simple Workflow Service** (**SWF**). It helps to distribute work across different components. It gives full control to developers over coordinating tasks and implementing processing steps without worrying about complexities such as keeping their state and tracking their progress.

Amazon SWF

Software workflows have been very popular and the preferred method to is break big tasks into sequential or parallel operational chunks depending on business requirements. Workflows mostly follow state machine concepts, where we have an orchestrator, execution steps in the form of states, and each state is executed through some events. Input/output and to/from states are managed by the orchestrator.

As defined by AWS, Amazon SWF helps developers to build, run, and scale background jobs that have sequential or parallel steps. It can be used in applications which need distributed asynchronous processing.

SWF web services help maintain the state of your workflow but they don't execute any software code, the logic of a workflow, or a state machine. SWF works on a polling mechanism, where your software source code has to poll for the tasks using SWF APIs. The software code will poll for new tasks and processes and provide its output back using SWF APIs.

Amazon SWF enables you to easily separate business logic from state management of your application that can be performed by human actions, web service calls, executable codes, and scripts.

SWF maintains the work tasks to be provided to your software code and keeps track of the workflow. SWF has two main parts: deciders and activity workers.

The decider application coordinates the execution of processing steps in a workflow. The flow of an activity task can be controlled by deciders. When change happens during the execution of a workflow, Amazon SWF will create a decision task. A decision task contains the workflow history and assign tasks to the decider. The decider will receive the decision task from Amazon SWF and analyze the workflow history to find out the next steps. Using decisions, the decider will communicate these steps back to Amazon SWF.

Activity workers are threads or processes to perform activity tasks which are part of the workflow. To use activity tasks, you must register them from the `RegisterActivityType` action or from the Amazon SWF console. The activity worker will poll Amazon SWF for a task which is appropriate for that worker to perform. Once the activity worker receives the task, it will process and complete it. Then it informs Amazon SWF of the result. After having completed the task, the activity worker will poll for another new task. It will continue until the workflow execution itself is complete. Activity workers can be running on a local machine, AWS EC2, or AWS Lambda.

As mentioned above, AWS SWF keeps track of the activity worker state. This tracking can be for activity workers taking a short time, or a long time (say for months) to finish its execution.

SWF is a reliable, scalable, and flexible solution.

AWS SWF can be used in following type of examples:

- **Order processing system**: Multiple tasks are required to be carried out in an order processing system. Each of these tasks can be programmed as an activity worker and decider applications can orchestrate the work between activity workers.
- **Video and audio encoding/decoding**: Large video or audio files can be broken into manageable chunks. These chunks can be encoded/decoded either in parallel or in sequential form. These processed chunks can be merged at the end of the process. In this encoding/decoding of each chunk, merging of all chunks can be looked as activity workers. The decider application will orchestrate which chunks are to be decoded/encoded in which sequence and when to merge processed chunks to a merged file.

AWS SWF provides the following methods for developers to communicate with it:

- **AWS SWF APIs**:
  - Specify the names of workflows (it can also be achieved using the Management console).
  - Start a new workflow. The *workflow execution* is kicked into action.
  - From the activity worker machine, to request and execute tasks in the cloud or on-premises.

- **AWS Flow Framework**:
    - Collection of libraries which assist developers to make it faster and easier to build applications with SWF.
    - It creates and executes your application's steps, keeps track of its progress, and helps define retry rules for failed steps.

We have two sections about AWS SWF:

- The *AWS SWF components* section gives info about SWF components
- The *AWS SWF examples* section provides step-by-step information about SWF examples

AWS SWF components

Now let's learn about a few of the components which are used in Amazon SWF:

- **Domain**: For workflow execution, a data domain is used as a logical container.
- **Workflow**: It represents code components. It defines the logical order of workflow activities and child workflows.
- **Decider**: It is a workflow worker. It polls for decision tasks and activities.
- **Activity**: One or more units of work in a workflow.
- **Activity worker**: Polls for activity tasks. In response, it runs activity methods.
- **Task List**: It issues requests to the workflow and activity workers. Decision tasks are tasks for workflow workers. Activity tasks are tasks for activity workers.
- **Workflow starter**: It starts workflow executions.

Amazon SWF orchestrates the operation of components, coordinating the flow, passing data into different components, heartbeat notifications, and handles timeouts behind the scenes.

Amazon SWF examples

We will see a few steps for the following examples:

- AWS SDK for Java using Apache Maven
- Workflow implementations
- Building and running a project

AWS SDK for Java using Apache Maven

Please perform the following steps to include AWS SDK for Java using Apache Maven:

1. Assuming that you have already installed Maven in your machine, create a new folder AWS SDK Example or any different name. Go to this folder and execute the following command to set up the environment:

   ```
   mvn archetype:generate -DartifactId=swfexample -DgroupId=com.packt
   -DinteractiveMode=false
   ```

2. To use AWS SDK for Java in your project, you need to add the dependency into the pom.xml file. For swf, it uses the aws-java-sdk-simpleworkflow module. Add the following code in the<dependencies> tag in your pom.xml file:

   ```
   <dependency>
   <groupId>com.amazonaws</groupId>
   <artifactId>aws-java-sdk-simpleworkflow</artifactId>
   <version>1.11.78</version>
   </dependency>
   ```

   Make sure that JDK 1.7+ versions can be supported by Maven. Add the following code into your pom.xml file before or after your <dependencies> block:

   ```
   <build>
     <plugins>
       <plugin>
        <groupId>org.codehaus.mojo</groupId>
         <artifactId>exec-maven-plugin</artifactId>
         <version>1.2.1</version>
         <configuration>
             <source>1.7</source>
             <target>1.7</target>
         </configuration>
       </plugin>
     </plugins>
   </build>
   ```

Workflow implementations

In this SWF example, we will create four different Java classes:

- `Types.java`: It has the project's domain, workflow, and activity type data which is shared with other components. It will help to handle registering these types with Amazon SWF.
- `Activity.java` (activity worker): It polls activity tasks and, in response, it runs activities.
- `Worker.java` (workflow worker or decider): Polls for decision tasks and schedules new tasks.
- `Starter.java` (workflow starter): Starts new workflow executions.

You need to import two classes, such as `AmazonSimpleWorkflow`, `AmazonSimpleWorkflowClientBuilder`, and the `simpleworkflow.model` package for this example.

Also create an instance of `AmazonSimpleWorkflowClientBuilder` to implement Amazon SWF in your application. You need to add this code for all classes:

```
Private static final AmazonSimpleWorkflow simpleWorkflow =
AmazonSimpleWorkflowClientBuilder.defaultClient();
```

In `Types.java`, add the following constants into the file, which will used throughout the application:

```
public final static String DOMAIN = "ExampleDomain";
public final static String TASKLIST = "ExampleTasklist";
public final static String WORKFLOW = "ExampleWorkflow";
public final static String WORKFLOW_VERSION = "1.0";
public final static String ACTIVITY = "ExampleActivity";
public final static String ACTIVITY_VERSION = "1.0";
```

SWF components can communicate with each other if they are in the same domain. The following code will create the method to register the domain:

```java
public static void registerDomain() {
    try {
        System.out.println("Register the domain '" + DOMAIN + "'.");
        simpleWorkflow.registerDomain(new RegisterDomainRequest()
            .withName(DOMAIN)
            .withWorkflowExecutionRetentionPeriodInDays("7"));
    } catch (DomainAlreadyExistsException e) {
        System.out.println("Exception: Domain Already exists!");
    }
}
```

Add the following function, which will help to register new activity types in your workflow:

```java
public static void registerActivityType() {
    try {
        System.out.println("Register Activity Type'" + ACTIVITY +"-" +
ACTIVITY_VERSION + "'.");
    simpleWorkflow.registerActivityType(new
RegisterActivityTypeRequest().withDomain(DOMAIN).withName(ACTIVITY)
.withVersion(ACTIVITY_VERSION));
    } catch (TypeAlreadyExistsException e) {
        System.out.println("Exception: Activity type already exists!");
    }
}
```

An activity type can be uniquely identified by its name and version.

Now register a new workflow type, which contains the logic of workflow execution:

```java
public static void registerWorkflowType() {
    try {
        System.out.println("Register Workflow Type '" + WORKFLOW + "-"
+ WORKFLOW_VERSION + "'.");
        simpleWorkflow.registerWorkflowType(new
RegisterWorkflowTypeRequest().withDomain(DOMAIN)
            .withName(WORKFLOW).withVersion(WORKFLOW_VERSION));
    } catch (TypeAlreadyExistsException e) {
        System.out.println("Exception: Workflow type already exists!");
    }
}
```

As with an activity type, a workflow type is also uniquely identified by its name and version.

Now add the `main` method to make this class executable and call register domain, activity type, and workflow type methods in it:

```
public static void main(String[] args) {
    registerDomain();
    registerWorkflowType();
    registerActivityType();
}
```

In `Activity.java`, it will poll for activity tasks which are generated by SWF in response to workflow decision.

Here we will implement a simple activity worker which drives a single activity.

Add the following method as an activity, which will take a string as input, concat with greetings, and return the result:

```
private static String greetings(String input) throws Throwable{
return "Hi, " + input + "!";
}
```

Now add the activity task polling method into the `main` method:

```
public static void main(String[] args) {
    while (true) {
    System.out.println("Polling for an activity task from the tasklist '"
+ Types.TASKLIST + "' in the domain '" + Types.DOMAIN + "'.");

    ActivityTask task = simpleWorkflow.pollForActivityTask(
      new PollForActivityTaskRequest().withDomain(Types.DOMAIN)
       .withTaskList(new TaskList().withName(Types.TASKLIST)));
    String task_token = task.getTaskToken();
  }
}
```

Now add the following code into the main method that polls for tasks and get the task token:

```
if (task_token != null) {
        String result = null;
        Throwable error = null;

        try {
        System.out.println("Executing the activity task. Input is '" +
            task.getInput() + "'.");
            result = greetings(task.getInput());
        } catch (Throwable th) {
            error = th;
        }
    }

if (error == null) {
   System.out.println("The activity task success. Result is '"
     + result + "'.");
   simpleWorkflow.respondActivityTaskCompleted(
     new RespondActivityTaskCompletedRequest()
     .withTaskToken(task_token).withResult(result));
   } else {
   System.out.println("The activity task failed. Error is '"
     + error.getClass().getSimpleName() + "'.");
   simpleWorkflow.respondActivityTaskFailed(
     new RespondActivityTaskFailedRequest()
      .withTaskToken(task_token)
      .withReason(error.getClass().getSimpleName())
      .withDetails(error.getMessage()));
   }
 }
```

If the task is successful then the worker responds to SWF by calling the respondActivityTaskCompleted() method with the RespondActivityTaskCompletedRequest object, which contains the task token and result.

If the task fails then the worker responds to SWF by calling the respondActivityTaskFailed() method with the RespondActivityTaskFailedRequest object, which contains the task token and error reason with the message.

In `Worker.java`, when the workflow worker receives a task, it will decide whether to schedule a new activity or not and take an action.

Now call the `pollForDecisionTask` method for continuous polling into the main method. Once the task is received, it will call its `getTaskToken` method to return a string to identify the task:

```
public static void main(String[] args) {
    PollForDecisionTaskRequest task_request =
      new PollForDecisionTaskRequest()
        .withDomain(Types.DOMAIN)
        .withTaskList(new TaskList().withName(HelloTypes.TASKLIST));

    while (true) {
        System.out.println("Polling for a decision task from the
tasklist '" + Types.TASKLIST + "' in the domain '" + Types.DOMAIN + "'.");
        DecisionTask task =
simpleWorkflow.pollForDecisionTask(task_request);
        String taskToken = task.getTaskToken();
        if (taskToken != null) {
          try {
              executeDecisionTask(taskToken, task.getEvents());
          } catch (Throwable th) {
              th.printStackTrace();
          }
      }
    }
  }
}
```

Add the `executeDecisionTask` method, which will take two parameters, string and list:

```
private static void executeDecisionTask(String taskToken,
List<HistoryEvent> events)
            throws Throwable {
  List<Decision> decisions = new ArrayList<Decision>();
  String workflowInput = null;
  int scheduledActivity = 0;
  int openActivity = 0;
  boolean completedActivity = false;
  String result = null;
}
```

In the preceding methods, we have set up some data members:

- `decisions`: This is a list of decisions with processing task results
- `workflowInput`: It has been provided by the `WorkflowExecutionStarted` event
- `scheduledActivity`: Count of scheduled activities
- `openActivity`: Count of open activities
- `activity_completed`: Boolean value of activity status; either it's completed or not
- `result`: String which holds the activity result

Now add the following code into the `executeDecisionTask` method to process `HistoryEvent` objects:

```
System.out.println("Decision task Execution for history events: [");
for (HistoryEvent historyEvent : events) {
    System.out.println(" " + historyEvent);
    switch(historyEvent.getEventType()) {
        case "WorkflowExecutionStarted":
        workflowInput =
historyEvent.getWorkflowExecutionStartedEventAttributes().getInput();
        break;
    case "ActivityTaskScheduled":
        scheduledActivity++;
        break;
    case "ScheduleActivityTaskFailed":
        scheduledActivity--;
        break;
    case "ActivityTaskStarted":
        scheduledActivity--;
        openActivity++;
        break;
    case "ActivityTaskCompleted":
        openActivity--;
        completedActivity = true;
        result =
historyEvent.getActivityTaskCompletedEventAttributes().getResult();
        break;
    case "ActivityTaskFailed":
        openActivity--;
        break;
    case "ActivityTaskTimedOut":
        openActivity--;
        break;
    }
```

```
}
System.out.println("]");
```

In the preceding code, we are more interested in the `WorkflowExecutionStarted` event because it indicates that execution has been started and provides initial input to the workflow.

The `ActivityTaskCompleted` event is sent once the scheduled activity is completed.

Add the following code after the switch statement to respond with the proper decision based on the task:

```
if (completedActivity) {
    decisions.add(
        new Decision()
    .withDecisionType(DecisionType.CompleteWorkflowExecution)
    .withCompleteWorkflowExecutionDecisionAttributes(
        new CompleteWorkflowExecutionDecisionAttributes()
            .withResult(result)));
} else {
        if (openActivity == 0 && scheduledActivity == 0) {
            ScheduleActivityTaskDecisionAttributes attrs =
            new ScheduleActivityTaskDecisionAttributes()
                .withActivityType(new
ActivityType().withName(Types.ACTIVITY).withVersion(Types.ACTIVITY_VERSION)
).withActivityId(UUID.randomUUID().toString())
.withInput(workflowInput);
            decisions.add(
            new Decision()
            .withDecisionType(DecisionType.ScheduleActivityTask)
            .withScheduleActivityTaskDecisionAttributes(attrs));
    }
}
```

If it is `ScheduleActivityTask` or `CompletedWorkflowExecution` decision, we add this information to the decision list which has been declared in the start of the method.

Add the following code to the `executeDecisionTask` method to return a list of decision objects:

```
simpleWorkflow.respondDecisionTaskCompleted(
        new RespondDecisionTaskCompletedRequest()
        .withTaskToken(taskToken).withDecisions(decisions));
```

In the preceding code, the `respondDecisionTaskCompleted` method will take task token and decision objects.

Add the `WORKFLOW_EXECUTION` constant and the main method to the `Starter.java` class. Create an instance of `startWorkflowExecution` which takes the `StartWorkflowExecutionRequest` object as input in the main method:

```
public static final String WORKFLOW_EXECUTION = "ExampleWorkflowExecution";

public static void main(String[] args) {
        String workflowInput = "Amazon SWF";
        if (args.length > 0) {
                workflowInput = args[0];
    }

    System.out.println("Workflow execution starting '" + WORKFLOW_EXECUTION +
  "' with input '" + workflowInput + "'.");

    WorkflowType wf_type = new WorkflowType()
  .withName(Types.WORKFLOW).withVersion(Types.WORKFLOW_VERSION);

    Run run = simpleWorkflow.startWorkflowExecution(new
  StartWorkflowExecutionRequest().withDomain(Types.DOMAIN)
      .withWorkflowType(wf_type).withWorkflowId(WORKFLOW_EXECUTION)
      .withInput(workflowInput).withExecutionStartToCloseTimeout("90"));

    System.out.println("Workflow execution started. Run id is '" +
  run.getRunId() + "'.");
    }
```

The `Run` object of `startWorkflowExecution` provides a Run ID. This ID is useful to identify a particular workflow execution in SWF's history.

 This Run ID is generated by SWF and does not have the same value as the workflow execution name.

Building and running a project

You can build using the `mvn package` command. It will generate a `swfexample-1.0-SNAPSHOT.jar` file in your target directory.

This example contains four different applications. They run independently.

 If you are using Windows, you have to execute all applications on different command lines. If you are using Linux, macOS, or Unix, you can execute all applications on the same Terminal window one after another.

You can set the classpath in two ways. One uses the `CLASSPATH` environment variable to specify the AWS SDK lib and the AWS SDK third-party lib as follows:

```
export CLASSPATH='target/swfexample-1.0-
SNAPSHOT.jar:/aws_sdk_path/lib/*:/aws_sdk_path/third-party/lib/*'
java com.packt.example.Types
```

Or you can use `java -cp option` when the application is running:

```
java -cp target/swfexample-1.0-
SNAPSHOT.jar:/aws_sdk_path/lib/*:/aws_sdk_path/third-party/lib/*
com.packt.example.Types
```

You need to register domain, workflow, and activity types before running workers and workflow starters by executing the following commands:

```
java -cp target/swfexample-1.0-SNAPSHOT.jar com.packt.example.Types
```

Once the domain, workflow, and activity type have been registered, you can start the activity and workflow workers:

```
java -cp target/swfexample-1.0-SNAPSHOT.jar com.packt.example.Activityjava
-cp target/swfexample-1.0-SNAPSHOT.jar com.packt.example.Worker
```

When your workflow and activity workers are polling, you can start the workflow execution. It will execute until the workflow returns a completed status:

```
java -cp target/swfexample-1.0-SNAPSHOT.jar com.packt.example.Starter
```

When you start the workflow execution, you can see the output delivered by both the workers and workflow execution. You will see the output on the screen when the workflow finally completes:

```
D:\AWS SDK Example\swf\swfexample>java -cp "D:\AWS SDK Example\AWS Tools and SDK\aws-java-sdk-
1.11.205\lib\aws-java-sdk-1.11.205.jar;D:\AWS SDK Example\AWS Tools and SDK\aws-java-sdk-1.11.
205\third-party\lib\*;D:\AWS SDK Example\swf\swfexample\target\swfexample-1.0-SNAPSHOT.jar" co
m.packt.example.Starter
Starting the workflow execution 'ExampleWorkflowExecution' with input 'Amazon SWF'.
Workflow execution started with the run id '224bGMBktPIudrtutup4M/kd8u0Orx0apxefEE7KRIs3Y='.
```

Troubleshooting Amazon SWF

The following are some common problems or issues you might get while developing or running workflows:

- Unknown resource fault
- Non-deterministic workflows
- Versioning problems
- Troubleshooting and debugging a workflow execution
- Lost tasks

Unknown resource fault

You will get an unknown resource fault when you try to perform some operation on a resource which is not available. The reason might be one of the following:

- Domain does not exist where you configure your worker. Register the domain using the service API or console to fix this.
- You try to create a workflow execution or activity tasks of types which are not registered. You must register workers with their types at least once before attempting to start executions.
- A worker attempts to complete a task which timed out. To fix this, you should consider adjusting the timeout. To achieve this, you should register a new version of the activity type.

Non-deterministic workflows

The implementation of your workflow must be deterministic. An exception will be thrown when the framework detects non-determinism while executing the workflow. Some common mistakes that can lead to non-determinism are the use of random numbers, system clock, and the generation of GUIDs. It will construct different values at different times, which will take your workflow to a different path each time it is executed.

Versioning problems

When you implement a new version of your workflow/activity or add a new feature, you should increase the version of the type by using the appropriate annotation. You can append the version number to the task list name. It will ensure that tasks belonging to different versions of the workflow and activities are assigned to the appropriate workers.

Troubleshooting and debugging a workflow execution

In the AWS SWF console, you can use the workflow history, which contains a complete and authoritative record of all the events that changed the execution state of the workflow execution. It is maintained by Amazon SWF but it will not help to diagnose problems. The Amazon SWF console will enable you to search for workflow executions and you can then drill down into individual history events. The `WorkflowReplayer` class is provided by the AWS Flow framework. This is used to reply a workflow execution and you can debug it locally. Using debugging tools, you can create breakpoints, step into code, and debug the workflow.

Lost tasks

This might happen when you shut down old workers and start new workers but tasks get delivered to old workers. It happens due to old race conditions which are distributed across several processes. To avoid this kind of situation, you should add a delay between shutting down old workers and starting new workers.

Summary

So far, we have completed implementations, examples, and best practices for different AWS services using AWS SDK.

In the next chapter, we will learn about the different phases of the release process in **Continuous Integration** (**CI**) and **Continuous Deployment** (**CD**) workflows. It will include the four major parts of CI/CD: source, build, test, and production.

3
Continuous Integration and Continuous Deployment Workflow

Development and Operations (**DevOps**) is the buzzword in current market trends; it is a practice/approach/methodology/process for continuous software development, testing, integration, deployment, and for managing environments.

In this chapter, we will cover **Continuous Integration** (**CI**) and **Continuous Deployment** (**CD**) workflows, and also see the difference between Continuous Delivery and Continuous Deployment. We will explore various types of tool to use in the DevOps process.

CI is the workflow strategy which ensures that everyone's code changes integrate with the current repository; it endeavors to catch bugs and reduce merge conflicts.

Continuous Delivery is the next step after CI, in which developers are developing software in such a way that they can release it at any time. Sometimes people are confused about **Continuous Delivery** (**CD**) and **Continuous Deployment** (**CD**), so we will discuss this later in this chapter.

Continuous Deployment is the next step after CI or Continuous Delivery. In this process, teams produce software in a short life cycle and then release it. It helps to release software faster and more frequently.

This chapter will cover the following topics:

- An overview of DevOps
- Continuous Integration – maintaining code repository
- Continuous Delivery – automating build and self-testing
- Continuous Deployment – automating production deployment
- Tools used for DevOps processes
- CI/CD on AWS

An overview of DevOps

Now, we know that DevOps is a contraction of DEVelopment and OPerationS. DevOps is the end-to-end life cycle of a product and is built based on a focus on business needs and shared goals within the organizations.

DevOps = Continuous Delivery + Continuous Integration + Continuous testing + Continuous Deployment

In traditional software development, a product/project has different phases of the **Software Development Life Cycle (SDLC)**. We will not go into too much detail about all the phases but it has phases such as development, integration, and implementation all the way to operation and maintenance. All the phases are siloed and the cycle is expensive and slow. One more problem is that if a client need changes during the development phase, it means you are delivering software that doesn't contain changes, or you need to start the process midway, which will take more time and money.

The Agile model helps to develop software by small iterations, and will adapt client changes better than the Waterfall model, thus helping to save time and money.

However, with the Agile approach, there is a lack of collaboration between the Dev team and the Ops team that slows down the development and release process. The DevOps methodology provides better collaboration, fast and continuous software delivery, with faster problem resolution and fewer problems to fix.

DevOps brings more flexibility with Continuous Delivery, CI, and the CD pipeline. It helps to provide a more automated release and fewer failures with customer needs, using effective tools and transparency.

People have some common misconceptions about DevOps such as:

- *Is DevOps a new thing?*: No. DevOps is not a new thing. It is an extension of the Agile model. Agile's concept was to embrace constant development changes. So, the DevOps concept is to embed those development changes within the operations process.
- *Is DevOps a product?*: No. DevOps it not a product. It is about the quality of your project/product or application.
- *Is DevOps a fad?*: No. Organizations that are adopting DevOps are deploying their code 30 times more frequently with 50% less failure for a new release. We cannot ignore this and that is the reason that DevOps is not fading and it will stay. Many companies are already using the DevOps approach or they have started to do so.
- *Is DevOps a tool?*: No. It is not a tool. It will help to connect or interact with other tools. It will help to drive your organization's goals and interact in such a way that it will help to establish transparency and improved communication throughout the process, within your organizations.

The goal of DevOps

The goal of DevOps is to:

- Increase the frequency and quality of deployment
- Reduce the frequency and severity of new release failures
- Shorten the lead time between fixes
- Provide a faster mean time to recovery
- Achieve a faster time to market

Reasons for integrating DevOps in your process

Now we know the goal of DevOps and in the next section, we will understand the reasons for integrating DevOps in your process. These are listed here:

- Faster identification of software defects.
- You can mitigate and identify software defects, at any stage, with better collaboration and communication between the Dev and Ops teams.
- Better resource management.

- The Dev and Test team are waiting constantly for resources to arrive, causing a delay in delivering the product in the software development stage.
- Reduction in human errors.
- Deploying frequent iterations helps to reduce human errors during the Dev and the Ops process in DevOps. It will help to implement multiple deployments in a defined timeline with a fewer failure rate.
- Enhanced version control.
- In all stages of the development life cycle, DevOps allows developers to leverage the dynamic infrastructure to emphasize the individuals. To achieve that, it will allow version control and automated coding options.

The benefits of DevOps

The benefits of DevOps are as follows:

- **Improved collaboration**: Dev and Ops teams have to collaborate (`https://aws.amazon.com/devops/what-is-devops/#communication`) closely to share responsibilities and combine their workflows under DevOps. It emphasizes values such as accountability and ownership to build more effective teams, and will save time and reduce inefficiencies by reducing the handover time between Dev and Ops.
- **Scale**: DevOps will help to scale, manage, and operate your Dev and infra process. Automation will also help to change systems efficiently, or to manage complex systems with reduced risk. Infrastructure as a Code will help you to manage development, testing, and production environments in an efficient and repeatable manner.
- **Speed**: DevOps gives you the ability to move faster as a business which means that you can innovate faster, adapt to the changing market better, and grow efficiently to drive business results. The DevOps model enables the Dev and Ops teams to achieve these business results.
- **Rapid delivery by automation**: DevOps enables you to innovate and improve your product faster by automating the process, which increases the frequency and pace of release. If you quickly release new features and fix bugs faster, you will respond to the customer's needs more efficiently and build competitive advantage. Continuous Integration and Continuous Delivery are practices which will automate the software release process from build to deployment.

- **Reliability**: DevOps will reliably deliver by ensuring the quality of application updates and infrastructure changes while maintaining a positive experience for end users. To test that each change is safe and functional, use practices such as Continuous Integration and Continuous Delivery. You can see real-time performance by monitoring and logging.
- **Security**: By using automated compliance policies, configuration management techniques, and fine-grained controls, you can adopt the DevOps model without sacrificing security. You can define and track compliance at scale without using infrastructure as code and policy as code.

You will achieve: Faster release + highest quality.

DevOps includes the following processes:

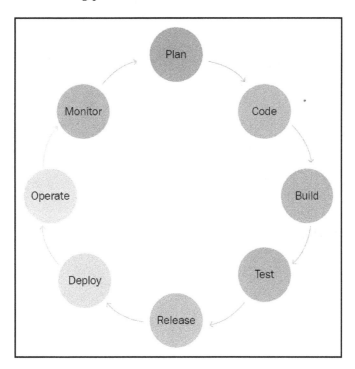

DevOps contains the following practices:

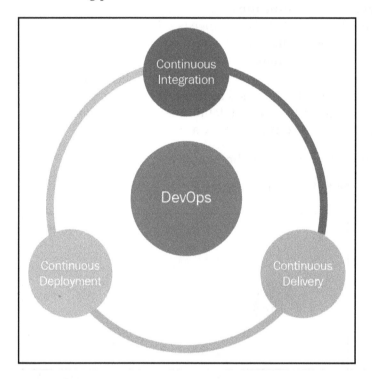

- Continuous Integration
- Continuous Delivery
- Continuous Deployment

Let's understand all these practices in brief.

Continuous Integration – maintaining code repository

CI originates with an extreme programming development process which is one of its original twelve practices. It doesn't require you to deploy any particular tools but it is useful if you use a CI server.

CI means the developer can constantly merge their work with the master/main/trunk branch, so it will be easier for the Test team to test the latest changes with the existing changes. It will help to test code as soon as possible and provide rapid feedback, so that any issue can be identified and fixed as soon as possible. In this process, most of the work is done by automated tests which are part of the unit test framework.

The following is a pictorial representation of CI. In this process, the Dev Team, Testing Team, and Software Configuration Team work together to integrate the latest code and make it available for the next process:

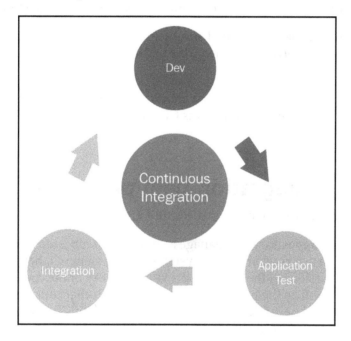

Now let's look at an example.

Let's say you check out the latest working copy from the source code management system on the main branch onto your local development machine. Here, when the developer copies the code from the main branch to their own local machine, it is called a checkout and the copy on the local machine is called the working copy. Once you take the latest code from the main branch then you can update it in your working copy.

Now, you complete your task on the working copy, where you can also add or change the automated test or alter the production code.

Once you complete your development, you can start to do the automated build on your local environment. It will take the local working copy for the source code, compile it, build it, make executables, and run the automated test. If the generated and tested build contains any errors or defects, then you should fix these and repeat all the processes (such as compile, build, create executable, and run the automated test) until you get a clean build without any error or defects.

Once that is done, you can update your code base with the latest code if anyone in your team has checked in the code into the main branch, and then you can rebuild the code. You need to fix any compilation issue and then commit your code with the main branch.

We cannot say that the code is integrated successfully until the build is executed from the main branch, without any errors or issues. This build can be executed manually or automatically.

If a bad build occurs at code level, it will be identified immediately and be fixed by the team. You will never get a failed build in this CI environment, so in your team you will get many builds a day.

Continuous Integration best practices

It's good practice to follow these best practices for CI:

- **Maintain a repository**: To manage a source code repository or master repository, you have to use version control systems. This system will help to manage different versions of the files and provide a history of the code. A master repository will be the buildable code from a fresh checkout and it doesn't require any additional dependencies. This repository contains the working version and all the changes should be integrated in this repository. You can also place the build server to monitor the code changes at any given time.
- **Build automation**: A single command is capable of building the entire system. The team should standardize the build script or build tool to trigger the build from the command. This build automation includes automating the source code integration, code compilation, unit and integration tests, and deployment on a production-like environment. You also need to keep a backup of the previous build in the version control system. If there is any failure on the build, then it can be reverted anytime to the previous versions, and the source code can be compared to find the reason for the failure.

- **Make a self-testing build**: To catch defects/bugs rapidly and efficiently, you have to include test automation in the build process. The result of running that automated test suite will give you information about any failed tests. If the test fails, it will fail the entire build.
- **Everyone commits frequently**: It will reduce the conflict if the developer commits regularly. It is good practice for CI if the developer commits changes at least once a day or several times a day. By doing this, the developer will see the real-time state of the test and health of the application.
- **Build from every commit**: A team gets more tested builds using frequent commits. It means the main repository will stay in a healthy state. There are two main ways you can do the build. One is a manual build and the second is using a CI server.

In a manual build, the developer kicks off the build on the Integration machine, using the main repository source code.

A CI server will monitor the repository. If there are any commits that have happened on the main repository, it will automatically check against the repository and start the build, and notifiy the result to the committer of the build.

- **Broken builds fixed immediately**: As a part of the CI, if any build fails, it should get fixed immediately. It means there should be the highest priority to fix the build. The fastest way to fix the build is to revert the code from the last known good build.
- **Faster build**: The build should be very fast, so if there is a problem with integration, it can be quickly identified. If it is more than 10 minutes, then the process becomes dysfunctional as people won't commit frequently. A large build will be broken into multiple small jobs and they will be executed in parallel.
- **Test on a clone of the production environment**: The production environment may differ from the test environment, so it might happen that a build on the test environment works properly but it will fail when deployed to the production environment. It will be costlier to create a replica of the production environment, so it is better instead to create a pre-production environment (*staging*). This environment is not tightly regulated but it has the same versions of the operating system, software, patches and libraries. In that way, the build will go into actual production without any dependency issue.

- **Latest deliverables available easily**: The team should know the latest build location. It's a good practice to keep the recent builds in the same place. It will help to do the early testing with the stakeholders and/or testers, to reduce the chances of more defects after deployment, and if errors are identified at the early stage then these can be fixed quickly.
- **Latest build results available for all**: Build information such as start/finish and its results, such as success/fail information, can be communicated with the team through email or the website, so that everyone is aware of the current situation. If the build fails, then it will notify the development team to take speedy action.
- **Deployment automation**: Deployment automation helps to deploy the build into production easily, by running the build on a local environment. As tests are executed on the staging environment, this deployment automation requires a minor increment in effort.

Continuous Delivery – automating build and self-testing

After fully implementing CI in the organization, you can move on to the next process and implement Continuous Delivery.

The following is a schematic of Continuous Delivery. In this process, the Dev Team, Testing Team, and Software Configuration Team work together to integrate the latest code and make it available for the acceptance test. Once this acceptance test has completed successfully, the product is available for delivery:

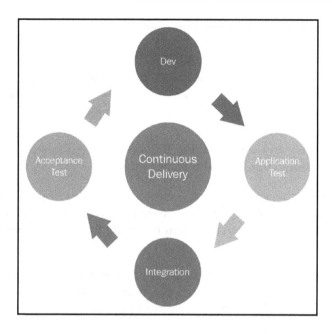

Continuous Delivery aims to deliver quality software in a very fast manner. It has the ability to continuously deliver changes, such as new features, bug fixes, and configuration changes into UAT, staging, and production. It also helps to deliver work in small batches frequently, so that issues can be uncovered at an early stage.

Continuous Delivery differs from Continuous Integration as it will feed the business logic for tests. For Continuous Integration it will do the unit test and unable to catch all the design issue. You can deliver the code for a code review in this process.

The following are the key differences between CI and Continuous Delivery:

Continuous Integration	Continuous Delivery
Can be done by one developer	Needs team collaboration
Continuous Delivery is not required for this process	Continuous Integration is required for this process
Continuous Integration is a continuous journey to get feedback and do the build	Continuous Delivery is a linear journey
You cannot directly push the build to production	You can directly push the build to production

You can do Continuous Delivery when:

- The product is deployable throughout its life cycle
- Working on new features, your team's priority will be keeping the software deployable
- Someone makes changes to the production readiness; you will get fast and automated feedback
- You can deploy any version of the software to environments such as UAT, staging, or production from the push-button

Continuous Delivery can be achieved by CI of the software developed by the team, building the executables and running automated tests to detect any issue. You can push the executable into a production-like environment to ensure that it will work in production. To do this, you can use the Deployment Pipeline.

Clients or business teams should be able to ask for the current working development version to be deployed to production, at any given time. This version has already passed the acceptance test, so there should be no objection from any of the team.

You can achieve Continuous Delivery with close and collaborative relationships between the teams involved in software delivery. You can also carry out extensive automation for all parts in the process using the Deployment Pipeline.

This Deployment Pipeline contains different stages such as Build Automation, Continuous Integration, Test Automation, and Deployment Automation. Let's go through all the stages in brief:

- **Build Automation**: This is the first process; the build happens automatically using tools rather than manually.
- **CI**: In CI, developers check in the code many times on a shared repository, the automated build will verify this check in, inform the team if there are any defects, issuers or errors, and carry out iterative and incremental software delivery.
- **Test Automation**: A new version of the application has been tested to ensure that it contains all the required functionalities with quality. It is important that it also verifies the security, performance, and compliance verified by the pipeline. This stage involves many automated activities.
- **Deployment Automation**: It should be automated to provide the reliable delivery of new functionalities to the users within minutes.

Continuous Delivery benefits

Now, let's look at the benefits of Continuous Delivery.

- **Less deployment risk**: You are deploying in chunks or small parts so there is less chance of something going wrong; if anything goes wrong it can be fixed easily.
- **Track the progress**: You can track the working progress as it is deployed in the production environment or production-like environment.
- **Feedback from user**: There is always a big risk with any software that you have developed something which is not useful. You will get quicker feedback from real users on how useful the software is, if you present this software earlier and more frequently to the user.

Once you implement the Continuous Integration–Continuous Delivery process, you will see the following benefits:

- Enhancement in teamwork
- Lower costs
- Higher quality with lower risk
- Quicker response to changes
- More frequent releases of the features
- Stability and reliability
- Reduction in manual efforts and time

Continuous Deployment – automating production deployment

Continuous Deployment (CD) is an extension of CI which is used to minimize the overall process time. Its use means it will help to reduce the time from the development team writing the new code to it being delivered to the real user in production environments. There will be no UAT process before production. Testing is done before the code gets merged to the main branch and it is performed on a clone of the production environment. Hence, the production branch is always stable and executables are ready to deploy to the production environment by an automated process. This process is an automated process and anyone can perform it by the single click of a button.

CI and Continuous Delivery is required prior to CD because, without it, the build or executables might produce an error in the production environment.

The following diagram displays of the CD processes:

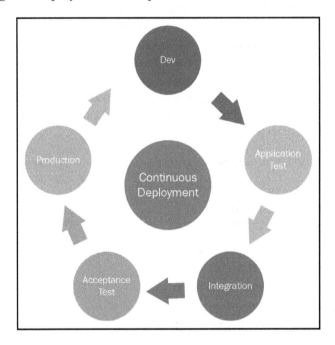

How they work together

In the CD process, you have to create several automated parts. You have to automate CI for the build server and Continuous Delivery for the staging server, which has the ability to deploy in a production environment.

The entire process can be automated from start to finish. Let's explore the different steps for that process:

1. After completing the work, the developer will check in the code to the branch.
2. The CI server will pick this change and merge it with the master branch, perform unit tests, and merge the code to the staging environment, based on test results.
3. The developer will deploy it to the staging environment and QA will test the functionality.

4. If it passes the QA test then the build will move to the production environment and the CI server will pick the code again, and determine if it's OK to merge into the production environment.
5. After successfully completing *Step 4*, it will deploy to the production environment.
6. This process changes on the basis of requirement and need.

In CD, changes are constantly tested, deployed, and released to the live or production environment, after successful verification. Code from development to release must be free flowing and it can be maintained and controlled by the Dev team. In the automation process, steps are implemented and executed without any cumbersome workflows.

People are very often confused with both CDs—Continuous Delivery or Continuous Deployment.

In Continuous Delivery, you are able to create the executable and you can deploy it to the production environment, but you need to do this manually when the business needs it.

In Continuous Deployment, you are able to create the executable and you can deploy it to the production environment, automatically.

In order to do Continuous Deployment, you must be doing Continuous Delivery.

The benefits of Continuous Deployment

- Your focus on the product will increase
- You can focus on actual testing and automate the repetitive tasks for better product quality
- You will get frictionless deployments, without compromising security
- You can scale the product from a single application and make it available as an Enterprise
- You can connect with existing tools and use the technologies into an easy going workflow
- There will be integration between teams and processes with a unified pipeline
- You can create workflows across the dev, test, and production environments
- You can get a single view across all applications and environments
- In a unified pipeline, you can provide traditional and cloud-native applications
- You can get overall productivity improvements

So far, you have understood the DevOps processes. Let's explore the tools used in the DevOps process.

Tools used for DevOps processes

The DevOps process consists of different kinds of tool to make the process smoother. It includes tools for source code management, configuration management, building and testing the systems, integration, application deployment, version control, and continuous monitoring.

Different tools are required for Continuous Integration, Continuous Delivery, and Continuous Deployment. You will need more or fewer tools, as per your application requires.

Here are some of the key tools and practices you need to know:

- **Source Code Management**: GIT, Bitbucket, Subversion
- **Build Automation Tools**: Maven, Ant, Gradle
- **Test Automation**: Selenium, JUnit, Cucumber
- **Continuous Integration**: Jenkins, Bamboo, Hudson
- **Configuration Management**: Puppet, Chef, Ansible
- **Continuous Monitoring**: Nagios, Ganglia, Sensu
- **Virtual Infrastructure**: Amazon Web Service, Microsoft Azure, Google Cloud Platform.

Source Code Management

In Source Code Management, a repository is a common place where the developer will check in and check out (download the code into a local system or environment) the code. This repository manages the various versions of source code that are checked in and available for checkout, so the developers will not overwrite other people's code.

This is the major component of Continuous Integration; some of the popular source code repository tools are Git, Bitbucket, and **Subversion** (**SVN**).

GIT

GIT is a distributed version control system to keep track of changes in any set of files between different people. In GIT, every developer's repository also contains the full history of all the changes.

The object format of GIT's files uses a combination of delta encoding for storing content differences, version metadata, compression and directory contents, explicitly. GIT has a significant performance benefit and it is secure with a SHA1 secure hashing algorithm.

Bitbucket

Bitbucket is owned by Atlassian and it is a web-based hosting service. It is used for development projects and source code that uses Mercurial or Git as a revision control system. Bitbucket has three different deployment models – Cloud, Bitbucket Server, and Data center.

Bitbucket can integrate easily with other Atlassian products such as Jira, Confluence, Bamboo, and HipChat.

Subversion (SVN)

Subversion (abbreviated SVN, after the command name svn) is a free and open source software versioning and revision control system, distributed under Apache License.

Subversion is used to manage current and historical versions of files and directories such as source code, web pages, and documentation. It also allows you to recover older versions of files and the history of the changed data. You can use different components after you install Subversion; components are tools and programs such as svn, svnversion, svnlook, svnadmin, svnsync, and a few others.

Build Automation tool

Build Automation is the process for automating the creation of the build, compiling the source code, packaging the code into executables, and running test automation.

Build tools can be differentiated into two types, such as task-oriented and product-oriented. Task-oriented build tools will describe the dependency in a specific set of tasks. Product-oriented build tools describe things in terms of products.

Popular tools are Maven, Ant, and Gradle.

Maven

Maven is used to simplify the build processes (its name comes from a Yiddish word meaning accumulator of knowledge). Now it is used to build and manage any Java-based projects. Its primary goal is to reduce the development effort. To achieve that goal, Maven deals with:

- Making the build process easy
- Providing a uniform build system
- Providing quality information for a project
- Providing best practices development guidelines
- Allowing new feature migration transparently

Ant

Apache **Another Neat Tool** (**ANT**) is a Java-based build tool for automating software build processes. Apache Ant is free, portable, open standard, and easy to understand.

In ANT, we have to provide project structure information into the build file, as well as provide the order for the information about what and when to do what through the code. You can execute ANT from the command line or integrate it into your IDE.

Gradle

Gradle is an advanced – general purpose, build management automation tool based on Groovy and Kotlin. It supports the automatic download of libraries or other dependencies. It uses a **Domain Specific Language** (**DSL**) instead of the traditional XML form to declare project configuration. It utilizes **Directed Acyclic Graph** (**DAG**) to determine the order of the task in which it will run.

Test automation

Test automation means that the test tool will execute the test case automatically and produce the test results. It saves the human effort of manual testing and has less scope for errors in the testing. It minimizes redundant manual work. Once the test script is ready, it can be run any number of times to test the same application.

In DevOps, testing focuses on automated tests within the build pipeline to ensure that the time you have a deployable build, you are confident that it is ready to be deployed.

You need to do the automated testing of the deployed code before it goes into the process of Continuous Delivery. Some popular tools are Selenium, JUnit, and Cucumber.

Selenium

Selenium is a portable software testing framework to perform web application testing, executed on multiple operating systems and browsers. It provides a record and playback feature to write tests without learning the test script language. It is compatible with popular programming languages such as Java, C#, Python, PHP, Perl, PHP, Ruby, and Automation Testing Framework. You can create scripts for the reproduction of bugs and regression testing.

JUnit

JUnit is an open source unit testing framework for the Java programming language. It is useful for the Java developer to write and run repeatable tests. It is important for **Test-Driven Development** (**TDD**). It promotes ideas such as *first testing then coding* which means set up the test data for the code, test it first, and then implement it. It allows you to write codes faster to increase product quality.

Cucumber

Cucumber is an open source tool to test other software. It is designed over the concept of **behavior-driven development** (**BDD**) and it runs automated acceptance tests. By running this acceptance test, it describes the behavior of the application. It has been written in the Ruby programming language; it supports other programming languages as well, as it has cross-platform OS support.

Continuous Integration

We have already learnt about CI, so we will discuss the tools used in CI, namely Jenkins, Bamboo, and Hudson.

Jenkins

Jenkins is an open source DevOps tool written in Java and run with different OS Systems. It is used to monitor the execution of repeated tasks. It provides CI and Continuous Delivery and is a server-based system, easily set up, and configured. It supports different SCM tools such as CVS, Git, Subversion, and Clearcase. It can also execute Apache Maven and Apache Ant, as per project needs. It helps to find the issue quickly and integrate project changes easily. It supports many plugins to build and test projects.

Bamboo

Bamboo is a CI and Continuous Delivery tool from Atlassian. It is used to do an automated build, test, and release. Bamboo supports builds in different languages using build tools and command line tools.

In Bamboo, if any events happen you will receive customized build notifications in email, messages, or pop-up windows in IDEs.

Hudson

Hudson is a tool for CI. It is written in the Java language and runs on the servlet container. It helps to build, test software projects, and monitor jobs continuously. It supports SCM tools including Git, SVN, CVS, and build tools including ANT, Maven, Gradle, as well as unit testing framework, and shell/batch scripts.

Configuration Management

Configuration Management is a way to improve the complete development, deployment, and operations pipeline. It is the process of standardizing configurations. It enforces these configuration states to infrastructure in an automated manner. Configuration Management is made up of an source code repository, an artifact repository and a configuration management database, which are used during the development and operation phase. Popular tools for configuration management are Puppet, Chef, and Ansible.

Puppet

Puppet is a Configuration Management Tool which runs on many Unix-like systems and Windows systems. A system configuration can be described by its own declarative language or a Ruby **Domain-Specific Language** (**DSL**). This information is stored in Puppet Manifests. Puppet follows the client server architecture, as well as being used as a stand-alone application. Puppet is model-driven, which requires limited programming knowledge. It is flexible and helps to increase productivity and manageability.

Chef

Chef is a Configuration Management Tool written in Ruby and Erlang to achieve speed, scale, and consistency. System configuration recipes can be written in pure-ruby or DSL. Chef is used to streamline the tasks for configuring and managing servers and can integrate with cloud-based platforms, such as **Amazon Web Services** (**AWS**), Google Cloud Platform, Microsoft Azure, and so on. It utilizes the **Master–Agent** model and the installation requires a workstation to control the master.

Ansible

Ansible is an open source platform for configuration management. It was written in Python and PowerShell. It will help to automate the entire application life cycle, so it will be easier for a team to speed up productivity and scale automation. Apart from other tools, Ansible uses an agent-less architecture. In this architecture, nodes are not installed and run background daemons to connect with controlling machine. It will reduce the overhead on the network. It uses the descriptive and easy language, YAML, to express description of system.

Continuous Monitoring

Continuous Monitoring will intelligently manage, analyze, and monitor hybrid applications, cloud on-premises, and network infrastructures. It is implemented with **Application Performance Management** (**APM**) to improve the stability of applications and monitor user experience. Monitoring and alerts at the application and operational level can give the ability to measure anything, so it spots patterns/trends and provides real business insight.

Some popular tools for Continuous Monitoring are Nagios, Ganglia, and Sensu.

Nagios

Nagios is an open source, computer software tool for monitoring and alerting. It is used to monitor and alert systems metrics, network services, applications, and infrastructure. It alerts the users when something goes wrong in the application and again alerts when the problem has been resolved. It provides remote monitoring.

Ganglia

Ganglia is an open source and highly-scalable distributed cluster monitoring tool for high-performance systems that supports clusters and grids. It provides monitoring of disks, CPU usage, memory, and other aspects for cluster health, and makes this information available offline. It also allows you to remotely and historically view statistics for all the monitored machines. You can integrate open source solutions, such as Logstash and Hadoop.

Sensu

Sensu is a free, open source, message-oriented architecture, and monitoring system which handles a cloud environment. It allows monitoring of applications, servers, and services. It is able to re-use existing Nagios plug-ins. You can write plug-ins and think notifications (handlers) for any languages.

Virtual Infrastructure

Virtual Infrastructures are infrastructures on the cloud or **Platform as a Service** (**PaaS**) provided by cloud vendors, such as Amazon Web Service and Microsoft Azure. With the help of Configuration Management Tools, you can create new machines programmatically using APIs provided by these infrastructures.

You can also use private clouds like vCloud provided by VMWare. This will allow you to run a private virtual cloud on top of the hardware in a data center.

You can combine virtual infrastructure with an automation tool that will give you the ability to configure servers automatically, build the environment, and run the tests.

Let's explore briefly how you can do the CI/CD in the AWS environment.

CI/CD on AWS

AWS provides Developer tools to work with CI/CD.

It has CodeCommit and CodeBuild to achieve CI in the AWS environment. We will discuss these tools in `Chapter 4`, *CI/CD in AWS Part 1 – CodeCommit, CodeBuild,* and *Testing*.

It also provides CodeDeploy and CodePipeline to achieve CI and Continuous Deployment in the AWS environment. You can develop, build, and deploy applications quickly using AWS CodeStar templates. We will discuss these tools in `Chapter 5`, *CI/CD in AWS Part 2 – CodeDeploy, CodePipeline, and CodeStar*.

Summary

So far, we have completed the different phases of release processes into the CI/CD workflow. It includes four major parts of CI/CD; source, build, test and production.

In the next chapter, we will discuss more about how we can achieve CI and CD on the AWS platform using Developer tools, such as CodeCommit and CodeBuild.

4
CI/CD in AWS Part 1 – CodeCommit, CodeBuild, and Testing

AWS with DevOps provides services to build software products reliably, rapidly, and delivers them using a set of flexible services. It simplifies the deploying of application code, automates the release process and provision, manages the infrastructure and monitoring of applications, and infrastructure performance. It also helps to automate manual tasks and manage complex environments, at any scale.

To achieve DevOps on the cloud, AWS provides Developer tools to securely store and version the source code and automatically build, test, and deploy applications.

AWS Developer tools provide services such as CodeCommit, CodeBuild, CodeDeploy, CodePipeline, CodeStar, and AWS X-Ray.

In this chapter, we will understand CodeCommit and CodeBuild services which are useful to commit the code into private Git repositories then build the code and test it.

At the end of the chapter, you will be aware of the AWS Developer tools, such as CodeCommit and CodeBuild.

In this chapter, we will cover the following topics:

- A brief overview of AWS for DevOps
- AWS CodeCommit – maintaining code repository
- AWS CodeBuild – automating the build

Let's explore each topic.

A brief overview of AWS for DevOps

You will get more benefits when you use AWS for DevOps.

The following are a few points:

- **Fast start**: AWS provides ready-to-use services without any setup or software installation. You must have an AWS account to use this service.
- **Fully managed**: It provides fully managed services that help us to focus more on the core products and worry less about the setup of the environment, installation, and infrastructure.
- **Highly scalable**: You can manage to scale from a single instance to multiple instances from AWS service. It will simplify your resources by configuring, provisioning and scaling with this services.
- **Programmable**: You can use all the services from APIs, SDKs, and the AWS command-line interface. You can also use AWS CloudFormation templates to model and provision your entire AWS infrastructure and AWS resources.
- **Automation**: AWS services helps to automate the build, quickly and more efficiently. Development and test workflows, deployments and container and configuration management can be automated using a manual task or process.
- **Secure**: You can use AWS **Identity and Access Management** (**IAM**) to secure the environment by setting up the user permissions, roles and policies. It gives granular control over the environment and gives access to the authorized person only.
- **Large ecosystem of partners**: A large ecosystems of partners is supported by AWS to integrate and extend AWS services. You can use your preferred open source or third-party tools to build a system on AWS.
- **Pay-As-You-Go**: AWS services have a **What You Pay is What You Use** (**WYPWYU**) kind of concept. You don't have to pay any upfront amount, suffer termination penalties, or commit to long-term contracts. You can purchase the service when you plan to use it and when you need it.

The following is a list of AWS Tools which provide different solutions for CI/CD:

AWS Tool Name	Solutions	Description
AWS CodeCommit	Version Control	It is used to store source code securely on private Git repositories
AWS CodeBuild	CI/CD	It is used to build and test code with continuous scaling
AWS CodeDeploy	CI/CD	Your code will deploy automatically
AWS CodePipeline	CI/CD	This is a Continuous Integration/Continuous Delivery Service from AWS
AWS CodeStar	CI/CD	Quickly develop, build, and deploy applications using templates
AWS X-Ray	Monitoring and Logging	Used to debug and analyze the applications
AWS Command Line Interface		You can manage your AWS resources by using this tool
AWS Cloud9 (New)		You can use Cloud IDE on your browser to write the code, run it and debug if necessary

Now, in this chapter we will dig more into the two tools: AWS CodeCommit and AWS CodeBuild.

AWS CodeCommit – maintaining code repository

AWS CodeCommit is a highly scalable and fully managed source control service under Developer tools in AWS. It is highly secure and helps companies to store source code on private GitHub repositories. It eliminates worry about scaling the infrastructure or your source code system.

AWS CodeCommit has the following benefits:

- **Fully managed**: It eliminates the need to host, maintain, back up, and scale own source control servers. It scales automatically, as per the needs for your project.
- **High availability**: It provides highly scalable, durable, and redundant architecture which is designed to keep your repositories accessible and available.
- **Store anything**: There are no size limits for the repository and it allows you to store any type of files. You can store different versions of application assets such as libraries and images with your code.
- **Secure**: It is fully integrated with AWS **Identity and Access Management (IAM)** to allow you to assign user-specific permission to the repositories.
- **Faster development life cycle**: AWS CodeCommit, keeps all the environments such as build, staging, and production close to the repositories. It will incrementally transfer the changes and not the whole application, so the speed and frequency of the application development life cycle increases drastically.
- **Existing tools usage**: With CodeCommit, you can use your preferred development environment plug-ins, graphical clients, existing Git tools, and Continuous Integration/Continuous Delivery system. All the Git commands are also supported by AWS CodeCommit.

AWS CodeCommit stores data in Amazon S3 and Amazon DynamoDB to provide high availability, scalability, and durability to your repositories. You can simply create a repository to store the code without any software to install, configure, and operate, or hardware provision to scale.

The following are some of the key features of AWS CodeCommit:

- **Collaboration**: It is designed for collaborative software development that allows you to commit, branch, and merge code to maintain control over a team's projects. It supports pull requests that provide a mechanism to request code reviews and discuss code with collaborators. You can create a new repository from AWS CLI, AWS SDKs, or AWS Management Console and start working with it using Git.
- **Encryption**: It is used to transfer files to and from through HTTPS and SSH. Your repositories are automatically encrypted at rest, as well as in transit through the AWS **Key Management Service (KMS)** using customer-specific keys.

- **Access control**: It uses AWS IAM to control and monitor who can access data and how, when, and where they can access it.
- **Highly available and durable**: It stores repositories in Amazon S3 and Amazon DynamoDB. Your data is highly available, durable, and stored across multiple facilities.
- **Unlimited repositories**: It allows you to create as many repositories as you need without any size limits. You can store and version any files with your code.
- **Easy access and integration**: You can manage your repositories from AWS CLIs, AWS SDKs, and AWS Management Console. You can use all Git commands and any Git or Git graphical tools to interact with your repository source files. It can easily integrate with development environment plug-ins or the Continuous Integration/Continuous Delivery system.
- **Notifications and custom scripts**: It uses the repository triggers to send notifications and creates HTTP webhooks with Amazon's **Simple Notification Service** (**SNS**) or invokes AWS Lambda functions to the repository events you choose.

Prerequisites of AWS CodeCommit

AWS CodeCommit provides the facility to add/update/delete any files to repository using AWS Management Console. But if you want to work across different branches or with multiple files than you can set up your machine to work with repositories. Configuring HTTPS Git Credentials is the simplest way to set up AWS CodeCommit. This HTTPS method for authentication will:

- Use a static username/password
- Work well with AWS CodeCommit-supported operating systems
- Be compatible with development tools or integrated development environments which Git credentials support

It means you can set up the connection with your repository by *using Git credentials* or *using other methods*. You need to go through the following options carefully and decide the best suitable method for your business requirements.

AWS CodeCommit setup using Git credentials

You can generate a static user name and password with HTTPS connections and Git credentials in IAM. These generated credentials can be used with Git, third-party development tools, and IDEs that supports the Git username and password authentication mechanism. This is the easiest as well as the simplest way to connect with AWS CodeCommit:

- **Setup Git credentials for HTTPS users**: To set up connections between the local computer and AWS CodeCommit repositories. You can follow this URL for more information: `https://docs.aws.amazon.com/codecommit/latest/userguide/setting-up-gc.html`.
- **Connections from IDE or Development tools using Git credentials**: To set up connections between Eclipse IDE and AWS CodeCommit repositories using Git credentials. Currently, AWS Cloud9, Eclipse, Visual Studio, IntelliJ, Xcode, and many other IDEs support Git credentials to integrate. You can follow this URL for more information: `https://docs.aws.amazon.com/codecommit/latest/userguide/setting-up-ide.html`.

AWS CodeCommit setup using other methods

You can use other methods due to operational reason if you do not want to use Git credentials. In this case, you can use the SSH protocol to connect to the AWS CodeCommit repository. With this SSH connection, you will create public and private key files on the local machine that will be used for SSH authentication from Git and AWS CodeCommit. You will store private key on your local machine and associate your public key with an IAM user.

For AWS CodeCommit, Git credentials might be easier and simpler than SSH as SSH requires you to create and manage public and private key files manually.

SSH Connection is varied depending on your local computer's operating system. You can distinguish SSH connections in the following ways:

- **AWS CLI not using by SSH users**: If you have public and private keys and you are aware of an SSH connection on your local computer. You can follow this URL for more information : `https://docs.aws.amazon.com/codecommit/latest/userguide/setting-up-without-cli.html`.
- **SSH connections on Unix, Linux, or MacOS**: Create a public-private key pair and set up connections on Unix, Linux, or MacOS operating systems. You can follow this URL for more information: `https://docs.aws.amazon.com/codecommit/latest/userguide/setting-up-ssh-unixes.html`.
- **SSH connections to AWS CodeCommit repositories on Windows**: To create a public-private key pair and set up connections on Microsoft Windows operating systems. You can follow this URL for more information: `https://docs.aws.amazon.com/codecommit/latest/userguide/setting-up-ssh-windows.html`.

If you don't want to configure IAM users and you want to set up the AWS CodeCommit repository then you can use the credential helper included in the AWS CLI which is the only method that supports federated access and temporary credentials. AWS CodeCommit might have some connectivity issues with the credential helper included with AWS CLI because some operating system, and Git version, have their own credential helpers.

So for easier usage you can configure GIT credential with HTTPS and create IAM users instead of using the credential helper.

There are different ways to setup AWS CLI's credential helper for Linux, macOS, Unix, and Windows.

Getting started with AWS CodeCommit

As you have already learnt about how to create a repository in AWS CodeCommit in previous steps, under the *Set up Git credentials for HTTPS users* topic. You will see how you can push the changes, browse the files which you pushed, and view the changes into files.

Once we log in to the AWS Console with valid credentials and navigate to the AWS CodeCommit, you will see list of the available repositories. You choose any repository, then it will show you the following screen:

In the AWS CodeCommit Console, the navigation pane contains the following features:

- **Code**: Read the contents or review the file in the repository.

  You can browse the content, review the files, and read the content of the file in the repository. Currently it is displaying the default branch content. You can change to a different branch by selecting it (here it is; **Branch: DevBranch**):

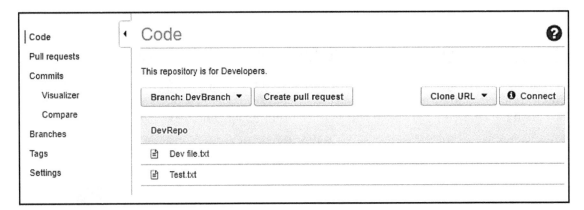

You can choose the file from the list to see its contents. Here, I have selected the `Test.txt` file:

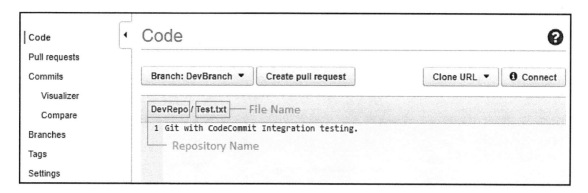

- **Pull requests**: This proposes a change on a repository or creates a pull request. Review the content and comments:

Once this request is created, you can see the list of all the Pull requests. You can also view **All open requests**, **All closed requests**, and all the open and closed requests you created:

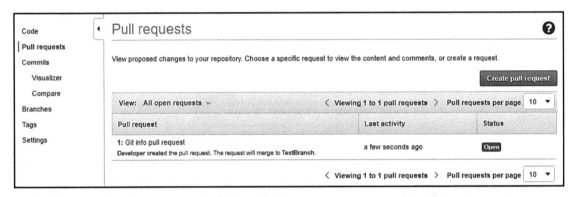

- **Commits**: Compare changes, review the history of commits, and browse code at specific commits.

You can identify who and when made the changes to the repository, by browsing the commit history of the repository.

You can view the history of commits in reverse chronological order. You can review the commit history by branch or by tag and get details such as author, date, and others.

As shown in the following screenshot, you can view the differences between a commit and its parent. You can also select how the changes should display, including show/hide whitespace changes, and whether to view the changes inline (**Unified view**) or side by side (**Split view**):

When you click on the **commit message**, you can see the changes on that file and add, review, or reply the comments:

- **Visualizer**: Review the information for the specific commit.

It will show you the commit graph with a commit message. This commit message is limited to displaying 80 characters.

You can also review the detailed information such as Commit ID and Parent ID about a particular commit. It provides links to navigate to view the differences between this commit and its parent:

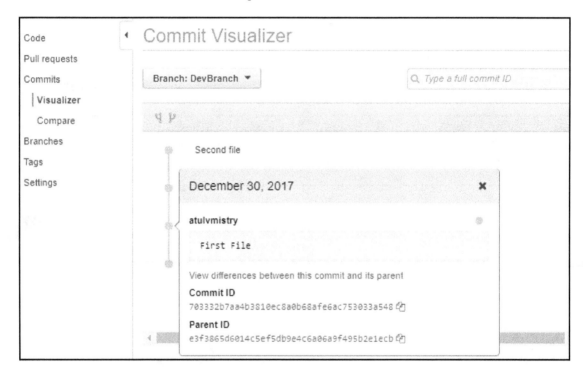

- **Compare**: See the difference between two commits.

  In Compare, you can view the differences between any two commits, including branches, tags, and commit IDs.

- **Branches**: Create and delete branch. View list of branch. Change default branch.

  You can create a new branch by selecting a **Create branch** link. You can select the **Create Pull request** which will redirect you to the **Pull requests** screen:

- **Tags**: View list of tags in a repository.

  It will show you the list of tags in your repository. It includes dates and messages of the latest commit, referenced by tag.

- **Settings**: Manage the settings of the repository.

  You can manage the settings for a current repository. It includes **Repository name**, its **Repository description**, **Default branch** name, and **Notification**, and creates triggers for repository events. If the repository is not required for cloning and sharing, then you can delete the repository by selecting the **Delete repository** button:

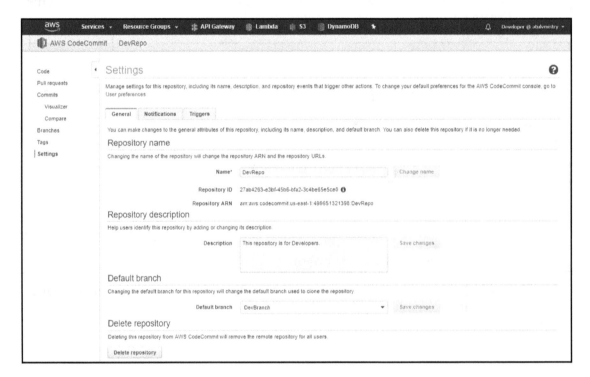

It will open the dialog box and you have to enter the name of the repository which you want to delete:

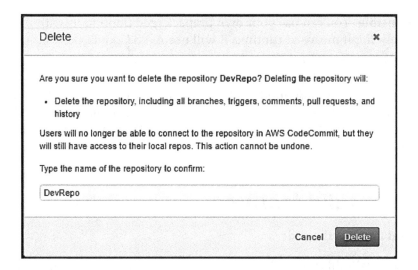

This is what we have learnt in AWS CodeCommit. In the next topic, we will learn about AWS CodeBuild.

AWS CodeBuild – automating the build

AWS CodeBuild is a fully managed AWS service that compiles source code, runs test cases, and produces ready-to-deploy software packages. It scales continuously and automatically to process multiple builds concurrently so you now need to provision, manage, and scale your own build servers.

AWS CodeBuild benefits

- **Fully managed service for build**: It eliminates the need to set up, update, patch, and manage build servers and software. There is no need to install, update, or manage any software.
- **Scale automatically**: It continuously scales to meet the requirements of the build volume. It immediately processes the build whenever you submit. It can run the separate build concurrently, so it means there are no build lefts in a queue.
- **Continuous Integration and Delivery enabled**: AWS CodeBuild is part of the AWS Code Service to create complete and automated software release workflows for CI/CD. You can integrate AWS CodeBuild into your existing CI/CD workflow.

- **Extensible**: You can use your own prepackaged build tools with AWS CodeBuild; it means at runtime, it will use AWS CodeBuild.
- **Pay as You Go**: You will pay for the number of minutes it takes to complete the build. It will not charge you when it is idle.
- **Secure**: In AWS CodeBuild, build artifacts are encrypted with customer-specific keys which are managed by the AWS **Key Management System** (**KMS**). It is also integrated with AWS IAM to assign user-specific granular permission to build projects.

AWS CodeBuild features

- **Build and test the code**:

  AWS CodeBuild runs builds in pre-configured build environments which contain the programming language, operating system, and build tools to complete the task. You specify your source code's location and select the settings for the build. AWS CodeBuild will build your code and store the artifacts in an Amazon S3 bucket, or upload to an artifact repository.

  AWS CodeBuild provides pre-configured build environments for Java, Node.js, Python, Go, Ruby, Android, and Docker.

  You can package the runtime and tools for your own build environment into a Docker image and upload to the public Docker Hub repository or Amazon EC2 **Container Registry** (**Amazon ECR**).

  You can specify the location of your Docker image when you create a new build project, and CodeBuild will pull the image to use it as the build project configuration.

- **Configuration setting**:

  You can specify commands such as run unit test, package the code, and install build to package, to be performed by AWS CodeBuild. YAML is a build-specific file that includes the command to be run at each phase of the build. CodeBuild helps you get started quickly with sample build specification files for some of the common scenarios.

You can select the best-suited compute type for your development needs. You might choose a higher CPU and memory compute for faster builds, or the minimum level of CPU and memory to complete the build.

AWS CodeBuild initiates builds in many ways. It can initiate builds after connecting with AWS CodeCommit, Amazon S3, or GitHub. It can also connect with AWS CodePipeline, which will automatically initiate a build whenever any commit happens.

- **Continuous Integration and Continuous Delivery Workflows**:

  AWS CodeBuild is part of the AWS Code Service to help CI/CD. It provides on-demand compute and a **What You Pay is What You Use (WYPWYU)** model to build and integrate your code more frequently and to help you to find and fix bugs at the development stage. It can easily integrate with your existing workflow using build commands, source integrations, or Jenkins integrations. It will easily plug with AWS CodePipeline to automate the build and test the code whenever new commits happen in the repository.

- **Monitoring**:

  You can view detailed build details from AWS Management Console, SDKs, AWS CLI, and APIs. AWS CodeBuild will show you build information such as Build ARN, Build project, Repository, start and end time, Status, and many more. CodeBuild streams build logs to Amazon CloudWatch log.

From AWS CodeBuild, you can create the build project using:

- AWS Management Console
- AWS CLI
- AWS SDKs

Let's explore these options starting with AWS Console.

Creating AWS CodeBuild project using AWS Management Console

Please perform the following steps to create the AWS CodeBuild project using AWS Management Console:

1. Log in with your AWS credentials and navigate to AWS CodeBuild Console.
2. If you see a welcome page, it means that there are no available Build projects. In that scenario, select **Get started**. Otherwise, it will redirect you to the AWS CodeBuild Console which is available with the projects along with repository information.

   Now, select **Build projects** from the left-side navigation pane, and then select **Create project**:

3. On the next screen you will see the **Configure your project** page. Specify your build **Project Name** here and make sure that it is unique. You can add description by clicking on the + sign which is not a mandatory field. You can add any project-related description over here. You will see different kinds of **Source provider** under **Source: What to build** and can select an appropriate one for the project. Following is the different kind of available Source provider, available fields, and description information:

Source provider	Field and description
Amazon S3	**Bucket**: Bucket name where you have stored your project source code. **S3 Object Key**: This is the ZIP file name, which contains the source code. **Insecure SSL**: This is an optional field. It will ignore SSL warning when it is enabled while connected to the project.
AWS CodeCommit	**Repository**: You can select the source code repository from the dropdown. **Git clone depth**: This is an optional field. Select the shallow clone with the number of commits or the full clone of your repository. **Build Badge**: This is an optional field. You will enable it, then your project's build status will be embeddable and visible.
Bitbucket	**Repository**: Click on the **Connect to Bitbucket** and it will redirect to the Bibucket website. After completing the configuration it will redirect to the AWS CodeBuild Console with the repository names. Select the appropriate repository for this project. **Git clone depth and Build Badge**: This information is the same as mentioned in the previous row.
GitHub	**Repository**: Click on the **Connect to GitHub** and it will redirect to the GitHub website. After completing the configuration it will be redirect to the AWS CodeBuild Console with the repository names. Select the appropriate repository for this project. **Git clone depth and Build Badge**: This information is the same as mentioned in the previous column.

You can select the source provider as per the availability of your code from the preceding options:

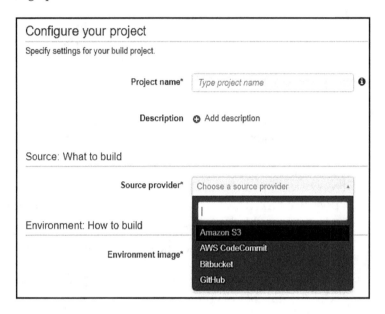

4. Now you can see the following two options for **Environment image** under **Environment: How to build**:

Use an image managed by AWS CodeBuild	You have to choose the appropriate Operating System which is managed by AWS CodeBuild from the drop down.
Specify a Docker image	It will provide you with two drop-down boxes: • **Environment Type**: To select the environment • **Custom Image Type**: Two options are **Amazon ECR** or **Other** In **Custom Image Type**, if you have selected **Other**, then you have to provide the **Custom image ID information** such as `<docker repository>/<docker image name>:<tag>`. In **Custom Image Type**, if you have selected **Amazon ECR**, then it will provide you with the drop down to select the **Amazon ECR Repository**.

5. For the **Build Specification**, you have two options to select:
- If your source code contains the build specification file then you can select **Use the buildspec.yml in the source code root directory**
- You can **Insert build commands** and it will execute these commands in the build phase:

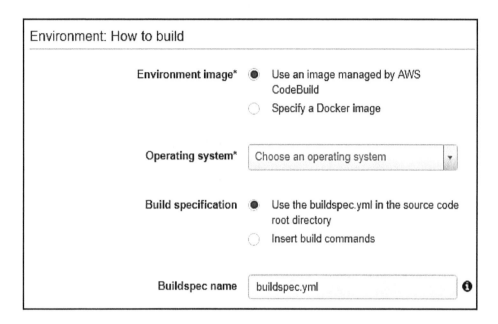

6. Select **Type** from the drop down, under **Artifacts: Where to put the artifacts from the build project** section. It provides you with the following options:

Amazon S3	If you leave **Name** blank then it will use the project name for the build output ZIP or folder. In **Path**, you can mention the **Artifacts Path**. In **Namespace type**, you can select the **Build ID** or **None**. Type the name of the output bucket into **Bucket name**. This is a mandatory field.
No artifacts	You can select this option when you don't want to create any build artifacts. It is useful to run build tests or to push the Docker image into the Amazon ECR Repository.

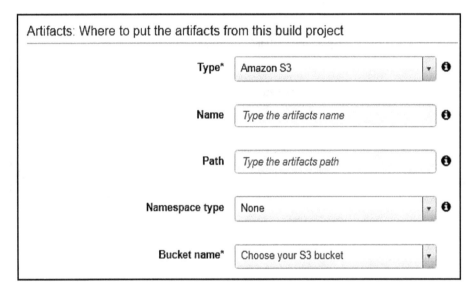

7. You can do following under **Cache**:

Amazon S3	You can use this option to store the cache. You can select the **Bucket** name from the drop down. You can add information for the **Path prefix** that is similar to directory name, and it is an optional field.
No cache	If you don't want to use cache.

Cache will save considerable build time as it will store reusable pieces of the build environment and can be used across builds:

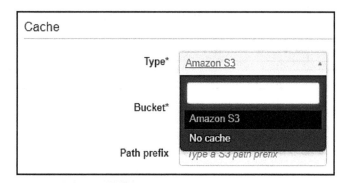

Under the **Service role** section, there are two options:

Create a service role in your account	Create a new service role if you don't have. Enter a value for **Role name** to create service role.
Choose an existing service role from your account	You can select an existing **Role name** from the dropdown.

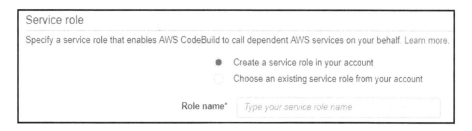

By default, this service role works with build projects only. When you use the console to associate this role name with another project, the role name is updated to work with the other build project. It can work with up to 10 build projects.

8. You can select **VPC** under the **VPC** section. It will provide you with two options:

No VPC	You are not using VPC.	
VPC ID	If you are using the VPC than select the following information from the dropdown:	
	Subnets	AWS CodeBuild will use these subnets to set up the VPC. You can select multiple subnets for high availability from different Availability Zones.
	Security Groups	AWS CodeBuild will use these **Security Groups** to work with the VPC. Make sure that outbound connections are allowed by selected **Security Groups**.

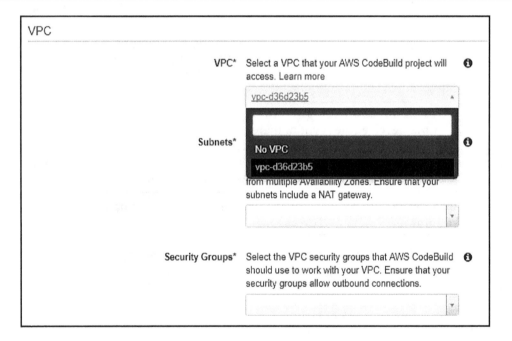

9. Now expand **Show advanced settings** and you can configure the following settings. The following fields are optional:

Timeout	You can specify between 5–480 minutes and it will stop after that if the build is not complete.
Encryption key	AWS is managing the **Customer Master Key** (**CMK**) for Amazon S3. It will help Amazon S3 to encrypt the output artifacts, so in this case you can leave it blank. But if you want to use the customer-managed CMK than you can provide the ARN. It will help the customer-managed CMK to encrypt the output artifacts.
Artifacts packaging	You can select ZIP if you selected **Amazon S3** for the **Artifacts type** earlier. It will create a ZIP file with build output. Else you can select **None**.
Compute type	Select the best suitable option for your application.
Environment variables	You can add environment variables by adding the name, value, and type. You can use **Add row** to add another environment variable. You can create a parameter for the type.
Tags	You can type the name and its value of tags to manage the configuration service and its cost. You can select **Add row** to add a new tag.

10. Choose **Continue**:

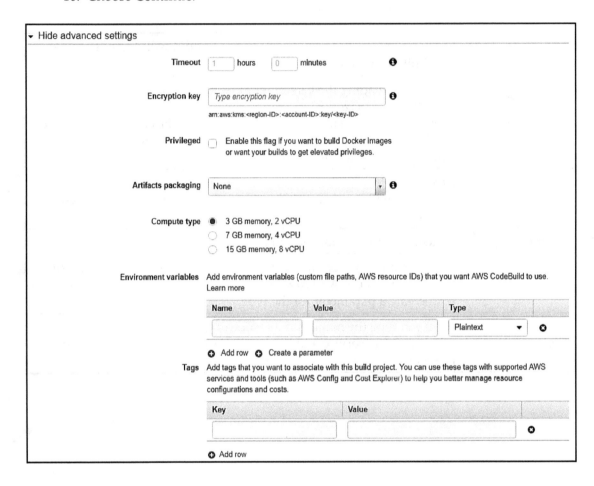

11. On the **Review** page, do one of the following:
      - Select **Save and build** to run the build.

    It will redirect you to the **Start new build** page where you can select
    the **Branch** name. It will display the **Source version** automatically. You can
    update the output Artifacts information under **Show advanced options**. The
    new environment variables will be added or updated under
    the **Environment variables** options:

You will see the build information once you click on the **Start build** button. It will display some information like Build, Build details and Phase details. Under the **Build details** section, you can click on the **Build artifacts** and navigate to the Amazon S3 bucket where your build is stored. You can see different phases of the build under **Phase details** such as **Name**, **Status**, **Duration**, and **Completed** time:

- Select **Save** to save the build project without running it.

  Navigate to the **Build** projects and select the projects you want to **Update**, **Delete**, or **Build history** by selecting **Actions**:

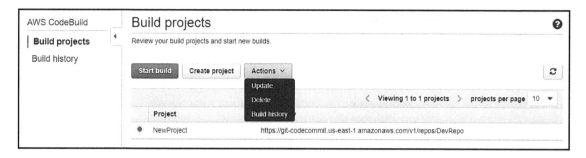

- Create the build project using AWS CLI.

I assume that you have already installed AWS CLI. If it is not installed, then you can download it from `https://docs.aws.amazon.com/cli/latest/userguide/installing.html` and install it. You can verify AWS CodeBuild services on AWS CLI by executing the `aws codebuild help` command.

You can create the project with AWS CodeBuild by executing this command on AWS CLI:

```
aws codebuild create-project --generate-cli-skeleton
```

It will display JSON-format data as the output. Save the output into the `create-project.json` file on the local machine and add values for the required field. It will look like the following file:

```
{
    "name": "TestCodeBuild",
    "description": "Description of TestCodeBuild ",
    "source": {
      "type": "CODECOMMIT",
      "location":
"https://git-codecommit.us-east-1.amazonaws.com/v1/repos/Your_Repo_
Name_Here",
      "buildspec": "",
      "auth": {
        "type": "OAUTH",
        "resource": ""
      }
    },
    "artifacts": {
      "type": "S3",
      "location": "S3-BUCKET-LOCATION",
      "path": "",
      "namespaceType": "NONE",
```

```
                    "name": "myprj1",
                    "packaging": "NONE"
                },
                    "environment": {
                        "type": "LINUX_CONTAINER",
                        "image": "aws/codebuild/java:openjdk-6",
                        "computeType": "BUILD_GENERAL1_SMALL",
                        "environmentVariables": [
                            {
                                "name": "your_environment_variable_name",
                        "value": "your_environment_variable_value"
                            }
                        ]
                },
                    "serviceRole": "arn:aws:iam::XXXXXXXXXXXX:role/service-
            role/codebuild-myprj-service-role",
                    "timeoutInMinutes": 10,
                    "encryptionKey": "arn:aws:kms:us-east-1:
            XXXXXXXXXXXX:alias/aws/s3",
                    "tags": [
                        {
                            "key": "tag-key",
                            "value": "tag-value"
                        }
                    ]
                }
```

The following table gives you information about different fields. In the table, **[R]** represents **Required** field and **[O]** represents **Optional** field:

name [R]	This is build project name. It must be unique.
description [O]	This is the description of the build project.
source-type [R]	Source code repository type. It has the following valid values: Amazon **S3/ CODECOMMIT/ BITBUCKET/ GITHUB**
source-location	It contains HTTPS URL. This URL contains the source code and build specification file for AWS CodeCommit, GitHub, and BitBucket. For Amazon S3, it contains the bucket name.
buildspec [O]	If the value is not provided or is empty then the source code must contain the `buildspec.yml` file in its root directory. If the value is provided, then it will be an inline build spec definition file or it has alternate build spec file path relative to the value of the built-in environment variable (CODEBUILD_SRC_DIR).

Auth	If you have selected GITHUB as source-type then specify OAUTH as value.
This artifacts object has the following output artifact settings:	
artifacts-type [R]	It is output artifact. CODEPIPELINE, NO_ARTIFACTS, and S3 are valid values.
artifacts-location [R]	If artifacts-type is set to S3 then specify output bucket name.
Path [O]	If artifacts-type is set to S3 then path inside artifacts-location.
namespaceType [O]	If artifacts-type is set to S3 then it has BUILD_ID and NONE as valid values.
artifacts-name [R]	If artifacts-type is set to S3 then it is name of build output ZIP file or folder.
Packaging [O]	If artifacts-type is set to S3 then ZIP and NONE are valid values. If ZIP is mentioned then it will create build output in ZIP file. If NONE is mentioned then it will contain the build output.
This environment object contains information about the project's build environment settings. It includes:	
environment-type[R]	Build environment type with valid value as LINUX_CONTAINER.
image [R]	Build environment is using the Docker image name. For example, AWS CodeBuild uses aws/codebuild/java:openjdk-6 for Java version 6.0.
computeType [R]	Build environment uses a different category based on the number of CPU cores and memory which includes BUILD_GENERAL1_LARGE, BUILD_GENERAL1_MEDIUM, and BUILD_GENERAL1_SMALL.
You can specify environment variables with this optional environmentVariable array. It includes:	
environmentVariable-name [O]	This is the name of the environmentVariables.
environmentVariable-value [O]	This is the value of the environmentVariables.
serviceRole [R]	This is the ARN of the service role used to interact with the service from AWS CodeBuild on behalf of the IAM user.
timeoutInMinutes[O]	You can specify 5 to 480 min. It the build is not completed than it will stop after the mentioned minutes.

encryptionKey [O]	Leave it blank if you want to use the AWS-managed **customer master key** (**CMK**) for Amazon S3 to encrypt the build output artifacts or type the ARN of the CMK, if you want to use customer-managed CMK to encrypt the build output artifacts.
Tags [O]	You can type the name and its value of tags to manage the configuration service and its cost. A tag is expressed by an array that contains a key- value pair.

After adding the value into the JSON file, execute the following command on AWS CLI:

```
aws codebuild create-project --cli-input-json
file://D:\AWS_CodeBuild\create-project.json
```

Once it executes the command successfully, you will see the following JSON response on AWS CLI:

```
{
    "project": {
        "name": "TestCodeBuild",
        "serviceRole": "arn:aws:iam:: XXXXXXXXXXXX:role/service-
role/codebuild-myprj-service-role",
        "tags": [
            {
                "value": "tag-value",
                "key": "tag-key"
            }
        ],
        "artifacts": {
            "packaging": "NONE",
            "name": "myprj1",
    {
        "project": {
            "name": "TestCodeBuild",
            "serviceRole": "arn:aws:iam:: XXXXXXXXXXXX:role/service-
role/codebuild-myprj-service-role",
            "tags": [
                {
                    "value": "tag-value",
                    "key": "tag-key"
                }
            ],
            "artifacts": {
                "packaging": "NONE",
                "name": "myprj1",
                "namespaceType": "NONE",
                "location": "S3-BUCKET-NAME",
```

```
                   "path": "",
                   "type": "S3"
              },
              "lastModified": 1514801454.38,
              "timeoutInMinutes": 10,
              "created": 1514801454.38,
              "environment": {
                   "computeType": "BUILD_GENERAL1_SMALL",
                   "image": "aws/codebuild/java:openjdk-6",
                   "type": "LINUX_CONTAINER",
                   "environmentVariables": [
                        {
                             "name": "your_environment_variable_name",
                             "value": "your_environment_variable_value"
                        }
                   ]
              },
              "source": {
                   "buildspec": "",
                   "type": "CODECOMMIT",
                   "location":
"https://git-codecommit.us-east-1.amazonaws.com/v1/repos/Repo-Name",
                   "auth": {
                        "resource": "",
                        "type": "OAUTH"
                   }
              },
              "encryptionKey": "arn:aws:kms:us-east-1:
XXXXXXXXXXXX:alias/aws/s3",
              "arn": "arn:aws:codebuild:us-east-1:
XXXXXXXXXXXX:project/TestCodeBuild",
              "description": "Description of CodeBuild"
         }
    }
```

You can verify the created build project on the AWS CodeBuild Console.

List of build project names

The following command will display the list of build project names:

```
aws codebuild list-projects --sort-by sort_by --sort-order sort_order --
next-token next_token
```

You need to change the placeholder:

- `sort_by`: It is a list of build project names. It has valid values:
    - `CREATED_TIME`: List of build project names based on the creation time of each build
    - `LAST_MODIFIED_TIME`: List of build project names based on the last modification time of each build
    - `NAME`: List of build project names based on the name of each build project
- `sort_order`: List of build project names. Valid values are `ASCENDING` and `DESCENDING`.
- `next_token`: If there are more than 100 items in the build project names list, then only the first 100 items are returned along with a unique string which is called `next_token`. For less than 100 items, it will not display `next_token`. For example, if you might run the following command:

```
aws codebuild list-projects --sort-by NAME --sort-order ASCENDING
```

You might get similar kind of output:

```
D:\AWS_CodeBuild>aws codebuild list-projects --sort-by NAME --sort-order ASCENDING
{
    "projects": [
        "NewProject",
        "TestCodeBuild"
    ]
}
```

Viewing the build project's details

The following command will display the build project's details:

```
aws codebuild batch-get-projects --names project_names
```

Before performing the preceding command you need to change the placeholder like:

- `project_names`: This is the required parameter. Specify the build project's name to view its details. A maximum of 100 build project names can be specified to view their details. You can separate those names with spaces.

For example, if you might run the following command:

```
aws codebuild batch-get-projects --names NewProject
```

You might get a similar kind of output. Ellipses (...) mean that the data has been omitted for brevity:

```
{
"projectsNotFound": [],
"projects": [
{
...
"name": "NewProject",
...
}
]
}
```

Updating the build project's details

To update the project on AWS CodeBuild, execute the following command on AWS CLI:

```
aws codebuild update-project --generate-cli-skeleton
```

It will display JSON-format data as output. Save the output into the update-project.json file on your local computer and update the values, as per the requirements mentioned in *Creating the build project using AWS CLI* section.

After adding the value into the JSON file, execute the following command on AWS CLI:

```
aws codebuild update-project --cli-input-json
file://D:\AWS_CodeBuild\update-project.json
```

Once it executes the command successfully you will see the JSON response mentioned in *Creating the build project using AWS CLI.*

Deleting the build project

The following command will delete the build project:

```
aws codebuild delete-projects --name project_names
```

Before performing the preceding command you need to change the placeholder like:

- `project_names`: This is the required parameter. Specify the build project's name that you want to delete. It will not display any message or error, if successful.

Summary

We have now finished looking at AWS CodeCommit and AWS CodeBuild, which are part of AWS Developer tools, to achieve version control and Continuous Integration and Continuous Deployment. I haven't covered the testing part here; it will be part of the next chapter, included with AWS CodePipeline.

In the next chapter, we will discuss more about AWS CodeDeploy, CodePipeline, and CodeStar to achieve **Continuous Integration (CI)** and **Continuous Deployment (CD)** on an AWS platform.

5
CI/CD in AWS Part 2 – CodeDeploy, CodePipeline, and CodeStar

In the previous chapter, we discussed AWS CodeCommit and CodeBuild. In this chapter, we will discuss other AWS code family tools such as AWS CodeDeploy, AWS CodePipeline, AWS CodeStar, and AWS X-Ray. AWS CodeDeploy is a fast, reliable, and consistent way to deploy the application.

AWS CodePipeline automates the deployment process to model and visualize the code for new updates and features. AWS CodeStar is used to develop, build, and deploy the application quickly on AWS from the AWS CodeStar console.

AWS X-Ray helps developers to easily debug and analyze the distributed applications.

In this chapter, we will cover the following topics:

- AWS CodeDeploy
- AWS CodePipeline
- AWS CodeStar
- AWS X-Ray

Let's explore each topic and see how they can be used to achieve CI/CD on AWS.

AWS CodeDeploy

The AWS CodeDeploy service will help to automate the deployment of a variety of different services that includes Amazon EC2 instances, AWS Lambda functions, and instances that are running on-premises. It scales from a single Lambda function to hundreds of thousands of EC2 instances. AWS CodeDeploy helps in the following ways to make deployment easier, as it:

- Releases new features quickly
- Avoids downtime for application deployment
- Handles complexity
- Eliminates manual operations

Now, we will find out more about the AWS CodeDeploy service with the following topics:

- AWS CodeDeploy benefits
- Compute platforms and deployment options for AWS CodeDeploy
- AWS CodeDeploy – a sample application deployment on a Windows Server

In the next section, we will discuss AWS CodeDeploy benefits.

AWS CodeDeploy benefits

The following are the benefits of AWS CodeDeploy. Let's understand each one of them very carefully:

- **Automatic deployment**: AWS CodeDeploy helps to deploy your code rapidly, reliably, and fully automatically. You can deploy your application consistently on different environments such as development, test, and production.
    - **Repeat deployments**: For a diverse group of instances, AWS CodeDeploy enables application deployment to be repeated easily, which means getting rid of manual deployment steps. It increases the reliability and speed of the delivery process. You can use AWS CodeDeploy to deploy applications by using a command-based install or using a file. You can also reuse existing code for the setup; your code for the setup can deploy consistently and test the updates on different environments for Lambda functions or Amazon EC2 instances.

- **On-premise deployments**: AWS CodeDeploy will allow you to automate deployments across different environments on any instances using it. It also includes your data center instances and it will enable you to deploy applications consistently using a single service.
- **Automatically scale**: AWS CodeDeploy allows you to integrate the deployment and scale activities that keep applications up to date in the production environment. AWS CodeDeploy can integrate with Auto Scaling for Amazon EC2 instances. With Auto Scaling, you can define the conditions to scale Amazon EC2 instance capacity. AWS CodeDeploy will notify you when new instances launch into the Auto Scaling group, and it will perform deployment operations on those instances, and then add them to the load balancer. For AWS Lambda, whenever response traffic is increased or decreased, it will integrate with AWS CodeDeploy to ensure that the latest code is deployed.

- **Minimize downtime**: It helps to avoid or minimize the downtime and maximize the availability of the application during deployment. It introduces the updates incrementally and helps to track the deployment's health, according to the configurable rules.
  - **Rolling and blue/green updates**: AWS CodeDeploy can perform the new revision upgrades without any downtime. It performs rolling updates for the Amazon EC2 instances group, where a few instances are taken offline for deployment at any time. It works progressively, so a few of the instances are available to serve the traffic continuously. You can use AWS Lambda functions to route the traffic gradually to a newer version from the older version. It also performs blue/green deployments where a new Amazon EC2 instance set is available with the new revision of code. With AWS CodeDeploy, you can reroute traffic to new instances from old production instances.
  - **Stop and rollback**: For any process, you can stop application deployment using AWS Management Console, AWS SDK, and AWS CLI, at any time. Once you have stopped the deployment, you can redeploy the same version later. Also, if you have rolled back the deployment, you can redeploy the previous version, later.

- **Deployment's health track**: The deployment's health track can work with rolling updates, so your applications will be highly available during the deployment phase. If bad updates are deployed, then your application will be down for an unspecified time. To keep applications highly available during the deployments, you need to track the health status of deployments. AWS CodeDeploy will monitor the deployment and it will stop if several available updates fail.

- **Control centrally**: You can use AWS Management Console or AWS CLI to launch the deployment and track its status. AWS CodeDeploy provides you with a detailed report. You can create push notifications from Amazon **Simple Notification Service** (**SNS**) to get live deployment updates.

  - **Control and monitoring**: AWS Management Console, SDKs, and AWS CLIs are used to launch, monitor, and control the deployments.

  - **Your deployment history**: AWS CodeDeploy tracks your deployment history and stores it. You can view the current deployed version by deployment groups, changed history, and past deployment's success rates. You can also view a deployment's success and failure from the history.

  - **Multiple groups for deployment**: You can deploy your application in multiple deployment groups. Deployment groups uses different configuration environments. Once it matches configuration with specific environments like staging or production environments. It will deploy the code to the staging environment and again deploy the same code after verification to the production environment.

- **Adopt easily**: AWS CodeDeploy works with any kind of application; it is platform, architecture, and language agnostic. A user will get the same experience while deploying to an Amazon EC2 instance or AWS Lambda. It can easily integrate with a continuous delivery tool chain or existing software release process. You can reuse your existing code for setup.

  - **Architecture and language agnostic**: AWS CodeDeploy uses a command-based or file-based install model to deploy the application. It uses a configuration file to map application files or AWS Lambda functions, known as an `AppSpec` file. This file is used to run tests, actions, and verification for each events in a life cycle.

- **Tool chain integration**: AWS CodeDeploy API can easily integrate application deployments with an existing delivery tool chain. AWS CodeStar, AWS CodePipeline, and other AWS services can provide built-in integration support with AWS CodeDeploy for CI/CD.

Compute platforms and deployment options for AWS CodeDeploy

AWS CodeDeploy supports the following compute platforms and deployment options to deploy the application.

Compute platforms

The compute platforms are as follows:

- **Amazon EC2/on-premises**: Amazon EC2 or an on-premises instance contains executable files, images, configurations files, and more
- **AWS Lambda**: AWS Lambda is used to deploy the updated or changed version of the function

Deployment options

The deployment options are as follows:

- **In-place deployment**: In this type of deployment:
    - The application in the deployment group for each instance is stopped
    - An updated application version is installed
    - A new application version is started and validated

 AWS Lambda cannot use this type of deployment.

- **Blue/green deployment**: This type of deployment is used for both the compute platforms. In this type of deployment, traffic is rerouted to a new set of instances from the old set of instances.

Now, let's deploy a sample application with AWS CodeDeploy to a Windows Server.

AWS CodeDeploy – sample application deployment on a Windows Server

In this sample application, you will use different AWS services such as IAM, Amazon EC2, Amazon S3, and AWS CodeDeploy. You will deploy a single page web application on a Windows Server using **Internet Information service (IIS)** as the web server on a single Amazon EC2 Windows instance. For that, you have to execute the following steps to deploy your applications successfully.

Step 1 – prerequisite configurations for AWS CodeDeploy

You need to complete the following prerequisite configurations before you start to use AWS CodeDeploy:

1. **Creating a custom AWS CodeDeploy policy for the IAM user**: You can attach the following IAM role to your existing user or new user to use AWS CodeDeploy. It will grant access for EC2/on-premises instances, Lambda functions, and other services:

```
{
  "Version": "2012-10-17",
  "Statement" : [
    {
      "Effect" : "Allow",
      "Action" : [
        "autoscaling:*",
        "codedeploy:*",
        "ec2:*",
        "lambda:*",
        "elasticloadbalancing:*",
        "iam:AddRoleToInstanceProfile",
        "iam:CreateInstanceProfile",
        "iam:CreateRole",
        "iam:DeleteInstanceProfile",
        "iam:DeleteRole",
        "iam:DeleteRolePolicy",
        "iam:GetInstanceProfile",
        "iam:GetRole",
```

```
                "iam:GetRolePolicy",
                "iam:ListInstanceProfilesForRole",
                "iam:ListRolePolicies",
                "iam:ListRoles",
                "iam:PassRole",
                "iam:PutRolePolicy",
                "iam:RemoveRoleFromInstanceProfile",
                "s3:*"
            ],
            "Resource" : "*"
        }
    ]
}
```

2. **Creating an IAM role for the Amazon EC2 instance**: You must create an instance profile to launch the Amazon EC2 instance, which is compatible with AWS CodeDeploy. It will give permission to access GitHub repositories or Amazon S3 buckets. You can create the policy from the following code and later create a role with this policy and attach it to your Amazon EC2 instance:

```
{
    "Version": "2012-10-17",
    "Statement": [
        {
            "Action": [
                "s3:Get*",
                "s3:List*"
            ],
            "Effect": "Allow",
            "Resource": "*"
        }
    ]
}
```

3. **Creating a service role for AWS CodeDeploy**: To access AWS resources, you have to create a service role in IAM and give permission for AWS resources. For AWS CodeDeploy, you have to provide permission to read the tags or group names for Auto Scaling that are associated with the EC2 instance. You can attach AWSCodeDeployRole, which is an AWS-supplied policy, to provide these permissions. You can use trust relationships to restrict the service role from accessing to some of the endpoints, such as with the following policy:

```
{
    "Version": "2012-10-17",
    "Statement": [
        {
```

```
                        "Sid": "",
                        "Effect": "Allow",
                        "Principal": {
                            "Service": [
                                "codedeploy.amazonaws.com"
                            ]
                        },
                        "Action": "sts:AssumeRole"
                    }
                ]
            }
```

Once you create this role, note down the value of the **Role ARN** field.

Step 2 – launch a Windows Server Amazon EC2 instance

You need to consider a few configuration settings when you create an instance of a Windows Server Amazon EC2. You have to select the proper IAM role for the EC2 instance that was created in *Step 1– prerequisite configurations for AWS CodeDeploy*:

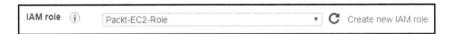

Add tags information when you create the EC2 instance. You will need this information when creating the deployment group for AWS CodeDeploy:

Under the **Configure Security Group** tab, select **HTTP** protocol with **RDP**:

After you have successfully launched the Amazon EC2 instance, please follow the instructions to connect it:

1. Select the Windows Server instance from the list, select **action** and click on **Connect**. Click on the **Get Password** button.
2. Now select **Choose File** and browse to the Amazon EC2 instance key pair associated with this instance and open it.
3. Click on the **Decrypt Password** button and save this.
4. You can connect the Windows instance using your favorite Remote Desktop Client or select the **Download Remote Desktop File** option and open it.
5. Choose **Connect**, if it prompts that the publisher of the remote connection can't be identified.
6. If you are using your Remote Desktop Client with `administrator` as a username, type the password that you have saved in previous steps.
7. Choose **Yes**, if it prompts that the identity of the remote computer cannot be verified.
8. Now, you will be able to see the Windows Server Amazon EC2 instance desktop.

 AWS CodeDeploy can't deploy on an Amazon EC2 instance if you stop or terminate it.

Step 3 – configure source content to deploy to the EC2 instance

For this sample application, you have to add a source file to the EC2 instance. You can create the following files under the `C:\Packt` directory or any other directory. If you use another directory name, use that name in the following steps:

1. **Sample web page**: Create a simple web page, `index.html`, under the `C:\Packt` directory and add the following contents:

```
<!DOCTYPE html PUBLIC "-//W3C//DTD HTML 4.01 Transitional//EN"
"http://www.w3.org/TR/html4/loose.dtd">
<html>
    <head>
            <title>Hi From Packt!!!</title>
    </head>
    <body>
```

```
            <h1>Hi From Packt!!!!!</h1>
        </body>
    </html>
```

2. **Script to run the application**: Now you need to create a script, `before-install.bat`, which AWS CodeDeploy uses to set up the web server on the Amazon EC2 instance. Add the following code into this `before-install.bat` and save it. This script will launch Windows PowerShell, which is a tool for task automation and configuration management and helps to install IIS:

```
REM Install Internet Information Server (IIS).
c:\Windows\Sysnative\WindowsPowerShell\v1.0\powershell.exe -Command
Import-Module -Name ServerManager
c:\Windows\Sysnative\WindowsPowerShell\v1.0\powershell.exe -Command
Install-WindowsFeature Web-Server
```

3. **Application specification file**: In addition to the preceding files, `index.html` and `before-install.bat`, you have to add an application specification file. It must be called `appspec.yml`.

   Now let's have a brief look at this file. This `appspec.yml` file uses a YAML-format and it describes:

   - The operating system where your instance is running, such as Linux or Windows
   - The source file location of the file you want to deploy and the destination file location where you want to deploy the file
   - The life cycle event hooks that specify which scripts are to be executed on the instance when deployed

   This `appspec.yml` contains the following sections:

4. **Header section (required)**: This contains `version` and `os` sections, where `version` is any arbitrary number to keep track of revisions, and `os` is the operating system instance for deployment and contains two options – `linux` or `windows`:

```
Version: 1.0
os: windows
```

5. **File section (required)**: This will execute during the install phase of life cycle events. It contains the source and destination of the files you want to install during the deployment:

```
files:
 - source: \index.html
   destination: c:\inetpub\wwwroot
```

6. **Permission section (optional)**: This section will assign permissions to files and directories after installation. It applies to Amazon Linux, Ubuntu, and RHEL instances; it does not include the Windows Server, so please don't include the following section in your `appsec.yml` file. It contains the following parameters:

- `object`: This is the required section, destination file, or directory where you want to set the permissions
- `pattern`: Specifies a pattern to set the permission for certain types of files
- `except`: Specifies exceptions for the preceding pattern
- `owner`: Owner of the object (if source settings is blank)
- `group`: Name of the group for the object (if source settings is blank)
- `mode`: Sets the permissions applied to the object (such as the `chmod` command)
- `acls`: Access control list entries applied to the object
- `context`: This applies to **Security-Enhanced Linux (SELinux)** enabled instances:
    - `user`: The SELinux user
    - `type`: The SELinux type name
    - `range`: The SELinux range specifier

            - `type`: Specifies if the object is a file or a directory:
                - `file`: Permissions will be applied only to an object's files
                - `directory`: Permissions will be applied recursively to all directories, and files that are within the object

You can set the permissions as in the following example and strictly it will not apply to this example as we are using Windows instances.:

```
permissions:
  - object: /var/www/html
    pattern: "*.html"
    except: [/var/www/html/index.html]
    owner: atul
    group: writers
    mode: 644
    acls:
      - u:vaibhav:rw
      - u:hiten:rw
      - m::rw
    context:
      user: unconfined_u
      type: httpd_sys_content_t
      range: s0
    type:
      - file
```

7. **Lifecycle event hooks (optional)**: The following section contains different deployment life cycle event hooks:
   - `ApplicationStop`: This will occur prior to the application being downloaded

When you deploy your application for the first time then it will not run because `appspec.yml` is not available.

   - `DownloadBundle`: The AWS CodeDeploy agent will copy version files to a temporary location listed here:
     - **On Windows Server Amazon EC2 instances**: `C:\ProgramData\Amazon\CodeDeploy\deployment-group-id\deployment-id\deployment-archive`
     - **On Amazon Linux, Ubuntu Server, and RHEL Amazon EC2 instances**: `/opt/codedeploy-agent/deployment-root/deployment-group-id/deployment-id/deployment-archive`

- `BeforeInstall`: Preinstall tasks, such as backing up the version or decrypting the files, can be specified in this event
- `Install`: The AWS CodeDeploy agent copies files to a destination folder from the temporary location using this event and it is reserved for it; you cannot use this event to run the scripts
- `AfterInstall`: You can change file permissions or application configurations when executing this event
- `ApplicationStart`: This event restarts those services that were stopped during an ApplicationStop event
- `ValidateService`: This event verifies that deployment has been successfully completed and this is the last event in the development life cycle.

It contains `location`, `timeout`, and `runas` parameters under the deployment life cycle event name. You can specify the location of the script filename that you want to run in `location`, the amount of time you want to execute the script in `timeout`, and the username in `runas`:

```
hooks:
  BeforeInstall:
    - location: \before-install.bat
      timeout: 900
      runas: root
```

The following are the environment variables that can be accessed from the hook scripts, during the deployment life cycle event:

- `APPLICATION_NAME`: The current AWS CodeDeploy application name, for example, `Packt_CodeDeploy_Demo`
- `DEPLOYMENT_ID`: The current deployment ID that has been assigned by AWS CodeDeploy, for example, `d-BLAG5O2SQ`
- `DEPLOYMENT_GROUP_NAME`: The current AWS CodeDeploy deployment group name, for example, `Packt_Deployment_Group`
- `DEPLOYMENT_GROUP_ID`: The current deployment group ID that has been assigned by AWS CodeDeploy, for example, `cc9904f4-6e55-46d4-a39f-ba6a80742335`
- `LIFECYCLE_EVENT`: The current deployment life cycle event name, for example, `ApplicationStart`

In this file, the location and number of spaces between each of the items are very important. If the spaces are incorrect, AWS CodeDeploy will produce an error, which is difficult to debug.

Step 4 – upload application to Amazon S3

In this step, we will see how to prepare and upload the source code to the location from where AWS CodeDeploy can deploy. It will cover these two steps:

- The provision of an S3 bucket with IAM user permission
- The preparation and bundling of the application's file, and push to the S3 bucket

Provision of S3 bucket with IAM user permission

I am assuming that you have created a new bucket or are using an existing bucket, and have also given access permission to this bucket and your IAM user. You must give the following permission through the S3 bucket policy, to upload files to any directory in the Amazon S3 bucket with the AWS account number, `123412341234`:

```
{
    "Statement": [
        {
            "Action": [
                "s3:PutObject"
            ],
            "Effect": "Allow",
            "Resource": "arn:aws:s3:::codedeploydemoapp/*",
            "Principal": {
                "AWS": [
                    "123412341234"
                ]
            }
        }
    ]
}
```

You must also attach the following policy to the S3 bucket policy to allow download requests from each Amazon EC2 instance:

```
{
    "Statement": [
        {
            "Action": [
                "s3:Get*",
```

```
                            "s3:List*"
                        ],
                        "Effect": "Allow",
                        "Resource": "arn:aws:s3::: codedeploydemoapp/*",
                        "Principal": {
                            "AWS": [
                                "arn:aws:iam::12345TESTING:role/CodeDeployUser"
                            ]
                        }
                    }
                ]
            }
```

To upload the revision to the S3 bucket, your account must have the proper permissions or you can specify them through the IAM policy. The following policy will allow the IAM user to upload the revisions in the codedeploydemoapp bucket:

```
{
  "Version":"2012-10-17",
  "Statement":[
      {
        "Effect":"Allow",
        "Action":["s3:PutObject"],
        "Resource":"arn:aws:s3::: codedeploydemoapp /*"
      }
  ]
}
```

Preparation and bundling of the application's file and pushing to the S3 bucket

Make sure you have all three files under your Packt folder that was created in *Step 3 – configure source content to deploy to the EC2 instance*:

```
C:\
  |-- Packt\
        |-- appspec.yml
        |-- before-install.bat
        |-- index.html
```

Open the CLI and switch to the C:\Packt folder. Now, execute the following command to create the application called Packt_CodeDeploy_Demo on AWS CodeDeploy:

```
aws deploy create-application --application-name Packt_CodeDeploy_Demo
```

Once you execute this command successfully, it will generate the application ID:

```
Administrator: Command Prompt

c:\Packt>aws deploy create-application --application-name Packt_CodeDeploy_Demo
{
    "applicationId": "94ed06e2-4a9a-4fff-9cf3-5bd2e91f9141"
}

c:\Packt>
```

Now, execute the following `push` command to bundle the file in the archive and upload the revision to Amazon S3. It will register the uploaded revision with AWS CodeDeploy:

```
aws deploy push --application-name Packt_CodeDeploy_Demo --s3-location
s3://packtdemo/PacktCodeDeploy.zip --ignore-hidden-files
```

It will create the ZIP archive file called `PacktCodeDeploy.zip` and upload the revision to the `packtdemo` bucket:

```
c:\Packt>aws deploy push --application-name Packt_CodeDeploy_Demo --s3-location s3://packtdemo/PacktCodeDeploy.zip --ign
ore-hidden-files
To deploy with this revision, run:
aws deploy create-deployment --application-name Packt_CodeDeploy_Demo --s3-location bucket=packtdemo,key=PacktCodeDeploy
.zip,bundleType=zip,eTag=ed5a870c5d2e5634b48e53df6933c962,version=45tZKZt8L0RUbHVi5IJwrdEiZiMSrIKP --deployment-group-na
me <deployment-group-name> --deployment-config-name <deployment-config-name> --description <description>

c:\Packt>
```

Step 5 – deploy application

In this step, you will deploy the revision that you uploaded to Amazon S3 in *Step 4– upload application to Amazon S3*. You can deploy this revision from AWS CLI or the AWS CodeDeploy console, and you can monitor the progress of your deployment. Once it deploys successfully, you can verify the results in the browser. Let's look at how we can do the following:

- Deploy and monitor the application from AWS CLI
- Deploy and monitor the application from AWS Management Console

To deploy and monitor the application from AWS CLI

To deploy the application, you need to create deployment groups. You can use the service role ARN that you created in *Step 1 – prerequisite configurations for AWS CodeDeploy*. From this service role, AWS CodeDeploy will get the permission to access the Amazon EC2 instance to expand its tags.

Now, call the `create-deployment-group` command to create the deployment group called `Packt_Deployment_Group`, associated with the application called `Packt_CodeDeploy_Demo`, the AWS instance tag called `PacktCodeDeployDemo`, and the deployment configuration called `CodeDeployDefault.OneAtATime` with the service role ARN:

```
aws deploy create-deployment-group --application-name Packt_CodeDeploy_Demo
--deployment-group-name Packt_Deployment_Group --deployment-config-name
CodeDeployDefault.OneAtATime --ec2-tag-filters
Key=Name,Value=PacktCodeDeployDemo,Type=KEY_AND_VALUE --service-role-arn
arn:aws:iam::XXXXXXXXXXXX:role/PacktCodeDeployServiceRole
```

This will create the deployment group and display the `deploymentGroupId`, as shown in the following screenshot:

Now, execute the `create-deployment` command with the application name `Packt_CodeDeploy_Demo`, the deployment configuration name `CodeDeployDefault.OneAtATime`, the deployment group name `Packt_Deployment_Group` that we created in the previous command, and the application revision name `PacktCodeDeploy.zip`, in the `packtdemo` S3 bucket:

```
aws deploy create-deployment --application-name Packt_CodeDeploy_Demo --
deployment-config-name CodeDeployDefault.OneAtATime
--deployment-group-name Packt_Deployment_Group
--s3-location bucket=packtdemo,bundleType=zip,key=PacktCodeDeploy.zip
```

This will generate the `deploymentID` that you can use to get the status of your deployment:

```
c:\Packt>aws deploy create-deployment --application-name Packt_CodeDeploy_Demo --deployment-config-name CodeDeployDefaul
t.OneAtATime --deployment-group-name Packt_Deployment_Group --s3-location bucket=packtdemo,bundleType=zip,key=PacktCodeD
eploy.zip
{
    "deploymentId": "d-H81YVFHVQ"
}
```

You can get the list of deployment IDs by calling the `list-deployments` command and passing the application name, `Packt_CodeDeploy_Demo`, and the deployment group name, `Packt_Deployment_Group`:

```
aws deploy list-deployments --application-name Packt_CodeDeploy_Demo --
deployment-group-name Packt_Deployment_Group --query "deployments" --output
text
```

You will see the deployment IDs generated by the previous commands:

```
Select Administrator: Command Prompt                                                                    —     □     ×

c:\Packt>aws deploy list-deployments --application-name Packt_CodeDeploy_Demo --deployment-group-name Packt_Deployment_G
roup --query "deployments" --output text
d-H81YVFHVQ       d-ZW2S5FOVQ        d-DMYJILHVQ
```

Now, to check the status of your deployment, (success or failure), execute the `get-deployment` command with the deployment ID:

```
aws deploy get-deployment --deployment-id d-H81YVFHVQ --query
"deploymentInfo.status" --output text
```

It will return the result as follows:

```
c:\Packt>aws deploy get-deployment --deployment-id d-H81YVFHVQ --query "deploymentInfo.status" --output text
Succeeded

c:\Packt>_
```

If the deployment status is failed, you can call the `list-deployment-instances` and `get-deployment-instance` commands to troubleshoot the problem. After a successful deployment, you can verify your installation from the public DNS address of your EC2 instance. To get the public DNS address, select your EC2 instance and in the description tab, you will see the value for your public DNS. Enter this DNS address in the web browser and you will see your `index.html`:

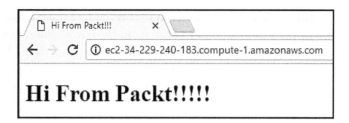

To deploy and monitor the application from AWS Management Console

In this section, we will follow these steps to deploy and monitor the application:

1. Log in to AWS Management Console and select the **AWS CodeDeploy** service.
2. It will display the **Get Started Now** button for a first time user. If any applications have already been created, then you will see the list of applications. Click on the **Create Application** button.
3. You will see the following screen. Type the value for the application name and deployment group name. The compute platform has two options: **EC2/On-premises** and **AWS Lambda**. The **In-place deployment** option has been selected as the deployment type for this demo application:

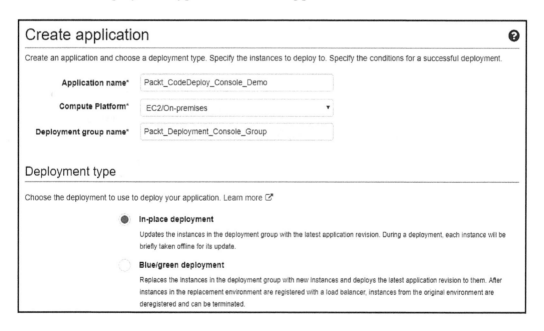

4. Under the **Environment configuration** section, select the **Amazon EC2 instances** tab. Add the appropriate key and value from the drop-down list for the **Tag group 1** section. You will see one instance, as it confirms that AWS CodeDeploy has found matching Amazon EC2 instances. Under the **Matching instances** section, it will display the status for the selected EC2 instance, as shown in the following screenshot:

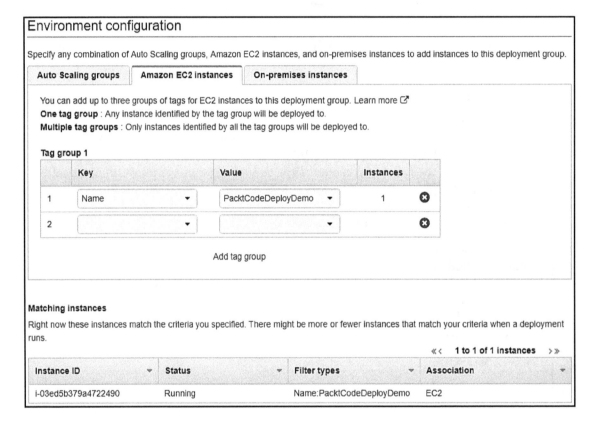

5. The **Deployment configuration** section is a set of rules, which specifies how fast an application will be deployed and success/failure conditions of the deployment. You can select from the default list or customize it by choosing the **Create Deployment Configuration** option. Here, we have selected the **CodeDeployDefault.OneAtATime** option:

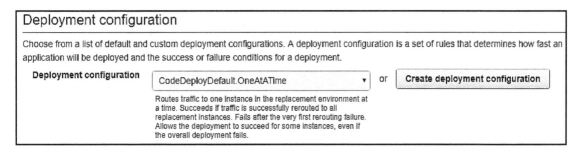

6. Under the advanced option, you can create triggers, alarms, and define conditions for the rollbacks.
7. Under the **Service role ARN** drop-down list, select the appropriate service role ARN, and then click on the **Create application** button:

8. Once the application has been created successfully, you will see the following screenshot:

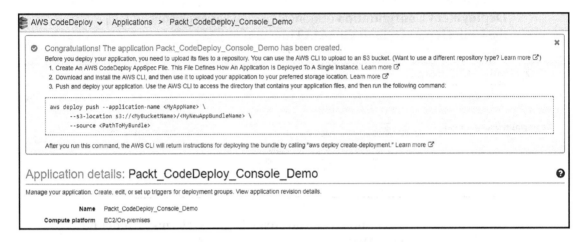

9. It will also create the deployment group. Now, select the newly created deployment group and select the **Deploy new revision** option from the **Actions** tab, as shown in the following screenshot:

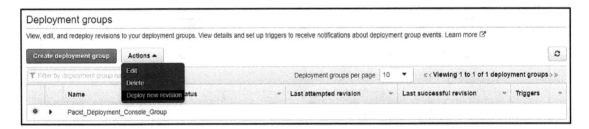

10. You will be redirected to the **Create deployment** screen where you have to select the information for the application, deployment group, and repository type. For the revision location, include the Amazon S3 revision file location URL. It will detect the file type as `.zip`, if it does not detect it automatically, then select it from the drop-down list. Select `CodeDeployDefault.OneAtATime` from the **Deployment configuration** drop-down list. Choose **Deploy** once you select/fill up all the information:

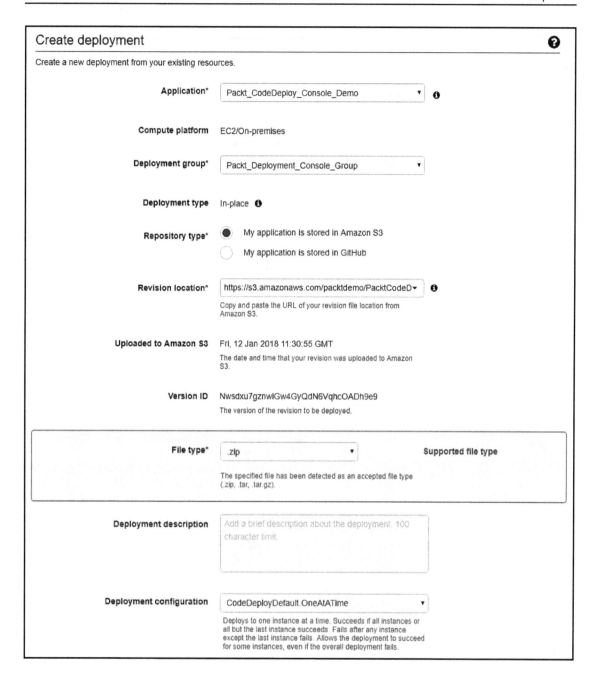

11. During the deployment, you can track the status and also stop it, if necessary:

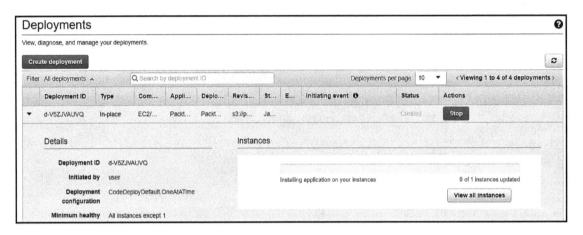

12. Once deployment is done successfully, you will see the following screen:

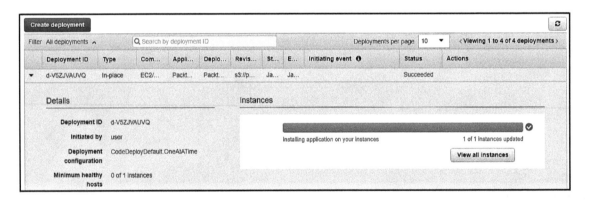

13. On the **Instance activity** section, you will see the deployment information, such as **Instance ID**, **Start time**, **End time**, **Duration**, **Status**, **Most recent event**, and **Events**:

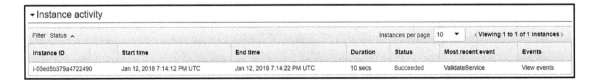

14. You will see the following screen when you click on the **View events** link. It gives details of all the events that have occurred during deployment:

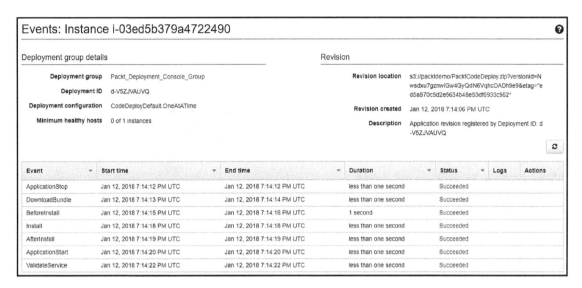

15. You can verify the installation the same way you did for AWS CLI.

Step 6 – update and redeploy application

To update and redeploy the application, you have to make changes to your code and push it to your Amazon S3 bucket. Once you update the code, then you have to execute the `create-deployment` command again to deploy new things. You can follow the preceding steps to complete the deployment.

Step 7 – clean up the application and related resources

Once you complete the preceding tutorial, you have to clean up the resources, such as Amazon S3, AWS CodeDeploy, and the Amazon EC2 instance. Here, you will see how to clean up the resources for AWS CodeDeploy. From AWS CLI, you can call the `delete-application` command to delete the `Packt_CodeDeploy_Demo` application from the AWS CodeDeploy. It will delete all the associated records for deployment groups and deployments:

```
aws deploy delete-application --application-name Packt_CodeDeploy_Demo
```

From the AWS CodeDeploy console, select the application that you want to delete. It will navigate to the application details page. Select the **Delete application** option and it will prompt you to enter the name of the application for confirmation. Enter the application name and then choose to delete:

Great!!! You have successfully completed deployment with AWS CodeDeploy using an Amazon EC2 Windows instance and Amazon S3. In the next tsection, we will discuss AWS CodePipeline.

AWS CodePipeline

AWS CodePipeline is a CI/CD service for a reliable and fast software release process. As per your release model, AWS CodePipeline will build, test, and deploy the code, if there is any code change. It enables the faster and reliable delivery of features and updates. AWS CodePipeline can easily integrate with AWS services and other DevOps platforms. This section on AWS CodePipeline is divided into the following topics:

- AWS CodePipeline benefits
- AWS CodePipeline features
- Creating an AWS CodePipeline from the console
- Creating an AWS CodePipeline from AWS CLI

AWS CodePipeline benefits

Let's start with AWS CodePipeline benefits, which are as follows:

- AWS CodePipeline allows you to rapidly deliver new features to users by automating the software release process.
- You can improve quality by easily testing each code change and catching bugs while they are simple and small to fix.
- AWS CodePipeline provides a graphical user interface to model different stages for the software release process.

- AWS CodePipeline is a fully managed service that connects to existing tools and systems. You can immediately start your software release process with AWS CodePipeline. There is no need to set up or provision for servers.
- AWS CodePipeline is easily extendable and adapts to specific needs. You can use existing pre-built AWS plugins or create your own custom plugins, at any step of the release process in AWS CodePipeline.

AWS CodePipeline features

The features of AWS CodePipeline are:

- **Workflow**: In AWS CodePipeline, you can define your workflow and describe how new code changes will progress. This pipeline has a series of stages that act as logical divisions in the workflow, and each stage has a sequence of actions to perform the task. It provides a graphical user interface to model and visualize your workflow and to create, manage, and configure your pipeline for the release process. You can execute your action in parallel to increase workflow speeds.
- **Integrations with AWS services**: AWS CodePipeline can use AWS CodeCommit or Amazon S3 to pull the source code. It can use AWS CodeBuild to run the build and tests. It can use AWS CodeDeploy, Amazon **Elastic Container Service (ECS)**, AWS Elastic Beanstalk, or AWS OpsWorks for deployment. It can update or delete the resources by providing AWS CloudFormation templates. It can use AWS Lambda, Amazon DynamoDB, and Amazon API Gateway for a serverless application model. You can trigger custom functions at any stage in your AWS CodePipeline.
- **Pre-built and custom plugins**: With AWS CodePipeline, you can integrate developer tools or your own custom systems. Developer tools can use for version control systems, build, test, and deployment. You can also create a custom action and register with AWS CodePipeline. This custom action allows hooking servers into a pipeline by integrating the AWS CodePipeline open source agent with servers. You can register existing build servers as a custom action.

- **Declarative templates**: AWS CodePipeline allows you to specify a release workflow, its stages, and actions for the pipeline structure from declarative JSON documents. These JSON documents enable you to start templates for creating a new pipeline, as well as to update existing pipelines.
- **Access control**: AWS CodePipeline uses AWS IAM roles, IAM users, and **Security Assertion Markup Language** (**SAML**) integrated directories to manage the access control. You can give permissions for who can make the changes to release the workflow or for who can control it.

Now let's understand how to create a pipeline from the AWS CodePipeline console.

Creating an AWS CodePipeline from the console

To create a pipeline from the console, you need to specify the source file location and information about the providers that you will use for the actions. You must include a Source stage with Build, or a Staging stage to create the pipeline. Through the pipeline wizard, AWS CodePipeline creates different stage names such as source, build, staging, which you cannot change. Later on, you can add more stages and give project specific names. AWS CodePipeline uses Amazon CloudWatch events to detect any code changes in your AWS CodeCommit source code repository. It means whenever any code changes occur, AWS CloudWatch will trigger events to start the pipeline automatically.

The steps to create AWS CodePipeline are as follows:

1. Log in to the AWS Management Console and select the AWS CodePipeline service.
2. It will display the **Get started** button for a first time user. If any pipelines have already been created, then you will see the list of pipelines. Select the **Create pipeline** button to create a new pipeline.
3. Specify your AWS CodePipeline name in the **Pipeline name** text field and click on the **Next step** button, as shown in the following screenshot:

The pipeline name must be unique within a region in a single AWS account.

4. In the **Source** step, select the source provider, provide the connection details for that source provider, and click on the **Next step** button. Currently, AWS CodePipeline supports the following three source providers:

- **Amazon S3**: This provides the full path of the object with the Amazon S3 bucket name and versioning enabled in the Amazon S3 **Location**, field such as s3://bucket_name/path/source.zip.
- **AWS CodeCommit**: In the **Repository name** field, select the repository from the drop-down list that you want to use as a source code repository and select the name of the branch from the drop-down list. Next, you can select the **Change detection options** section if you want to start the build automatically from the Amazon CloudWatch Events, or for AWS CodePipeline to check changes, periodically. In this example, we have selected the **AWS CodeCommit** option.

If you ask AWSCodePipeline to check changes periodically, this will provide a slower and less configurable experience, and it is not recommended.

- **GitHub**: Click on the **Connect to GitHub** button and log in with your GitHub credentials. I assume you have GitHub credentials and a source code repository. Once you successfully logged in, you can see the repository in the drop-down list on the source page. Select the repository that you want to use for the source location and then select the branch from the drop-down list, as shown in the following screenshot:

5. In the **Build** step, select the build provider that you want to use or are already using, provide the necessary information, and click on the **Next step** button. Currently, AWS CodePipeline provides the following options for the build provider:

- **No Build**: You can skip the Build stage.
- **Add Jenkins**: You must specify the provider name, server URL and project name to use the Jenkins instance as the build provider.
- **AWS CodeBuild**: For AWS CodeBuild, you can choose the **Select an existing build project** or **Create a new build project** option. For an existing project, you can select the project name from the drop-down list. For a new build project, you can refer to Chapter 4, *CI/CD in AWS Part 1 – CodeCommit, CodeBuild, and Testing*, and create a project. We will use this option for our demo project.
- **Solano CI**: You can select **Connect** to link Solano CI and AWS CodePipeline:

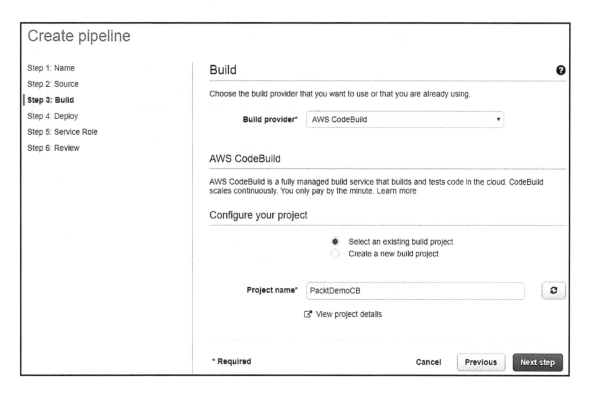

6. In the **Deploy** step, select the deployment provider to deploy your instance, provide necessary information, and click on the **Next step** button. Currently, AWS CodePipeline provides the following options for deployment:

> - **No Deployment**: You can skip the Deployment stage and add later.
> - **Amazon ECS**: You can select an existing Amazon ECS cluster in the cluster name. You can select an existing service running on that cluster in the service name. You can also create a new cluster and service, if you don't have any. In image filename, mention the JSON filename that describes the Amazon ECS container service name, image, and tag.

 Make sure you have two Amazon ECS instances. One is the primary instance and the other is to accommodate new instances.

> - **AWS CloudFormation**: In the **Action mode** dropdown, you can select any of the following options:
>   - **Create or update a stack**: Enter the stack name, template filename, and IAM role name. Optionally, you can select the configuration filename and select IAM capabilities.
>   - **Create or replace a change set**: Enter the stack name, change set name, template filename, and IAM role name. Optionally, you can select the configuration filename and select IAM capabilities.
>
> - **AWS CodeDeploy**: You can select an existing application name and deployment group for AWS CodeDeploy or create a new application from the AWS CodeDeploy console.
> - **AWS Elastic Beanstalk**: You can select an existing application name and environment name for AWS Elastic Beanstalk or create a new application from the AWS Elastic Beanstalk console.
> - **AWS OpsWorks**: You can select a stack name and app. Optionally, you can select the layer to which the target instance belongs:

7. In the **Service Role** step, select the role name from the drop-down list, if you have already created an IAM service role for AWS CodePipeline. If you don't have any service role, you can create a new role by clicking on the **Create role** button, which will navigate you to the IAM console to create a new role and redirect you to the same page. You can select the newly created role and click on the **Next step** button, as shown in the following screenshot:

8. In the **Review** step, review the pipeline configuration, and then select **Create pipeline** to create the pipeline. Select the **Previous** button to go back and edit the choice. Select the **Cancel** button to exit the wizard. You will see the following success message once you create it, and you can see the pipeline in the console. It will start automatically once created:

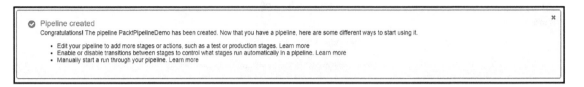

Now, select the pipeline and click on the **Release change** button. It will start the processing and show you the succeeded/failed message. If it has failed, then you can click on the **Details** link to debug it and fix it. Once it has been fixed, then you can click on the **Retry** to execute the same stage again. You can verify your deployment once it is successful. You can click on the **Edit** button next to the **Release change** button to update the existing pipeline. You can add a new **Stage**, **Action**, or edit the existing stage or actions. In the following screens, I have added a new **Test** stage and specified an approval type, **Manual approval**, as shown in the following screenshot:

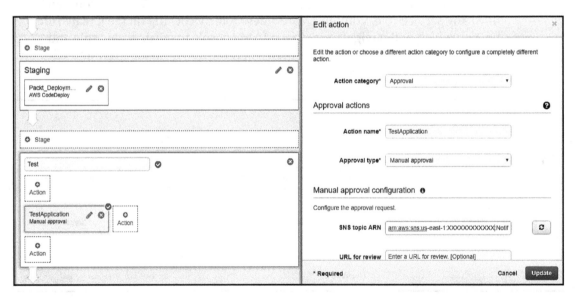

It means that during the process execution, it will stop at this stage and send an email, as configured in the SNS topic, as shown:

Once the team has tested all the test cases, then it can review and approve the **Test** stage. Once that has been approved, the next stage will execute automatically.

In the next step, we will create the pipeline using AWS CLI.

Creating an AWS CodePipeline from AWS CLI

You can use AWS CLI to create an AWS CodePipeline. For that, you need to create a JSON file with a pipeline structure and then execute the `create-pipeline` command with the JSON file as the input parameter. You can execute the `get-pipeline` command to get the JSON structure of the existing pipeline, and modify it to create the JSON file. If you don't have any existing pipeline, then you can use the AWS CodePipeline wizard to create a pipeline and use that JSON structure.

 The `create-pipeline` command will not create an Amazon S3 bucket.

There are two ways to create a pipeline from CLI, which are as follows:

JSON file creation

In a command prompt or terminal, run the `get-pipeline` command and copy the output to the JSON file. For example, if a pipeline is called `PacktPipelineDemo`, then you can type the following command:

```
aws codepipeline get-pipeline --name PacktPipelineDemo >mypackt.json
```

The output of this command is stored in the `mypackt.json` file. Open this file in a text editor and change the value to reflect the structure you want. You must change the pipeline name. Apart from that, you should consider using the same Amazon S3 bucket where artifacts are stored, the source location, deployment provider, and other details. Once you have modified the changes, then you must manually create the AWS CloudWatch Event rules to detect the changes.

Execution of the create-pipeline command

Now, execute the `create-pipeline` command with the `-cli-input-json` parameter. Here, the parameter should be the JSON file you have created. To create the `PacktPipelineSecondDemo` pipeline, you must specify this name in the JSON file as the value parameter.

You must include `file://` before the JSON filename,
`aws codepipeline create-pipeline --cli-input-json file://mypackt.json`
This command will return the entire pipeline structure. You can verify your pipeline from the AWS CodePipeline console or use the `get-pipeline-state` command.

We have successfully completed AWS CodeDeploy and AWS CodePipeline. Now, we will look at AWS CodeStar.

AWS CodeStar

AWS CodeStar provides tools to develop, build, and deploy applications quickly. It has many project templates for developing applications on AWS Lambda, Amazon EC2, and AWS Elastic Beanstalk, with support for many popular programming languages, including Java, PHP, JavaScript, Python, and Ruby. AWS CodeStar provides preconfigured delivery tools to develop, build, test, and deploy applications for faster delivery. It supports built-in security policies for easy access of your project. It provides project dashboards to monitor application activity centrally, and manage development tasks easily. AWS CodeStar can integrate with Atlassian JIRA. Atlassian JIRA is a third-party project management and issue tracking tool. From the AWS dashboard, you can create and manage JIRA issues.

Some of the AWS CodeStar features are as follows:

- You can use your favorite **Integrated Development Environment** (IDE) such as Visual Studio, Eclipse, or AWS CLI. After creating your project in AWS CodeStar, you can directly use your code in AWS Cloud9, a cloud-based IDE from AWS.
- AWS CodeStar uses the AWS **Identity and Access Management** (IAM) service that provides built-in, role-based security policies for easy and secure access for the team, and also manages a developer's identities. It allows you to share the projects using different access levels, such as owners, contributors, and viewers.
- AWS CodeStar uses AWS CodeCommit to securely store application code. You can also choose to store source code in the GitHub repository in your GitHub account.
- AWS CodeStar uses AWS CodeBuild to compile and package the source code and AWS CodePipeline for the software release process.
- You can automate the deployments by integrating AWS CodeDeploy and AWS CloudFormation with AWS CodeStar for the easy update of application code, and deployment to Amazon EC2 and AWS Lambda.
- AWS CodeStar includes a dashboard to easily track and manage end-to-end development for your projects. From the project dashboard, you can manage activity for a CI/CD pipeline, include wiki projects and integrate with Amazon CloudWatch, and Atlassian JIRA software. From all these integrations, you can centrally manage JIRA issues and monitor application activity.

Now, let's explore how to create a project in AWS CodeStar.

Creating a project in AWS CodeStar

The steps for creating a project in AWS CodeStar are as follows:

1. Log in to AWS Management Console and select the **AWS CodeStar** service.
2. It will display the **Start a project** button for the first time user. If any projects have already been created, then you will see the tile of projects with a dashboard, code, and team link. Select the **Create a new project** button to create a new project.
3. For a first time user, it will show the **Create service role** dialog box. You have to select the **Yes, create role** option to create the role. It will give full access for AWS CodeStar to create and manage resources, and grant other IAM users permission to access these resources. It will show the project templates for starting AWS projects. You can filter or select the following, or choose a template. Here, we have selected the **Static Website** template:

   - Application category, such as web application, web service, Alexa Skill, static website
   - Programming language, such as C#, Go, HTML5, Java, Node.js, PHP, Python, Ruby
   - AWS services, such as AWS Elastic Beanstalk, Amazon EC2, AWS Lambda:

4. The following screenshot is the **Project details** screen. Add a value for the **Project name** field. The **Project ID** field will populate automatically. You can change this project ID by clicking on the **Edit** button. It will be used to name the AWS resources included in the AWS CodeStar project. AWS CodeStar will store the source code in AWS CodeCommit or GitHub. Provide the repository name generated by AWS CodeCommit or GitHub. Click on the **Next** button:

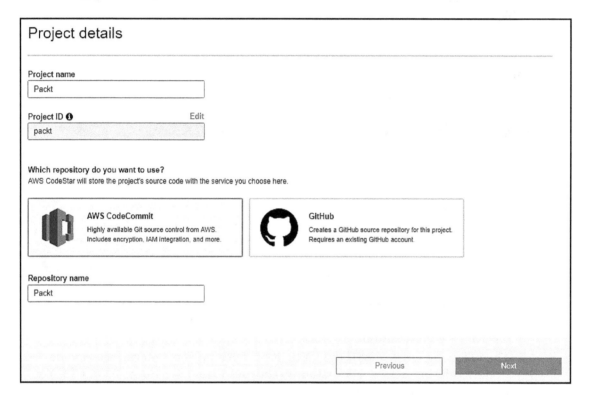

5. The following screenshot is the **Review project details** screen. This page will display all the AWS services you need for this project with tools. The **Edit Amazon EC2 configuration** option will be provided to change the Amazon EC2 configuration. Click on the **Create Project** button after reviewing the project details:

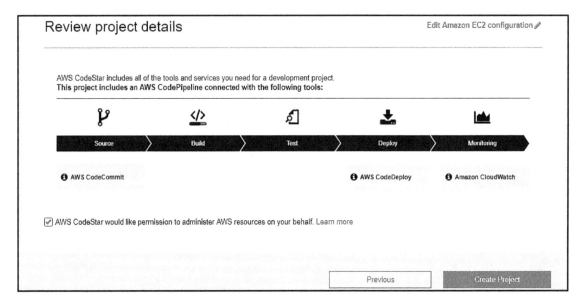

6. Now the project has been created. It will show you the **Select template** screen to configure user settings, such as the IAM user name, display name, and email. Click on the **Next** button.

7. The following screenshot is the set up tools screen where you can select your preferred IDEs, such as **AWS Cloud9**, **Eclipse**, **Visual Studio**, or AWS CLI. You can skip this section if you don't want any IDEs:

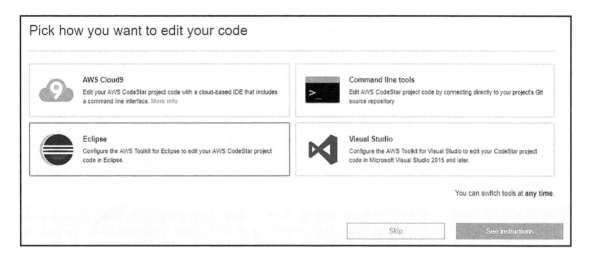

8. Once you select your preferred IDE and select **next**, it will redirect you to the AWS CodeStar dashboard. In the dashboard, you can see the AWS CodeStar project information with IDE. You can add an additional tile with the **Add tile** dropdown. It provides options such as JIRA issue tracking, Team wiki, Continuous deployment, Application activity, Application endpoints, AWS Cloud9 environments, and GitHub issue tracking:

This is the continuous screen and you can see the **Team wiki tile**, **AWS Cloud9 environments**, and **Application endpoints** sections:

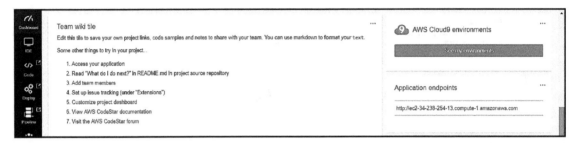

This is the continuous screen and you can see **Commit history**, **Application activity**, **JIRA**, and **AWS CodePipeline** details:

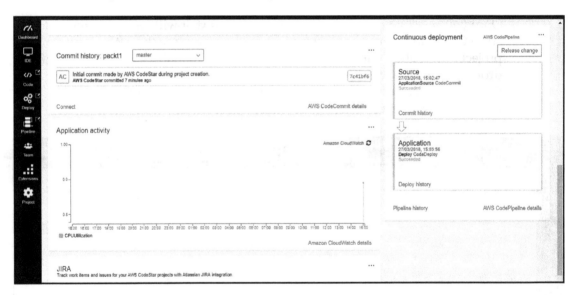

9. To verify the deployment, you can click on the **Application endpoints** section and you will see the following screen. The application has been created and deployed successfully:

10. You can rename or delete the application from the AWS CodeStar console. When you rename the application, it will open the dialog box and ask for the new or updated name. When deleting the application, it will open the confirmation dialog box and ask for the project ID. It will also delete the associated resource that has been generated by AWS CodeStar:

You have completed AWS CodeStar. In the next section, we will look at AWS X-Ray.

AWS X-Ray

AWS X-Ray is used by developers to debug and analyze the distributed, production applications that are built using the microservice architecture. AWS X-Ray helps to identify and troubleshoot the root cause of any performance issue, or any errors in an application. AWS X-Ray will show a map of the application's underlying context by getting an end-to-end view of a request that can travel through the application. AWS X-Ray can be used to analyze applications in any kind of environment, such as development or production, from simple applications to complex applications. This section on AWS X-Ray has been divided into the following topics:

- AWS X-Ray benefits
- Key features of AWS X-Ray
- An AWS X-Ray example from the console

AWS X-Ray benefits

The following are the benefits of AWS X-Ray:

- AWS X-Ray supports the tracing of user requests. It provides tracing features, to follow the request path and pinpoint the performance issue in an application.
- AWS X-Ray has annotations to append metadata to the traces. It helps with tagging and filtering trace data to discover specific patterns and diagnose issues.
- AWS X-Ray helps to identify performance bottlenecks. It aggregates the data that has been generated by the service and provides you with a view of the applications performance.
- AWS X-Ray provides the service maps that are used to see the relationships between your services and resources, used in the application in real time. You can easily detect high latencies occurring in the application, as well as you can visualize the nodes, and edge latency distribution for services that will help to drill down the service and paths that impact the application performance.
- AWS X-Ray can work with Amazon EC2, Amazon **Elastic Container Service** (**ECS**), AWS Lambda, and AWS Elastic Beanstalk. Applications that are written in Java, Node.js, and .NET and deployed on these services can be used with AWS X-Ray.
- AWS X-Ray can work for simple as well as complex applications, in a development or in a production environment. You can trace the requests for multiple AWS accounts, AWS Regions, and **Availability Zone** (**AZ**) with AWS X-Ray.

Key features of AWS X-Ray

The following are the key features of AWS X-Ray:

- AWS X-Ray is simple to set up. You can integrate X-Ray SDK with an application and install an X-Ray agent. For AWS Elastic Beanstalk, you have to integrate the X-Ray SDK with the application only, as the X-Ray agent is pre-installed.
- With AWS X-Ray, you will get an end-to-end, cross-service view of requests that are made to your application. It supports applications running on various AWS services, it captures metadata for requests made to MySQL, PostgreSQL, Amazon DynamoDB, Amazon **Simple Queue Service** (**SQS**), and Amazon SNS. It also supports applications written in different languages such as Java, Node.js, and .NET.
- AWS X-Ray creates service maps with trace data of your application to drill down into issues or a specific service. It also helps to visually detect nodes.
- AWS X-Ray can add annotations to specific components or services in an application. You can filter the data for traces.
- AWS X-Ray can be used with the AWS Management Console, AWS SDKs, and AWS CLI. AWS SDK provides interceptors to trace incoming requests, client handlers to call other services, and HTTP clients to call other internal and external web services. You can programmatically access services with AWS X-Ray APIs to custom analytics dashboards, and easily export trace data, or ingest data into tools.
- AWS X-Ray is easily integrated with AWS IAM to control which users and resources have permission, and how they can access traces.

Now let's look at an example of AWS X-Ray.

Creating an AWS X-Ray example from the console

The following are the steps to create an AWS X-Ray example using AWS Management Console:

1. Log in to AWS Management console and select the AWS X-Ray service.
2. It will display a getting started page for the first time user. If any projects have already been added then it will navigate to the **Service map** tab. Select **Getting started** to create a new project.

3. In **Step 1: Options**, select to launch a sample application or instrument your application. If you select the **Instrument your application** option, then in **Step 2: Language**, you have to select your programming language, such as Node.js, Java, C# .Net, Python, and Go. In the same flow, in **Step 3: Implementation**, it will provide you with the instructions to add or modify your code for implementation, and then run the AWS X-Ray Daemon because AWS SDK will not send data directly to AWS X-Ray. For this example, select the **Launch a sample application (Node.js)** option. It will skip **Step 2: Language** and forward to **Step 3: Implementation**:

4. In the implementation step, click on the **Launch sample application** button:

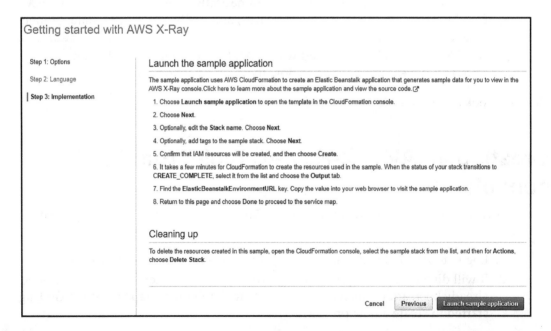

5. It will navigate to the AWS CloudFormation **Create stack** screen. In the **Select Template** option, you can create the stack as per your needs. For that you can design a template or choose a template. Select the **Specify an Amazon S3 template URL** option and click on the **Next** button:

A stack is a group of resources that is managed as a single unit.

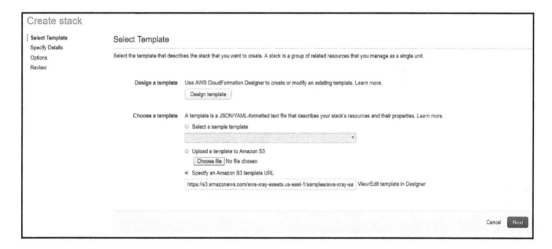

6. It will navigate to the **Specify Details** page. Type the stack name and select the parameters such as **subnet** and **VPC** to launch the AWS EC2 instance, and click on the **Next** button:

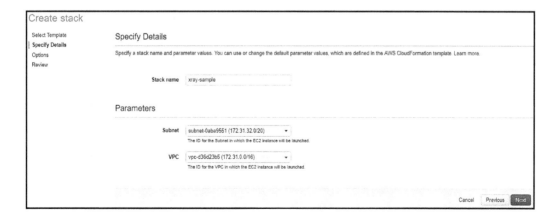

7. On the **Options** page, you can add the key-value pair for tags. Also, add a few more things such as permissions, rollback triggers, and so on, and click the **Next** button.

8. On the **Review** page, verify your information and select the checkbox to acknowledge that AWS CloudFormation might create IAM resources, and click on the **Create** button. It will create a stack for you.

9. You can select the stack name and it will show you all the events. If your stack fails then you can check the events for error messages and fix. You can go to the **Outputs** tab and select the URL for `ElasticBeanstalkEnvironmentURL`:

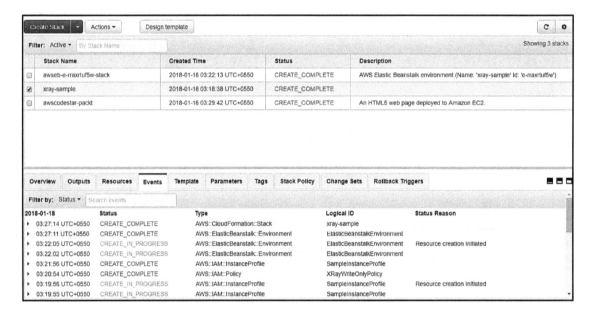

10. It will open the sample application. Click on **Start/Stop** a few times:

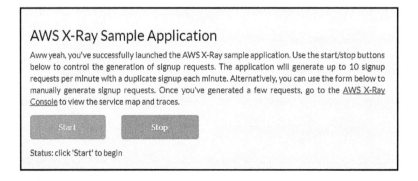

11. Now, on the AWS X-Ray screen, the **Done** button will be enabled. Select that button and it will navigate to the AWS X-Ray service map. You can see the service call graph:

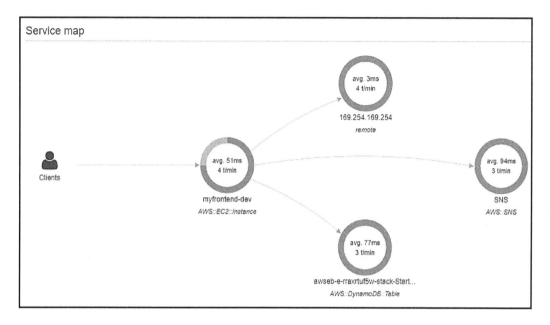

12. Click on the **Traces** option and you will see the overview of the traces to identify the impact. It provides you with different groups through options such as **URL**, **StatusCode**, **Method**, **User**, and so on:

13. To identify the performance bottlenecks, click on the corresponding ID from the trace list:

14. To check for any exceptions, select the group by **StatusCode**. It will show you the success/failure StatusCode in response. Select the StatusCode for the failed response and click on the ID in the trace list. It will navigate you to the trace details page. You will see the error icon under status; you can click on that icon for error details:

15. Once you verify, you can delete the stack from the AWS CloudFormation and it will clean up the resource that has been created.

Summary

So far, we have looked at AWS CodeDeploy, AWS CodePipeline, AWS CodeStar, and AWS X-Ray, which are part of the AWS Developer tools that help you implement CI/CD. In the next chapter, we will discuss how to manage user authentication from AWS Cognito.

User Authentication with AWS Cognito

6

In the previous chapter, we discussed the AWS Code family of tools, such as AWS CodeDeploy, AWS CodePipeline, AWS CodeStar, and AWS X-Ray.

In this chapter, we will discuss the AWS Cognito service for simple and secure user authentication for mobile and web applications.

Amazon Cognito is a user authentication service that enables user sign-up and sign-in, and access control for mobile and web applications, easily, quickly, and securely. In Amazon Cognito, you can create your user directory, which allows the application to work when the devices are not online and to save data on the user's device and synchronize it. It gives a consistent application experience to the user, regardless of the device.

Amazon Cognito supports, to scale, millions of users and authenticates users from social identity providers such as Facebook, Google, Twitter, Amazon, or enterprise identity providers, such as Microsoft Active Directory through SAML, or your own identity provider system.

With Amazon Cognito, you can concentrate on developing great application experiences for the user, instead of worrying about developing secure and scalable application solutions for handling the access control permissions of users and synchronization across the devices.

In this chapter, we will cover the following topics:

- Amazon Cognito benefits
- Amazon Cognito features
- Amazon Cognito User Pools
- Getting starting with Amazon Cognito User Pools
- Amazon Cognito User Pool creation from the console
- Amazon Cognito example for Android with mobile SDK
- Amazon Cognito Federated Identities
- Creating a new Identity Pool from the console
- Amazon Cognito Sync

Let's explore each topic and see how it can be used for user authentication from AWS.

Amazon Cognito benefits

- Amazon Cognito is a fully managed service and it provides User Pools for a secure user directory to scale millions of users; these User Pools are easy to set up.
- Amazon Cognito User Pools are standard-based identity providers, Amazon Cognito supports many identity and access management standards such as OAuth 2.0, SAML 2.0, OAuth 2.0 and OpenID Connect.
- Amazon Cognito supports the encryption of data in transit or at rest, and multi-factor authentication.
- With Amazon Cognito, you can control access to the backend resource from the application. You can control the users by defining roles and map different roles for the application, so they can access the application resource for which they are authorized.
- Amazon Cognito can integrate easily with the sign-up and sign-in for the app because it provides a built-in UI and configuration for different federating identity providers. It provides the facility to customize the UI, as per company branding, in front and center for user interactions.
- Amazon Cognito is eligible for HIPAA-BAA and is compliant with PCI DSS, SOC 1-3, and ISO 27001.

Amazon Cognito features

Amazon Cognito provides the following features:

- Amazon Cognito Identity
  - User Pools
    - Federated Identities
- Amazon Cognito Sync
- Data synchronization

Let's understand these features in detail.

Amazon Cognito User Pools

Amazon Cognito User Pools helps to create and maintain a directory for users and adds sign-up/sign-in to mobile or web applications. Users can sign in to a User Pool through social or SAML-based identity providers. It provides a secure, simple, low-cost option and scales to millions of users.

Enhanced security features such as multi-factor authentication and email/phone number verification can be implemented for your application. With AWS Lambda, you can customize your workflows for Amazon Cognito User Pools such as adding application specific logins for user validation and registration for fraud detection.

Getting started with Amazon Cognito User Pools

You can create Amazon Cognito User Pools through Amazon Cognito Console, AWS **Command Line Interface** (**CLI**), or Amazon Cognito **Application Programming Interface** (**API**). Now let's understand all these different ways of creating User Pools.

Amazon Cognito User Pool creation from the console

Please perform the following steps to create a **User Pool** from the console.

1. Log in to the AWS Management console and select the **Amazon Cognito** service.

2. It will show you two options, such as **Manage your User Pools** and **Manage Federated Identities**, as shown:

Amazon Cognito

Amazon Cognito makes it easy for you to have users sign up and sign in to your apps, federate identities from social identity providers, secure access to AWS resources and synchronize data across multiple devices, platforms, and applications.

Manage your User Pools   Manage Federated Identities

Add Sign-up and Sign-in

With Cognito Your User Pools, you can easily and securely add sign-up and sign-in functionality to your mobile and web apps with a fully-managed service that scales to support hundreds of millions of users.

Federate User Identities

With Cognito Federated Identities, your users can sign-in through social identity providers such as Facebook and Twitter, or through your own identity solution, and you can control access to AWS resources from your app.

Synchronize Data Across Devices

With Cognito Sync, your app can save user data, such as preferences and game state, and sync that data to make your users' experiences consistent across their devices and when they are disconnected.

3. Select **Manage Your User Pools**. It will take you to the **Create a user pool** screen. You can add the **Pool name** and create the **User Pool**. You can create this user pool in two different ways, by selecting:
   - **Review defaults**: It comes with default settings and if required, you can customize it
   - **Step through settings**: Step by step, you can customize each setting:

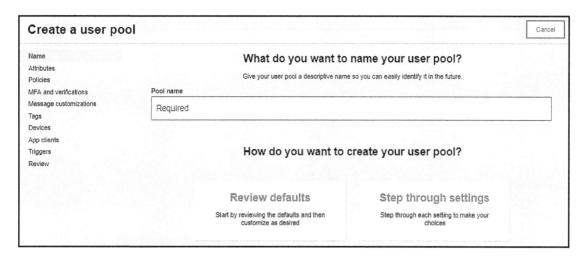

4. When you select **Review defaults**, you will be taken to the review **User Pool** configuration screen and then select **Create pool.**

5. When you will select **Step through settings**, you will taken to the **Attributes** screen to customize it. Let's understand all the screens in brief:

   - **Attributes**: This gives the option for users to sign in with a username, email address, or phone number. You can select standard attributes for user profiles as well create custom attributes.

   - **Policies**: You can set the password strength, allow users to sign in themselves, and stipulate days until expire for the newly created account.

   - **MFA and verifications**: This allows you to enable Multi-Factor Authentication, and configure require verification for emails and phone numbers. You create a new IAM role to set permissions for Amazon Cognito that allows you to send SMS message to users on your behalf.

   - **Message customizations**: You can customize messages to verify an email address by providing a verification code or link. You can customize user invitation messages for SMS and email but you must include the username and a temporary password. You can customize email addresses from SES-verified identities.

- **Tags**: You can add tags for this User Pool by providing tag keys and their values.
- **Devices**: This provides settings to remember a user's device. It provides options such as **Always**, **User Opt In**, and **No**.
- **App clients**: You can add app clients by giving unique IDs and an optional secret key to access this User Pool.
- **Triggers**: You can customize workflows and user experiences by triggering AWS Lambda functions for different events.
- **Reviews**: This shows you all the attributes for review.

6. You can edit any attribute on the **Reviews** screen and then click on **Create pool**. It will create the **User Pool**.

7. After creating a new User Pool, navigate to the **App clients** screen. Enter the **App client name** as `CognitoDemo` and click on **Create app client**:

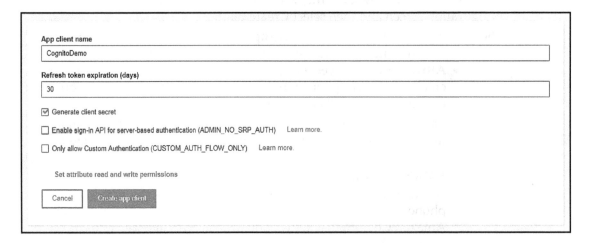

8. Once this **Client App** is generated, you can click on the **show details** to see **App client secret**:

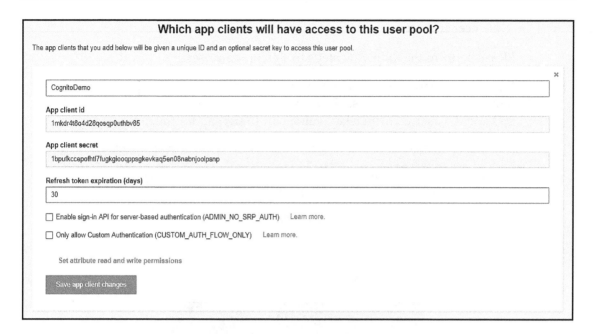

9. **Pool Id**, **App client id**, and **App client secret** are required to connect any application to Amazon Cognito.

In the next section, we will explore an Amazon Cognito User Pool example to sign up and sign in the user.

Amazon Cognito example for Android with mobile SDK

In this example, we will perform some tasks such as create new user, request confirmation code for new user through email, confirm user, user login, and so on.

- **Create a Cognito User Pool**:

    To create a User Pool with the default configuration, you have to pass parameters to the CognitoUserPool constructor, such as application context, userPoolId, clientId, clientSecret, and cognitoRegion (optional):

    ```
    CognitoUserPool userPool = new CognitoUserPool(context, userPoolId,
    clientId, clientSecret, cognitoRegion);
    ```

- **New user sign-up**:

Please perform the following steps to sign up new users:

Collect information from users such as username, password, given name, phone number, and email address. Now, create the `CognitoUserAttributes` object and add the user value in a key-value pair to sign up for the user:

```
CognitoUserAttributes userAttributes = new CognitoUserAttributes();

String usernameInput = username.getText().toString();
String userpasswordInput = password.getText().toString();
userAttributes.addAttribute("Name", name.getText().toString());
userAttributes.addAttribute("Email", email.getText().toString());
userAttributes.addAttribute("Phone", phone.getText().toString());

userPool.signUpInBackground(usernameInput, userpasswordInput,
userAttributes, null, signUpHandler);
```

To register or sign up a new user, you have to call `SignUpHandler`. It contains two methods: `onSuccess` and `onFailure`.

For `onSuccess`, it will call when it successfully registers a new user. The user needs to confirm the code required to activate the account. You have to pass parameters such as Cognito user, confirm state of the user, medium and destination of the confirmation code, such as email or phone, and the value for that:

```
SignUpHandler signUpHandler = new SignUpHandler() {
    @Override
    public void onSuccess(CognitoUser user, boolean
signUpConfirmationState, CognitoUserCodeDeliveryDetails
cognitoUserCodeDeliveryDetails) {
        // Check if the user is already confirmed
        if (signUpConfirmationState) {
            showDialogMessage("New User Sign up successful!","Your
Username is : "+usernameInput, true);
        }    }

    @Override
    public void onFailure(Exception exception) {
        showDialogMessage("New User Sign up
failed.",AppHelper.formatException(exception),false);
    }
};
```

You can see on the `User Pool` console that the user has been successfully signed up but not confirmed yet:

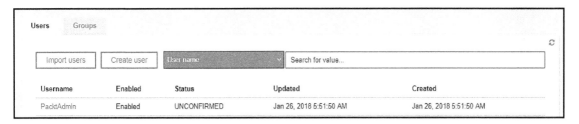

- **Confirmation code request**:

  After successfully signing up, the user needs to confirm the code for sign-in. The confirmation code will be sent to the user's email or phone. Sometimes it may automatically confirm the user by triggering a Lambda function. If you selected automatic verification when you created the User Pool, it will send the confirmation code to your email or phone. You can let the user know where they will get the confirmation code from the `cognitoUserCodeDeliveryDetails` object. It will indicate where you will send the confirmation code:

```
VerificationHandler resendConfCodeHandler = new
VerificationHandler() {
    @Override
    public void onSuccess(CognitoUserCodeDeliveryDetails details)
{
        showDialogMessage("Confirmation code sent.","Code sent to
"+details.getDestination()+" via "+details.getDeliveryMedium()+".",
false);
    }

    @Override
    public void onFailure(Exception exception) {
        showDialogMessage("Confirmation code request has failed",
AppHelper.formatException(exception), false);
    }
};
```

In this case, the user will receive an email with the confirmation code:

---

* New Packt User Sign Up Verification Code ★

no-reply@verificationemail.com Today at 11:21
To atulvmistry@yahoo.com

Greetings. Thanks for sign up to Packt. Your Sign up verification code : 018672. Please enter this code for successful login.

The user can complete the sign-up process after entering the valid confirmation code. To confirm the user, you need to call the GenericHandler. AWS SDK uses this GenericHandler to communicate the result of the confirmation API:

```
GenericHandler confHandler = new GenericHandler() {
    @Override
    public void onSuccess() {
        showDialogMessage("Success!",userName+" has been
confirmed!", true);
    }

    @Override
    public void onFailure(Exception exception) {
        showDialogMessage("Confirmation failed", exception, false);
    }
};
```

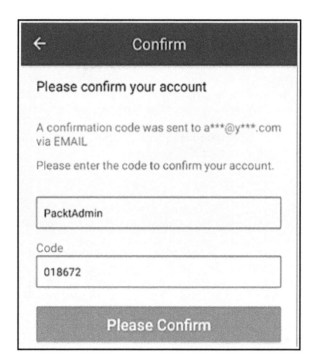

Once the user confirms, it will be updated in the Amazon Cognito console:

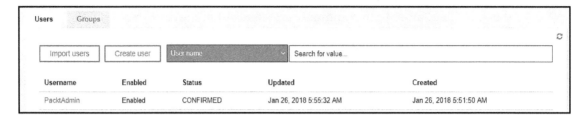

- **Sign in user to the app**:

  You must create an authentication callback handler for the user to sign in to your application. The following code will show you how the interaction happens from your app and SDK:

```
// call Authentication Handler for User sign-in process.
AuthenticationHandler authHandler = new AuthenticationHandler() {
    @Override
    public void onSuccess(CognitoUserSession cognitoUserSession) {
        launchUser();
// call Authentication Handler for User sign-in process.
AuthenticationHandler authHandler = new AuthenticationHandler() {
    @Override
    public void onSuccess(CognitoUserSession cognitoUserSession) {
        launchUser();
    }

    @Override
    public void
getAuthenticationDetails(AuthenticationContinuation continuation,
String username) {
        // Get user sign-in credential information from API.
AuthenticationDetails authDetails = new
AuthenticationDetails(username, password, null);
        // Send this user sign-in information for continuation
continuation.setAuthenticationDetails(authDetails);
        // Allow user sign-in process to continue
continuation.continueTask();
    }

    @Override
    public void getMFACode(MultiFactorAuthenticationContinuation
mfaContinuation) {
        // Get Multi-factor authentication code from user to sign-
in
```

```
        mfaContinuation.setMfaCode(mfaVerificationCode);
        // Allow user sign-in process to continue
        mfaContinuation.continueTask();
    }

    @Override
    public void onFailure(Exception e) {          // User Sign-in
failed. Please check the exception
        showDialogMessage("Sign-in failed", e);
    }

    @Override
    public void authenticationChallenge(ChallengeContinuation
continuation) {
        /** You can implement Custom authentication challenge
logic
        * here. Pass the user's responses to the continuation.
        */
    }
};
```

- **Access AWS resources from application user**:

A user can access AWS resource from the application by creating an AWS Cognito Federated Identity Pool and associating an existing User Pool with that Identity Pool, by specifying **User Pool ID** and **App client id**. Please see the next section (*Step 5*) to create the Federated Identity Pool with Cognito.

Let's continue with the same application; after the user is authenticated, add the user's identity token to the logins map in the credential provider. The provider name depends on the Amazon Cognito User Pool ID and it should have the following structure:

```
cognito-idp.<USER_POOL_REGION>.amazonaws.com/<USER_POOL_ID>
```

For this example, it will be: `cognito-idp.us-east-1.amazonaws.com/us-east-1_XUGRPHAWA`.

Now, in your credential provider, pass the ID token that you get after successful authentication:

```
// After successful authentication get id token from
// CognitoUserSession
    String idToken = cognitoUserSession.getIdToken().getJWTToken();

  // Use an existing credential provider or create new
```

```
    CognitoCachingCredentialsProvider credentialsProvider = new
CognitoCachingCredentialsProvider(context, IDENTITY_POOL_ID,
REGION);

 // Credentials provider setup
    Map<String, String> logins = new HashMap<String, String>();
    logins.put("cognito-idp.us-east-1.amazonaws.com/us-east-1_
XUGRPHAWA", idToken);
    credentialsProvider.setLogins(logins);
```

You can use this credential provider to access AWS services, such as Amazon
DynamoDB, as follows:

```
AmazonDynamoDBClient dynamoDBClient = new
AmazonDynamoDBClient(credentialsProvider)
```

You have to provide the specific IAM permission to access AWS services, such as
DynamoDB. You can add this permission to the Federated Identities, as
mentioned in the following *Step 6,* by editing the **View Policy Document**. Once
you have attached the appropriate policy, for example
AmazonDynamoDBFullAccess, for this application, you can perform the
operations such as create, read, update, and delete operations in DynamoDB.

In the next section, we will look at how to create the Amazon Cognito Federated Identities.

Amazon Cognito Federated Identities

Amazon Cognito Federated Identities enables you to create unique identities for the user
and, authenticate with Federated Identity providers.

With this identity, the user will get temporary, limited-privileged AWS credentials. With
these credentials, the user can synchronize their data with Amazon Cognito Sync or
securely access other AWS services such as Amazon S3, Amazon DynamoDB, and Amazon
API Gateway.

It supports Federated Identity providers such as Twitter, Amazon, Facebook, Google,
OpenID Connect providers, or SAML identity providers, unauthenticated identities. It also
supports developer-authenticated identities from which you can register and authenticate
the users through your own backend authentication systems.

You need to create an Identity Pool to use Amazon Cognito Federated Identities in your
application. This Identity Pool is specific for your account to store user identity data.

Creating a new Identity Pool from the console

Please perform the following steps to create a new Identity Pool from the console:

1. Log in to the AWS Management console and select the **Amazon Cognito Service**.
2. It will show you two options: **Manage your User Pools** and **Manage Federated Identities**.
3. Select **Manage Federated Identities**. It will navigate you to the **Create new identity pool** screen. Enter a unique name for the **Identity pool name**:

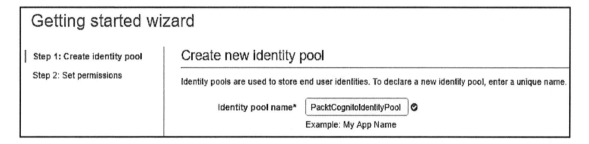

4. You can enable unauthenticated identities by selecting **Enable access to unauthenticated identities** from the collapsible section:

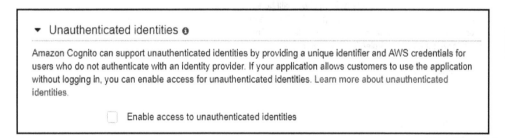

5. Under **Authentication providers**, you can allow your users to authenticate using any of the authentication methods. Click on **Create pool**.

 You must select at least one identity from Authentication providers to create a valid Identity Pool.

Here Cognito has been selected for a valid Authentication provider by adding **User Pool ID** and **App client id:**

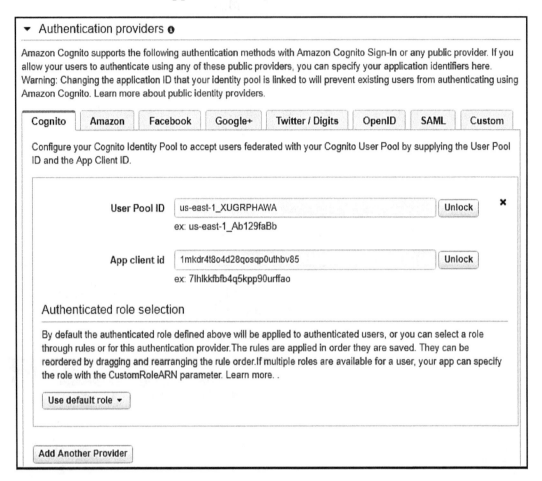

6. It will navigate to the next screen to create a new IAM role by default, to provide limited permission to end users. These permissions are for Cognito Sync and Mobile Analytics but you can edit policy documents to add/update permissions for more services. It will create two IAM roles. One for authenticated users that are supported by identity providers and another for unauthenticated users, known as guest users. Click **Allow** to generate the Identity Pool:

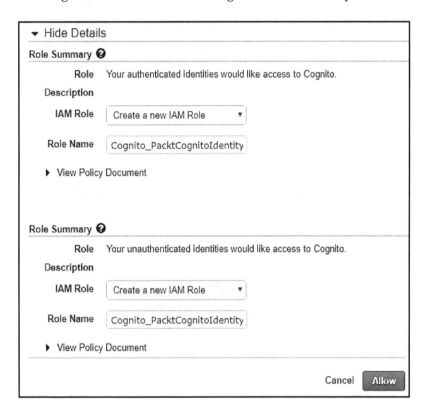

7. Once the Identity Pool is generated, it will navigate to the **Getting started with Amazon Cognito** screen for that Identity Pool. Here, it will provide you with downloadable AWS SDK for different platforms such as Android, iOS - Objective C, iOS - Swift, JavaScript, Unity, Xamarin, and .NET. It also provides sample code for **Get AWS Credentials** and **Store User Data**:

You have created Amazon Cognito Federated Identities. In the next section, we will look at Amazon Cognito Sync.

Amazon Cognito Sync

Amazon Cognito Sync is an AWS Service used to synchronize the data across client devices, platforms, and operating systems.

Amazon Cognito Sync supports cross-device sync and the offline access of a user's application-related data. It can be used to synchronize a user's profile data as well as across mobile and web applications, without requiring your backend system.

It contains a client library to cache data locally that is used to read and write data, without any device connectivity status. You can synchronize the data when the device is online and you can set push synchronization to notify other devices whenever any update is available.

It provides a client library to enable the cross-device sync of application-related data. If a user is using your app on a phone and later on switches to a tablet or other devices, the persisted application information is available on other devices.

The client libraries cache the user information locally which means the app can read and write data, regardless of any device connectivity, and it will synchronize the user data when the device comes online. You can set up the push sync, then it will notify other devices immediately about the availability of new updates.

Amazon Cognito saves end-user data as key-value pairs in datasets. This data is associated with Amazon Cognito Identity and it can be accessed across different devices and logins. The synchronize method is invoked to sync the data between an end user's device and Amazon Cognito. The maximum size of each dataset is 1 MB, and you can associate an identity with up to 20 datasets.

As we discussed, a client of Amazon Cognito Sync creates a local cache for identity data and the app talks to this cache, when it reads and write keys. All of your changes made on the device are available immediately on the device, even if you are offline. When you call the synchronize method, it will pull the changes from the service to the device and it will push the local changes from the device to the service, so the changes are available for other devices to synchronize.

You need to create a credential provider to initialize the Amazon Cognito Sync client. This credential provider gets temporary AWS credentials to enable the app to access your AWS resources.

You can use the following code to initialize the Amazon Cognito Sync client in Android.

You need to import the Amazon Cognito package:

```
import com.amazonaws.mobileconnectors.cognito.*;
```

Now, initialize the Amazon Cognito Sync Manager by providing the Android app context, an AWS region, and an Amazon Cognito credential provider:

```
CognitoSyncManager client = new CognitoSyncManager
  (getApplicationContext(), Regions.YOUR_REGION, credentialsProvider);
```

With Amazon Cognito, your app's profile data is organized into datasets. This dataset is the granular entity to perform the sync operation and it is a unique string. Read and write operations on datasets will affect the local store, until the synchronize method is invoked.

The following code will create a new dataset or open an existing dataset:

```
Dataset dataset = client.openOrCreateDataset("my_dataset_name");
```

Amazon Cognito datasets function as dictionaries and are accessible through keys with values.

 Dataset values affect only the local cached copy, until you call its synchronize method.

```
String value = dataset.get("myKey");
// You can call put to put the key in dataset
dataset.put("myKey", "my value");
// You can call remove to remove the key from dataset
dataset.remove("myKey");
```

You can call `synchronize` to compare Amazon Cognito Sync store data with local cache data. Amazon Cognito Sync will pull the remote changes, conflict the resolution, if any, and update the values on the service which are pushed from the device. You can call synchronize dataset by calling its synchronize method:

```
dataset.synchronize(syncCallback);
```

When connectivity is available immediately, `synchronizeOnConnectivity()` will behave as `synchronize()` and if it's not available, it will monitor for connectivity change and perform a sync when connectivity is available.

When `synchronizeOnConnectivity()` calls multiple times, then only the last synchronize request is kept and callback will fire.

This method will not perform sync and callback will not fire, if the dataset or the callback has collected garbage.

To delete the dataset from Amazon Cognito, you first remove the dataset from local storage and then call the `synchronize()` method:

```
dataset.delete();
dataset.synchronize(syncCallback);
```

Now, let's understand how to handle a callback.

You can implement the `SyncCallback` interface to receive a notification in the app. Your app can make the decision to delete the local data, merge authenticated and unauthenticated profiles, and resolve the synchronization conflicts. You can implement the following methods:

- `onSuccess()`: It will trigger when a dataset is downloaded successfully from the sync store:

  ```
  @Override
  public void onSuccess(Dataset dataset, List<Record> newRecords) {}
  ```

- `onFailure()`: It will call if an exception occurs during synchronization:

  ```
  @Override
  public void onFailure(DataStorageException dse) {}
  ```

- `onConflict()`: It might happen that the same key has been modified in the local store and in the sync store. This `onConflict()` method helps to handle this kind of conflict situation. If you do not implement this method, then Amazon Cognito Sync will use the most recent changes:

  ```
  @Override
  public boolean onConflict(Dataset dataset, final List<SyncConflict>
  conflicts) {
      List<Record> resolveRecord = new ArrayList<Record>();
      for (SyncConflict conflict : conflicts) {
          // Taking remote records to resolve conflicts
          resolveRecord.add(conflict.resolveWithRemoteRecord());
      }
      dataset.resolve(resolveRecord);

      // synchronize() will retry after conflicts resolved
      return true;
  }
  ```

- `onDatasetDeleted()`: Once the dataset is deleted, it should also delete the local dataset, and the Amazon Cognito client uses the `SyncCallback` interface to confirm it. What you can do with the local data is that you can tell the client SDK by implementing the `onDatasetDeleted()` method:

```
@Override
public boolean onDatasetDeleted(Dataset dataset, String
datasetName) {
    // Return true to delete local dataset copy
    return true;
}
```

- `onDatasetsMerged()`: All the datasets are merged when two unconnected or disconnected identities are linked together. You can notify the application to merge by calling the `onDatasetsMerged()` method:

```
@Override
public boolean onDatasetsMerged(Dataset dataset, List<String>
datasetNames) {
    // Return false if Dataset merge outside the synchronization
callback
    return false;
}
```

 You can use default `SyncCallback` for empty implementation for all, if you don't want to implement all the callbacks.

In Amazon Cognito, the association between the device and identity can track automatically. You can sure that every instance of the identity is notified when it identifies any changes using **push synchronization** or **push sync**. Push sync confirms that whenever any changes occur in sync store data for a particular identity, then it will automatically send the silent push notification to other devices associated with that identity.

 JavaScript, Xamarin, and Unity do not support Push Sync.

To enable **Push Sync** for your application, you need to create and configure an Amazon SNS app for the supported platform and select the service role in the **Federated Identities** page for **Push Synchronization**:

You can use the following keys for the push notification payload:

- **source**: `cognito-sync` is the differentiating factor between notifications
- **identityPoolId**: The Identity Pool ID, used for validation or additional information
- **identityId**: Identity ID within the pool
- **datasetName**: Name of the dataset which was updated
- **syncCount**: The sync count for the remote dataset

Summary

So far, we have looked at AWS Cognito with User Pools, Federated Identities, and Cognito Sync.

In the next chapter, we will discuss three main architectures: EC2 instance with Load Balancer, Docker, and Serverless, and look at the differences between them.

7
Evaluating the Best Architecture

In the previous chapter, we looked at how the AWS Cognito service provides simple and secure user authentication for mobile and web applications.

In this chapter, we will discuss traditional web hosting, and web hosting on the cloud using AWS, and look at the best architecture for the application. We will also look at the comparison between EC2 instances with load balancer, Docker, and serverless architecture, such as Amazon Lambda, and evaluate the results.

Most traditional web hosting comes in two types: dedicated and shared, and it depends on one machine only. In dedicated web hosting, clients have to pay upfront for one or more servers from the service provider, and they have full control of the resources. For shared web hosting, clients have to pay for a set of shared space and resources, on a server with other clients. This form of web hosting is popular with small and medium size businesses.

Cloud web hosting is in demand and is the most popular. It provides different kinds of services for the customer. It is high performance, scalable, reliable, secure, and affordable; it helps to avoid a single point of failure by spreading the resources, such as RAM, disk, and CPU, on multiple connected servers. It utilizes the resource to its maximum extent to help with the **Return on Investment** (**ROI**).

Currently, there are many players in the market for cloud computing, such as AWS, Microsoft Azure, Google Cloud, and many others. But AWS has dominated the market and it offers more and variety of services than others.

Amazon Elastic Compute Cloud is a well-known AWS service that provides resizable compute capacity to run applications on the cloud. It provides a console, AWS CLI, or AWS SDK to create the virtual machines and easily configure their capacity. Amazon EC2 offers different types of instances for different requirements and costs.

Docker is a container-based platform for modern applications. It is used to build, test, deploy, and manage the applications on-premises and in the cloud, as well from development to production. Docker is a packaged software in standardized units known as containers. It comes in two forms: Docker **Community Edition** (**CE**) for developers to build the applications, and Docker **Enterprise Edition** (**EE**) for multi-architecture operations. It is reducing the infrastructure cost by 50% or more. AWS provides container-managed services called Amazon **Elastic Container Service** (**ECS**) for Docker.

AWS Lambda is an event-driven compute service and is also known as serverless architecture. It executes the code in response to events without provision, or manages the servers. Your code will scale automatically when it needs to, from a few requests per day to thousands of requests per second. It will charge when the code is running.

In this chapter, we will cover the following topics:

- The comparison of traditional web hosting versus web hosting on the cloud using AWS
- The AWS Well-Architected framework
- Amazon EC2 instances and Elastic Load Balancer
- Docker with Amazon EC2 Container Service (Amazon ECS)
- Serverless architecture with Lambda
- Use cases for different architectures
- Controlling and optimizing costs

Now let's start with the first topic and look at traditional and cloud web hosting.

The comparison of traditional web hosting versus web hosting on the cloud using AWS

Now, in this section we will look at traditional web hosting and web hosting on the cloud, using Amazon Web Services. Let's start with traditional web hosting.

Traditional web hosting

Traditional web hosting is mainly shared or dedicated hosting.

In shared hosting, you are sharing the server resources with other websites. It is used by small to medium-scale websites because of the cost-effectiveness and low maintenance.

The drawbacks of shared hosting are:

- **Performance**: Your website will share server resources such as storage, CPU, and bandwidth with other websites, so if other websites get more user traffic, it will slow down your website.
- **Lack of control**: You are not the owner of the server. You can use only the available resources on the server and can't install any software, as per your needs.

Challenges with traditional hosting

In traditional web hosting, you need to purchase additional resources as the website traffic grows. It is a very expensive and complex proposition to keep websites highly available and scalable. To achieve this, you have to implement complex solutions that will ensure a high level of availability, and also require you to implement accurate traffic forecasts to provide a high level of customer service. Sometimes, there is low utilization of your expensive hardware because of less traffic to your website, which means that you are maintaining idle or underused hardware, with high operating costs.

For example, you can go for shared hosting if your website has 10,000 users. In the same way, you can go for dedicated hosting if you have 100,000 users, and you can add more servers as the number of users grows. You need to keep purchasing the servers as the traffic grows. Now, the real problem starts here. The traffic decreases and the extra servers that you have purchased aren't being used. In today's world, hardware is becoming a commodity, but on the other hand, the value of this server deprecates more than 50% over a year. It means that you are getting a very small, or negative Return of Investment (ROI) on your investment of an extra server.

As per the following example, a traditional web hosting application generally implements three tiers of architecture, a Presentation layer (User Interface layer), an Application layer (Business layer), and a Data layer (Persistence layer). This architecture also contains built-in performance, availability, and failover features:

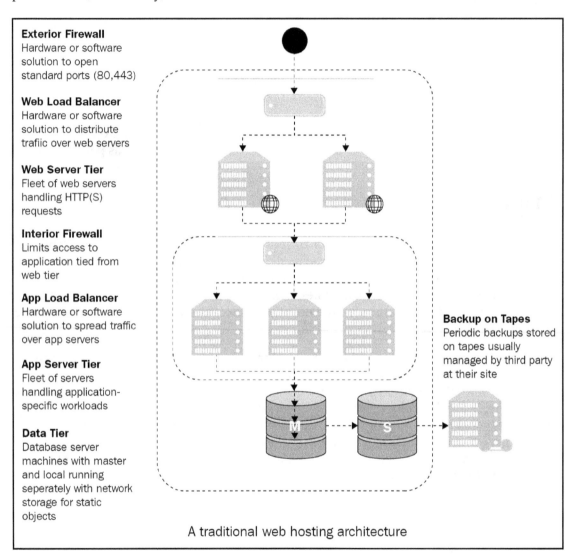

Exterior Firewall
Hardware or software solution to open standard ports (80,443)

Web Load Balancer
Hardware or software solution to distribute trafiic over web servers

Web Server Tier
Fleet of web servers handling HTTP(S) requests

Interior Firewall
Limits access to application tied from web tier

App Load Balancer
Hardware or software solution to spread traffic over app servers

App Server Tier
Fleet of servers handling application-specific workloads

Data Tier
Database server machines with master and local running seperately with network storage for static objects

Backup on Tapes
Periodic backups stored on tapes usually managed by third party at their site

A traditional web hosting architecture

Cloud hosting

Cloud computing provides high availability and scalability that traditional hosting can't provide. Cloud hosting companies rent out their server space as needed and on an on-demand basis. Instead of paying upfront for a server, you will pay for what you actually use. Cloud hosting is more resilient and elastic. It will not affect the performance and bandwidth of your application or website, if there is a problem with any other application or website.

Cloud hosting scales more quickly than traditional hosting. The cloud server will scale up and down automatically, if the traffic to the website or applications, increases or decreases. It will also add and remove the server space automatically.

In short, cloud hosting provides you with highly available, scalable, flexible, and low-cost hosting solutions without any maintenance.

Now, let's look at why cloud hosting is a better choice over traditional hosting:

- Highly available:
    - **Cloud hosting**: It guarantees no single point of failure and maximum network uptime. If one server fails and is unable to take a request than another server will take over the workload of the failed server, because all the servers are interconnected.
    - **Traditional hosting**: Due to single server setup, there are risks of downtime and hardware failure for your application and website.
- Pay as you need:
    - **Cloud hosting**: You will not invest in any of the infrastructure. You pay for the resource or service that you actually use.
    - **Traditional hosting**: You have to pay a fixed amount for the service, whether you use it or not. If you have set up your own infrastructure, then it will cost more for the initial setup, as well as for maintenance.
- Security:
    - **Cloud hosting**: It will secure your data at different levels, such as network, application, data, and physical. It will also ensure the safety of the data through identity management, data isolation, storage, encryption, firewalls, and backups.

- **Traditional hosting**: You share the resources with other websites on the same server, and there is the risk that if one website has been hacked, then it is easier to access other websites, too. You can maintain a dedicated server to store your sensitive information but the costs for this are very high.

- Scalability:

  - **Cloud hosting**: It is simple and quick to allocate resources. You can add/reduce or remove resources, such as RAM, CPU, memory, and storage from the network of multiple servers.
  - **Traditional hosting**: It might have rigid specifications and limited resource to add/reduce or remove any resources immediately.

- Multi-location:

  - **Cloud hosting**: Hosting servers are present across the globe and can be accessed from anywhere.
  - **Traditional hosting**: Servers are located at a fixed place, so you have to select the location of the server wisely, as it plays a major role in loading the website.

- Disaster recovery and backup:

  - **Cloud hosting**: It provides a disaster recovery feature so that data is backed up automatically to interconnected servers.
  - **Traditional hosting**: It doesn't offer disaster recovery, as it provides a single server to host the application or website. You are responsible for backing up the data periodically.

- Integration:

  - **Cloud hosting**: You can customize or integrate applications with the latest technologies as per your business needs. This includes the upgrading of servers and the latest releases of software.
  - **Traditional hosting**: You cannot customize or upgrade automatically.

Now, if you have decided to go for the cloud than you need to find a suitable architecture. In the next section, we evaluate AWS solutions. For that, we will deploy the application on-premises, present the AWS cloud architecture, and discuss its key components.

The AWS solution for common web hosting

For your running web application, you might face some architectural and infrastructure issues, and for that, AWS provides cost-effective and reliable solutions. The following are some of the benefits of using AWS:

- **Handle peaks in cost-effective way**:

    In the traditional hosting model, you have to take care and handle peak capacity by provisioning additional servers. This wastes resources during off-peak periods.

    If you host the application on AWS, then it will provision the additional servers during the peak hours, and constantly adjust the cost and capacity to meet the actual traffic patterns.

    For example, as shown in the diagram that during the peak hours from 9 A.M. to 3 P.M., it has maximum inbound traffic. So, if we consider the traditional hosting model, it will waste the resources in the remainder of the day. In contrast, in the AWS scenario, it will automatically scale and provision the resource, when it needs to, during actual traffic trends. It will not waste the resources and saves more than 50% on costs:

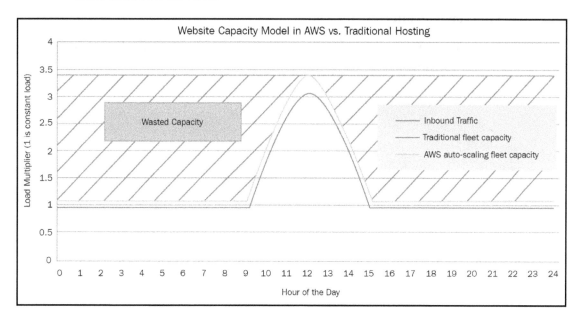

- **Solution for unexpected spikes**:

  During unexpected traffic spikes, the traditional hosting model is unable to respond on time. It often happens that web applications are not able to handle the unexpected spikes and go down.

  With AWS, it automatically scales on demand for the unexpected traffic spikes, launches the server quickly and in case of normal traffic, it will take the servers offline.

- **An On-Demand solution for different environments**:

  In traditional web hosting, you need a different environment, such as preproduction, beta, testing, and production, to ensure the quality of the web application. The hardware costs of these different environments are relatively high. It might also happen that you are not using hardware to its optimum capacity and very often the expensive hardware sits unused.

  In the AWS Cloud, you can provision a different kind of environment when you need it. It also enables you to quickly switch between different environments, with little or no service outages and with small configuration changes.

- **AWS cloud architecture for web hosting**:

  The following figure shows a classic web application using an AWS Cloud Computing infrastructure:

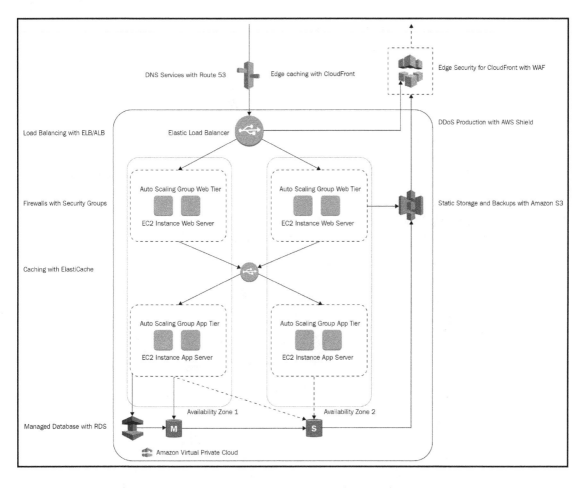

The following is the list of resources used in the preceding architecture:

- **Elastic Load Balancing (ELB) and Application Load Balancer (ALB)**: To decouple services and redundancy, these spread the load across Amazon EC2 Auto Scaling groups and multiple Availability Zones.
- **Amazon S3 for Static Storage**: Enables you to store simple HTTP-based objects for backups and static content, such as executable scripts, images, videos.
- **Amazon RDS to Manage Database (DB)**: Creates highly available, multi-AZ DB architecture.
- **Amazon ElastiCache for Caching**: Provides a caching service to remove load from applications and databases with Memcached or Redis. It will lower the latency for frequent requests.

- **Amazon Route53 for DNS Services**: Simplifies domain management.
- **Amazon CloudFront for Edge Caching**: Caches the content to decrease the latency for customers.
- **Amazon CloudFront with AWS WAF for Edge Security**: Filters malicious traffic, such as XSS and SQL injection, to provide edge security through customer-defined rules.
- **Security Groups with Firewall**: Web and application servers will get the host-level firewall for the instance.
- **AWS Shield for DDoS Protection**: Your infrastructure safeguards automatically against the DDoS attacks.

If we consider different kinds of architecture such as traditional hosting on the cloud, Docker, and serverless architecture, then it can be split in the following ways:

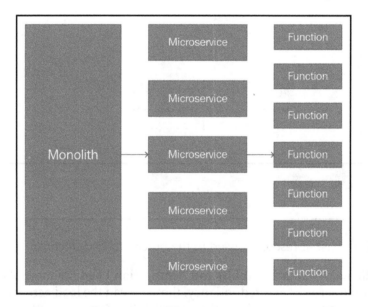

Now, let's look at the AWS Well-Architected framework, provided by AWS.

AWS Well-Architected framework

The AWS Well-Architected framework provides best practices that you will learn and implement to design a secure, cost-effective, and reliable application.

This framework is divided into five pillars, as follows:

- **Operational excellence**:
    - To deliver business values, systems should be able to run and monitor
    - The supporting process and procedures improve continually
- **Security**:
    - Provides risk assessments and mitigation strategies while delivering business values to protect systems, information, data, and assets
- **Reliability**:
    - The system should be capable of recovering from service/infrastructure disruptions, by acquiring resources dynamically to meet demand, and from transient network issues, or mitigating disruptions such as mis-configurations
- **Performance efficiency**:
    - To meet system requirements, it should use computing resources efficiently
    - It should also maintain the same efficiency whenever there are changes to demand and changes to technologies
- **Cost optimization**:
    - It should be able to eliminate suboptimal resources or avoid unneeded costs

The following are some of the general design principles which have been identified by the AWS Well-Architected framework, to facilitate good design in the cloud:

- You can eliminate the guessing capacity for your infrastructure needs, as it will automatically scale up and down, as per your requirements.
- You can create a production-like test environment to test your systems and, once you have completed the testing, you can decommission the resources. You will pay only when your test environment is running.

- You can automate the experiment for any architecture change easily, by creating or replicating the system at low cost.
- With traditional architecture, it is difficult to change the architecture continually and take advantage of the latest technology. In the cloud, you can automate and test the new technology on demand, which allows you to evolve over time with innovations, and take advantage of it, as a standard practice for your business.
- You can collect the data on the cloud and see how the different architectural choices affect the behavior of the workloads; this will help you in making fact-based decisions.
- You can schedule such a process regularly, in order to simulate some events in a production environment. This helps to improve the organizational experience of dealing with that sort of event.

All five pillars contain design principles, definitions, best practices, and key AWS services. We will not go into much detail about those; instead we will look at the real-time use cases with their challenges and see how AWS solves the problems.

Now, let's briefly look at the EC2 instance with Elastic Load Balancer, Docker, and AWS Lambda, with its benefits and drawbacks.

Amazon EC2 instance and Elastic Load Balancer

Amazon Elastic Compute Cloud (**Amazon EC2**) is a web service that provides a virtual server on the cloud. It eliminates your costs in investing in hardware up front and gives you the facility to develop and deploy your application faster. You can launch as many or as few Amazon EC2 instances as per your business requirements, configure security and networking, and manage the storage. It will boot new server instances in minutes and allow you to quickly scale your capacity up or down, as the requirements change or if there are unexpected spikes.

For Amazon EC2 instances, you will pay for the capacity that you actually use. It provides tools to build applications that are failure resilient, and isolates the developers from common failure scenarios.

Amazon EC2 common terms are as follows:

- **Instances**: Virtual compute environments
- **Instance types**: Different configurations such as CPU, storage, memory, and networking capacity for instances
- **Amazon Machine Images (AMIs)**: Preconfigured templates for instances
- **Key-Value Pairs**: Secure login information for instances
- **Instance store volumes**: To store temporary data, it will be deleted when you stop or terminate instances
- **Amazon EBS volumes**: Persistent storage volumes for data using **Amazon Elastic Block Store** (**Amazon EBS**)
- **Security groups**: A firewall that enables you to specify the protocols, ports, and source IP ranges that can reach instances
- **Elastic IP addresses**: Static IPv4 addresses for dynamic cloud computing
- **Tags**: Metadata that you can create and assign to Amazon EC2 resources

EC2 purchasing options are as follows:

- **On-Demand Instances**: Low cost, flexible without any upfront cost, long-term commitment, and unpredictable workload cannot interrupt the application.
- **Reserved Instances**: Provides capacity reservation, offers discount on instances for one year or three year terms, steady or predictable usage applications.
- **Spot Instances**: Spot instances enables bid. You can use spot instances when you have applications with flexible start and end times. You need large additional capacity on an urgent basis. Useful for saving costs up to 90% than on-demand instance.
- **Dedicated Hosts**: Physical and dedicated EC2 servers. Used for existing server-bound software licenses and regulatory requirements.

Amazon EC2 provides 32 instance types with five categories for different use cases. These instance types are combinations of CPU, memory storage, network capacity, and graphic hardware, to provide you with more flexibility for your applications. Each instance type has one or more instance size to allow you to scale the resources:

General Purpose		
Instance Family	**Features**	**Use Case**
T2	• Balance of memory, compute, and network resource • Governed by CPU credit, burstable - CPU, consistent performance	• Website and web applications • Development, test, and staging environments • Microservice and code repo
M5	• Powered by light-weight Nitro system • New larger instance size • Higher EBS performance on smaller instance sizes	• Small and mid-size databases • Data processing tasks that require additional memory • Running backend servers for enterprise applications
M4	• Support for enhanced networking • By default, EBS-optimized without additional cost	• Same as use case for the M5 instance

Compute Optimized		
Instance Family	**Features**	**Use Case**
C5	• By default, EBS-optimized • Runs each core using Intel Turbo Boost Technology • New larger instance size	• High-performance web servers and computing • Machine/deep learning inference • Highly-scalable multiplayer gaming
C4	• By default, EBS-optimized without additional cost • Higher networking performance • Requires Amazon VPC, Amazon EBS and 64-bit HVM AMIs	• High-performance, frontend fleets, web servers • Batch processing, distributed analytics • High performance science and engineering applications

Memory Optimized		
Instance Family	**Features**	**Use Case**

X1E	• High frequency processors • Up to 3,904 GiB of DRAM-based instance memory • Ability to control processor C-state and P-state configurations	• High-performance databases and memory-intensive applications • Certified by SAP to run next-generation Business Suite • Data Mart Solutions on HANA
X1	• One of the lowest prices • Ability to control processor C-state and P-state configuration • By default, SSD storage, and EBS-optimized without additional cost	• In-memory databases • Big data processing engines • High-performance computing (HPC)
R4	• High frequency processors • DDR4 Memory • Enhanced networking support	• High-performance databases, data mining, analysis • Applications performing real-time processing of unstructured data

Accelerate Computing

Instance Family	Features	Use Case
P3	• High-frequency Intel processors • Provides enhanced networking within a Placement Group • Supports NVLink for peer-to-peer GPU communication	• Machine/deep learning • High-performance computing • Speech recognition, autonomous vehicles, drug discovery
P2	• High-frequency Intel processors • Provides enhanced networking within a Placement Group • Supports GPUDirect™ for peer-to-peer GPU communications	• Machine learning and high-performance databases • Computational fluid dynamics and finance • Seismic analysis, molecular modeling and genomics
G3	• Enables NVIDIA GRID Virtual Workstation features • Each GPU features an on-board hardware video encoder • Enabling low-latency frame capture, encoding, and high-quality interactive streaming experiences	• 3D visualizations and rendering • Graphics-intensive remote workstation • Application streaming and video encoding

F1	• High-frequency processors • NVMe SSD Storage • Support for enhanced networking	• Genomics research and financial analytics • Real-time video processing • Big data search and analysis, and security

Storage Optimized

Instance Family	Features	Use Case
H1	• Up to 16 TB of HDD storage • High disk throughput • ENA enabled enhanced networking	• MapReduce-based workloads, distributed file systems • Network file system and big data workload clusters • Log or data processing applications
I3	• High-frequency processors • High random I/O performance and high sequential read throughput • Supports Bare Metal instance type	• NoSQL and in-memory databases • Scale-out transactional databases • Data warehousing, Elasticsearch and analytics workloads
D2	• HDD storage and high disk throughput • Consistent high performance at launch time • Support for enhanced networking	• Massively Parallel Processing (MPP) data warehousing • MapReduce and Hadoop distributed computing • Distributed file and network file systems

The following is the architecture for any simple application, where the applications are running on Amazon EC2 instances. In the next section,we will look at the architecture for Amazon ECS and AWS Lambda:

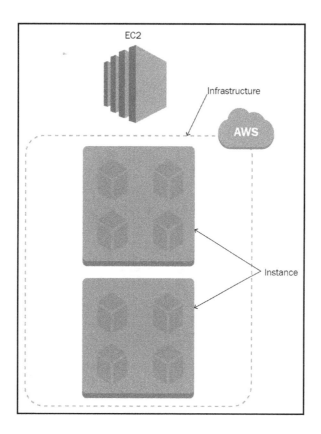

Benefits and drawbacks of Amazon EC2

The following are the benefits and drawbacks of Amazon EC2:

Benefits:

- You can provision new servers instantly
- Provides variety of instance types and is ready to launch any OS or software without setup
- You can run servers in multiple regions from a standard EC2 console

- Provides programmatic and API access
- It provides high availability and capacity planning in multiple availability zones, in each region
- You can bid for spot instances at a cheap price for cost savings on scalable workloads
- Long-term pricing is available at discounted rates
- ELB makes load balancing easy to set up

Drawbacks:

- All servers are virtual and large instance types with better provision might encounter performance issues, compared to a dedicated server
- Expensive at On-Demand rates
- Cross-region communication is not available
- VPN access is not available if connected to an internal network
- Networking is not flexible

Now let's understand the Elastic Load Balancing that is used to distribute the load on an EC2 instance.

Elastic Load Balancing

Elastic Load Balancing (**ELB**) is a service from AWS to balance the load automatically. It will help distribute incoming traffic, and scales the resources automatically, to meet demand. Users enable it within a single or multiple-availability zones to maintain application performance.

ELB offers features including:

- Automatically detecting the unhealthy Amazon EC2 instances
- Spreading incoming traffic to healthy channels
- **Secure Sockets Layer** (**SSL**) certificates are centrally managed
- Public key authentication
- Supports for IPv4 and IPv6

Elastic Load Balancer supports the following three types of load balancers:

- **Application Load Balancers**: Best suited for HTTP and HTTPS traffic and advanced request routing
- **Network Load Balancers**: Best suited for TCP traffic and to get extreme performance
- **Classic Load Balancers**: Connection and request level, load balancing across multiple Amazon EC2 instances

It contains the following benefits:

- **Highly Available**: Incoming traffic will be distributed between multiple targets such as Amazon EC2 instances, IP address, containers; it must be received from healthy targets
- **Elastic**: It is capable of handling any quick changes in network traffic. It provides deep integration with Auto Scaling
- **Secure**: It provides security features such as integration with certificate management and SSL decryption
- **Flexible**: It allows an IP address to route the incoming request to application targets
- **Monitoring and auditing**: The Elastic Load balancer provides real-time monitoring of the application and its performance, with Amazon CloudWatch metrics, request tracing, and logging
- **Hybrid Load Balancing**: The Elastic Load balancer offers to load balance across on-premises resources and AWS resources using the same load balancer

Now, let's look at Docker and Docker on AWS, using the Amazon EC2 Container Service.

Docker with the Amazon EC2 Container Service (Amazon ECS)

Docker is a technology to build, run, test, and deploy distributed applications, easily and quickly on Linux-based containers. In Docker, your application will be packaged with all of its dependencies, into a standardized unit. This standardized unit is known as a container. This container includes system tools, libraries, and code to run the applications. You can scale and deploy applications in any environment and know that your code will run.

It helps users by providing highly reliable and low-cost ways to build, run, test, and deploy the distributed applications, at any scale, by running Docker on AWS. Docker comes in two licensing models: subscription-based Docker **Enterprise Edition** (**EE**), open source Docker **Community Edition** (**CE**), and AWS supports both these models.

It provides a few benefits such as:

- Docker users ship software 13 times more frequently than non-Docker users because developers will ship only isolated services as needed
- It improves productivity by reducing the time to set up new environments or troubleshoot between different environments
- Docker-based applications move seamlessly from local machines to production environments on AWS
- You can easily deploy small containerized applications or identify issues, if any, or roll back the deployments, if necessary
- Docker contains built-in security capabilities and out-of-the box configurations to provide safer delivery across the application life cycle.
- Docker helps to streamline operations and optimizes the infrastructure resources to save more than 50% in total costs

Use case of Docker

- You can use Docker where you need Continuous Integration, and accelerate application delivery by standardizing the environments and removing the conflicts between different language stacks and versions.
- Docker will use big data processing as a service. It will package the data into containers to be executed by non-technical users.
- You can use Containers-as-a-Service to build, run, and managed the distributed applications and the content and infrastructure.

We will look at Containers in the next section.

Containers

A container is a standalone, lightweight and executable package that is a piece of software; it includes everything required to run it such as runtime, code, system libraries, and system tools.

It is available for Linux and Windows-based applications, and is containerized software that will always run the same way, in any of the environments. It will isolate the software from the surroundings.

Containers and virtual machines have the same benefits for resource isolation and allocation; both function differently, as Containers virtualize the operating system and not the hardware. Containers are more efficient and portable, compared to virtual machines.

In the next section, we will look at the Amazon EC2 Container Service.

Amazon ECS

Amazon ECS is a container-managed service to run, stop, and manage Docker containers, quickly and easily on a cluster. It is highly scalable and you can host clusters on serverless infrastructure. You can also use Amazon EC2 to host your task to gain more control, and manage by using Amazon EC2 launch types, such as the Fargate launch type and the EC2 launch type.

With Amazon ECS, by using simple API calls you can launch and stop the container-based applications. You can also get the cluster state from a centralized service and give access to other Amazon EC2 features.

EC2 is a remote virtual machine where as ECS is a logical grouping of EC2 instances. If you launch an ECS instance without adding an EC2 instance, then it doesn't make any sense. ECS is a cluster of EC2 instances and it uses Docker to instantiate containers on these EC2 hosts.

With Amazon ECS, you will get a consistent deployment and build experience. It is also used to **Extract-Transform-Load** (**ETL**) the workloads, and to manage and scale the batch. We will discuss this more in `Chapter 9`, *Amazon EC2 Container Service*.

In the following figure, we can see how the different services run in containers on ECS instances:

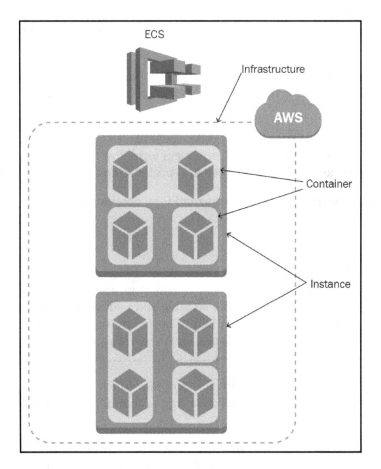

The Amazon ECS benefits are:

- Easy to use.
- Amazon ECS and Docker CLI are tightly integrated to simplify development and production workflow.
- With the Amazon EC2 container service, you can launch your own container and not share the resource with other customers. It has great level of isolation and will provide you with a highly reliable and secure application. It is highly secure as permissions and the users' access can be controlled using AWS IAM.

- No upfront fees or commitments. You pay only for the amount of data you store in your repositories, and data transferred to the internet.
- Easy to manage the cluster without the need to scale or install any software. You have full control, and visibility for the cluster and can easily integrate it with any of your applications or schedulers.
- You can connect easily with an existing application.
- You can easily integrate with other AWS services such as IAM, CloudTrail, AWS **Virtual Private Cloud** (**VPC**), Elastic Load Balancer, to offer a containerized services or applications-based solution.
- With Amazon ECS, you can launch multiple containers without any complexity in much less time.
- AWS ECS removes the complexity for container management and you just need to launch the cluster of container instances.
- In ECS, you can create task definitions by defining the tasks using a declarative template. In this file, you can define CPU requirements, the Docker repository, and memory and shared data volumes. It will also control the application version.
- ECS offers a set of simple APIs for the integration or extension of services to create, as well as delete, the clusters. You can register/deregister tasks and launch/terminate containers.
- The Amazon ECS service scheduler will add or remove the container from ELB automatically.
- Amazon ECS provides capabilities to monitor containers and clusters. You can set the AWS CloudWatch alarms.

Amazon ECS drawbacks:

- Lack of insight about registry use
- It is quite difficult to work with a Docker client because it requires you to create a temporary token
- It is expensive, if the container is not deployed on AWS

Now, let's look at the serverless architecture with AWS Lambda.

Serverless architecture with Lambda

AWS Lambda is a compute service. It is called a serverless architecture because you will not provision or manage any servers. Your code will execute whenever you need it. It will scale automatically to 1,000 requests per second.

You will pay for the compute time that you consume to run the code; there is no extra charge when the code is idle. You can virtually run the code for any type of application and backend service, with zero administration.

AWS Lambda provides high-availability compute infrastructure to perform the administration of resources. This includes operating systems and server maintenance, automatic scaling, capacity provisioning, code monitoring, and logging.

You need to write your code in an AWS Lambda supported language; currently AWS Lambda supports Java, Node.js, C#, Go, and Python.

AWS Lambda is also known as event-driven architecture. It will execute the code in response to any events, such as if file is uploaded or downloaded into an Amazon S3 bucket, or data is added or removed from an Amazon DynamoDB table. Amazon API Gateway is used to run your code in response to an HTTP request. AWS SDKs are also used to invoke the code by using API calls.

Serverless applications can be built using the Lambda functions, by triggering events and deploying them automatically through AWS CodeBuild and AWS CodePipeline.

AWS Lambda console, AWS CLI, and AWS **Serverless Application Model** (**SAM**) are used to create and test the AWS Lambda-based applications.

Event-based, server-side logic that runs on stateless compute containers which will ephermal and managed by a third party, is known as serverless. It is also known as **Function-as-a-Service** (**FaaS**) and AWS Lambda is a popular implementation of this.

In the following architecture, we can see how the different functions run on AWS Lambda:

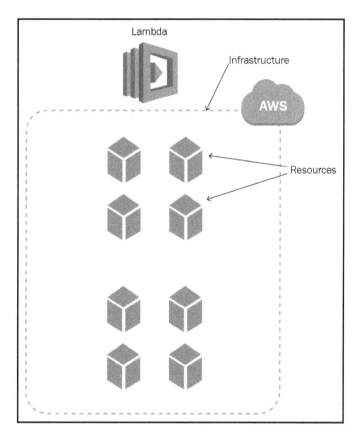

Now, we will look at the benefits and drawbacks of AWS Lambda.

Serverless benefits using AWS Lambda:

- There is a clear separation between the infrastructure services and applications that are running on top of the platform.
- FaaS provides an automatic scaling functionality to reduce operational management overheads and compute cost.
- Lower operational and development costs.
- It doesn't need to implement any code for scaling, and administrators do not need to add or upgrade any servers.

- Technical resources can innovate at a rapid pace.
- It will aid quicker software release and reduce the time to market.
- You will pay for the bills when the AWS Lambda function is called.
- Developers can work in an Agile way and focus on the development of the product for faster delivery.
- Fits with microservices so it can be implemented as a function.
- Reduces software complexity.
- Simply package and easily deploy without any system administration.
- No need to worry about infrastructure security.
- AWS Lambda functions are stateless.
- AWS Lambda will scale automatically for instances and spin them up. If there are massive changes in scale, you need to inform AWS.
- Your risk is reduced by not relying on a single machine to serve your app and execute the code. AWS Lambda automatically swaps it out, if one machine goes down.

Serverless drawbacks using AWS Lambda:

- FaaS adds some latency so is not the best solution for high-performance applications.
- AWS Lambda functions are time boxed and it has a default timeout of three seconds and is configurable up to 300 secs or 5 min. So, you will spend more time orchestrating and organizing the functions. Tasks with large amount of data will exceed the runtime limits.
- In traditional applications, it can be handled by launching another microservice, or by calling a custom tool. AWS Lambda doesn't provide these options.
- AWS Lambda functions are stateless, so don't store data locally. It might be a limitation for the Lambda function.
- You don't have control of your system and it is completely dependent on a third-party. It is difficult to change the platform or provider without making any changes to your applications. It also depends on the platform availability, its API, and costs to change.
- Giving up system control when implementing APIs leads to system downtime, loss of functionality, forced API upgrades, cost changes and unexpected limits.
- Serverless is not suitable for long-running applications.

- Service providers run the software for different customers on the same physical server to utilize the resources more efficiently. It might create security issues, if the customer's platform or code has any potential bugs and it affects your data. It also affects the availability and performance of your application.
- In serverless platforms, AWS Lambda needs to initialize the resources (to start containers or spin up instances) to handle the first request for the function. This problem is known as cold function or cold start. You can keep your function in an active state by sending requests periodically.

Now, let's look at a few use cases with different architectures.

Use cases for different architectures

Use cases for Amazon EC2 service:

Use case 1
Challenges: • Service administration   • Contact the service provider to ramp up more servers   • Minimum usage commitments with existing service provider   **Reasons to choose Amazon Web Services**:   • It can automatically distribute incoming traffic between Amazon Elastic Compute Cloud (EC2) instances   • No need to contact service provider if need to scale up or down additional servers   • Use Amazon CloudWatch to monitor the resources and easily supervise Amazon EC2 instances from AWS Management Console, AWS CLI, or AWS SDK   **Benefits**:   • Save the expense of one or more operation position   • Flexible and responsive to prepare for more growth
Use case 2

Challenges:
- Control costs and an infrastructure that allows you to start from small and scale as needed
- More cost-effective than an on-premises hosted solution
- Service availability issue because of **Distributed Denial-of-Service** (**DDoS**) attacks

Reasons to choose Amazon Web Services:
- Availability, security, cost-effectiveness, and disaster recovery
- Resilient against DDoS attacks and increased performance
- Integrate Amazon CloudFront with AWS **Web Application Firewall** (**WAF**) to detect and filter malicious web requests

Benefits:
- Improves significant defense against DDoS attacks
- Increases availability of service using AWS Firewall Protection
- Scales out IT infrastructure cost-effectively in multiple regions
- Using AWS service it reduced 70% management time

Use case 3

Challenges:
- As per the business requirements, demand will grow quickly and it will spike during some events
- Purchasing resources to support these spikes will be a sizable cost burden for business
- Dedicated technical engineer to maintain all the resources
- Resources are unused or underused during non-peak hours

Reason to choose Amazon Web Services:
- Amazon EC2 instance runs the commerce suite to enable customers to use the application
- Amazon CloudFront distributes content to users with high-speed data transfer and low latency to improve the performance
- Amazon Elastic Block Store (Amazon EBS) to store web server logs

Benefits:
- Developers are able to create and update instances on the fly to innovate quickly for new software
- Automates the business by scaling the infrastructure process to support peak time
- Supports the spikes five times more than normal, without reduction in availability or performance and manual intervention
- Achieved 99.999% AWS infrastructure availability with 1.5 seconds of an average page loading time

Use cases for Amazon ECS service:

Use case 1
Challenges: • To implement microservices on Docker containers • Developers are using Docker and Docker Compose in the local environment but few developers are experienced to deploy the Docker Containers in the production environment **Reasons to choose Amazon Web Services**: • Amazon EC2 Container Service (Amazon ECS) is a highly scalable container-managed service; it provides container orchestration and cluster management • Enables developers to build and deploy Docker Compose applications on Amazon ECS **Benefits**: • Amazon EC2 Container Service (Amazon ECS) eliminates installing and maintaining cluster and container-managed software • It is really very fast to implement • Environment will be consistent by using Docker with Amazon ECS • Amazon ECS provides 99.9% service availability
Use case 2

Challenges:
• Company was running every application on instance only; it was manually required to run the startup scripts and installations
• Instances were out of sync because of different configuration settings
• Company moved to Docker because of better configuration management and applications are defined with Docker Compose for consistency
• Want to move to the production environment with new Docker-based architecture but it needs to manage and schedule containers at scale

Reasons to choose Amazon Web Services:
• Amazon EC2 Container Service (Amazon ECS) provides cluster management and container orchestration as a service
• Different services are deployed on Amazon ECS clusters such as API, Applications, CDNs
• Each service has a task definition that indicates the version of the container to run, cluster to choose, and how many containers can deploy
• It is using Elastic Load Balancing and Amazon Route53 to discover the service; ELB registers each service and Amazon Route 53 points for local entry to each ELB

Benefits:
• Amazon ECS helps to manage the placement of containers across multiple Availability Zones on different Amazon EC2 instances to provide high availability
• It is easy to run new services by adding Docker files and create task definitions and associate with a cluster
• Amazon ECS also manages the complexity of launching new containers and monitors that it should continually run. The developer will concentrate on deployment without worrying about the application availability or deployment downtimes.

Use cases for Amazon Lambda:

Use case
Challenges: • Company was using Amazon EC2 for their business logic and configurations for real-time bids on video ads across multiple exchanges; Amazon EC2 also used for transcoding the video ads in real-time • It was difficult for the developers to manage the cluster of EC2 instances despite using AWS Elastic Beanstalk to manage, provision, and scale EC2 instances; developers need to manage the elements such as selection of instance types, its scaling, deployment logic, and software configuration • To quickly scale the business, developers need to focus on tasks without worrying about the IT infrastructure **Reasons to choose Amazon Web Services**: • Company has implemented their business logic using AWS Lambda for real-time ad bidding; Amazon API Gateway is used from the video player to trigger the Lambda function • AWS Lambda used in real-time to transcode video ads **Benefits**: • With AWS Lambda, developers focus on their tasks without worrying about the IT infrastructure • Code written is never changed, so no need to rewrite the code again if the system changes; it leads to productivity gains • Company usually allocates two-three technical resources which usually takes 8–10 resources because of code reusability

In the next section, we will discuss how to control and optimize the infrastructure cost.

Controlling and optimizing costs

For cost optimization, you have to select the appropriate purchasing instance option, and the right instance type for your application workload. As we have discussed in detail about different instance types, you can select the right one to optimize performance.

Once you finalize the instance type, then you have the option to purchase a reserved instance. This is an upfront commitment but reduces costs drastically.

Reserved instances are offered for 1 year or 3 year commitments. If your requirements change before this time period, then you can use the EC2 Container Service to increase instance usage or sell your reserved instance into the AWS marketplace.

You can also use Auto Scaling to reduce the cost. Let's say your workload runs during business hours, then you can configure Auto Scale to launch new and appropriate instances for that known predictable load, and reduce the instance by Auto Scaling after office hours.

You can use spot instances. Spot instances are available at a discounted rate compared to on-demand pricing. Generally, you can use this spot instance to complete Amazon EMR Hadoop jobs.

As we know, Amazon ECS provides platforms for EC2 instances where you host your Docker containers. From a cost-optimization perspective, you can use Amazon ECS with under-utilized Reserved Instance. In Amazon ECS, you can place the containers on instances, as per your schedule.

AWS Lambda is known as server-less computing, so you will eliminate the need for running instances and administrative overhead of operating systems.

It is appropriate for the workloads that respond to events. In this case, no design decision needs to be permanent; you can assess new products and services that are the best fit for your requirements.

So, for very light workloads, AWS Lambda is less expensive compared to Amazon EC2.

You can consider the following points to estimate the cost of your Amazon EC2 instance:

- The resource will charge when it runs
- Consider the machine configuration that you select for Amazon EC2 instances, such as AWS region, operating system, memory, number of cores, and so on
- You can select the best suited instance purchase type such as On-Demand instances, reserved instances, spot instances, or dedicated hosts
- Consider the number of instances that will handle the peak loads
- Use Elastic Load Balancer to distribute the traffic between Amazon EC2 instances
- You can monitor the Amazon EC2 instance using Amazon CloudWatch
- Use Auto Scaling to automatically scale AWS EC2 instances as per the defined conditions

The following are some tips to optimize the architecture:

- You can choose reserved instances for cost optimizations
- Remove unused resources
- Downgrade the under-utilized resources
- Stop the resources while they are idle or not in use

You can use Amazon-provided tools for cost optimization such as EC2 Right Sizing solution and AWS Trusted Advisor. This utility can run any time for maximum upto last two weeks. EC2 Right Sizing solution will analyze all EC2 instances for maximum CPU utilization lower than 50%, and help to find the cost-effective instance type. AWS Trusted Advisor will alert you for low utilization thresholds. Both tools will help to lower the cost.

Summary

So far, we have looked at the three main architectures, such as EC2 instance with load balancer, Docker, and serverless architecture, and reviewed the benefits, drawbacks, and use cases related to them.

In the next chapter, we will look into traditional web hosting with Amazon EC2 with Elastic Load Balancing.

8
Traditional Web Hosting – Amazon EC2 and Elastic Load Balancing

In the previous chapter, we discussed traditional web hosting, web hosting in the cloud using AWS, and the architecture for the application. We also saw a comparison between EC2 instances with a load balancer, Docker, and serverless architecture such as Amazon Lambda, as well as use cases for these architectures.

In this chapter, we will discuss Amazon EC2 best practices and troubleshooting. Also, we will cover the advanced topics of Elastic Load Balancing (ELB), auto scaling, and fault tolerance. We will monitor and optimize the infrastructure cost. Lastly, we will deploy a practical real-world example of a CI/CD application with EC2 instances and a load balancer.

In this chapter, we will cover the following topics:

- Amazon EC2 best practices and troubleshooting
- Elastic Load Balancing, auto scaling, and fault tolerance
- Monitoring and optimizing the cost of the infrastructure
- Continuous Integration (CI) and Continuous Deployment (CD) workflow

Now, let's start with the first topic and understand best practices and troubleshooting for Amazon EC2.

Amazon EC2 best practices

Here are some of the best practices to get the maximum benefit from your Amazon EC2 instance:

- You can use approved AMIs and not the blacklisted AMIs to launch AWS EC2 instances.
- You can create an **Amazon Machine Image** (**AMI**) from an existing instance and save the configuration as a template. You can use this template to launch instances in the future. This instance should be encrypted to meet compliance and security requirements.
- Make sure that you are using custom resource tags with proper naming conventions to track AWS resources.
- Optimize cost by removing any unassociated Elastic IP addresses and unused Amazon Machine Images.
- Take frequent backups of EBS volumes using Amazon EBS Snapshots.
- For high availability and to handle failover, you can launch your Amazon EC2 instance inside an Auto Scaling Group.
- You can also attach an Elastic IP address or network interface to handle the failover.
- Make sure that you will not reach the limit set by AWS for Amazon EC2 instances. You can request prior if you want to update the limit.
- Your security group doesn't allow all public traffic. It should be granular, and have less permissive rules defined.
- You should understand the involvement of the root device for backups, recovery, and data persistence.
- Make sure that on your Amazon EC2 instances you are secure by updating and patching the applications and operating systems.
- Ensure that your Amazon EC2 instance is distributed evenly across multiple Availability Zones in a region.
- Make sure that the IAM Roles and User instance profiles have been granted appropriate permissions to manage AWS resources and APIs for Amazon EC2 instances.
- You can monitor your Amazon EC2 instancer closely by enabling its detailed monitoring.

- Make sure that there are no idle or underutilized Amazon EC2 instances. You can stop or terminate these instances for cost optimizations. You can also identify overutilized Amazon EC2 instances and upgrade them for faster response times.
- You should store temporary data on your instance store. This data will be deleted when you stop or terminate the instance.
- You should use different EBS volumes for operating systems and your data. Make sure that data will be persisted after instance termination on your volume.
- When you restart the instance, your application should handle dynamic IP addressing.

Troubleshooting instances

Following are some of the troubleshoot problems that might happen with your instance.

Instance terminates immediately

It is always a best practice to check the status after you launch an instance; it should be in the running state after the pending state, and not in the terminated state. Here are possible reasons to terminate the instance immediately after launch:

- Your EBS volume limit was reached. This is a soft limit and you can increase it by submitting a request to AWS Support.
- A corrupted EBS snapshot.
- You launch the instance from the instance store-backed AMI, and that AMI is missing a required part of the file, such as `image.part.xx`.

Instance termination reasons:

From the Amazon EC2 console, AWS CLI, or API, you can get the reason for instance termination.

For that, log on to the Amazon EC2 console, navigate to **Instances**, and select your instance. Under the **Description** tab, check **State transition reason** and **State transition reason** message. Or, you can execute this command on AWS CLI: `awsec2 describe-instances --instance-id instance_id`. Here you have to replace `instance_id` with your instance ID. This will return a JSON response. Check the code and message under the **StateReason** tag.

Errors when connected to an instance

Here is a possible error message when you try to connect to the instance:

Connection timed out:

If you get an error message such as **Network error: Connection timed out** or **Error connecting to [instance], reason: -> Connection timed out: connect** while connecting to your instance, try the following:

- Check the security group rule to allow traffic from public IP addresses on the proper port.
- In your **Virtual Private Cloud** (**VPC**), check the route table for a subnet that sends all traffic outside the VPC to an internet gateway.
- In your VPC, verify the network **Access Control List** (**ACL**) for that subnet to allow inbound and outbound traffic from local IP addresses to the proper port.
- If you have a firewall on your machine, or it is on a corporate network, ask the administrator whether it allows inbound and outbound traffic from a computer on port 22 for Linux instances, or 3389 for Windows instances.
- If the instance doesn't have a public IP address, you can associate an Elastic IP address with it.
- Use an appropriate username for the AMI. Some common username include `ec2-user` for Amazon Linux AMI, `ubuntu` is Ubuntu AMI, `root/ec2-user` for SUSE Linux/RHEL5 AMI, and `fedora/ec2-user` for Fedora AMI.
- Verify the CPU load on the instance if the server is overloaded. You can adjust this in the following ways:
  - You can scale the load automatically with Elastic Load Balancing or Auto Scaling if it is viable
  - You can move to a new and larger instance type if the load is growing steadily

User key not recognized by server:

You will get a **Permission denied** error if you are trying to connect with a key that is not recognized or not the format required by the server.

Host key not found, Permission denied (publickey), or Authentication failed, permission denied:

If you get an error message such as **Host key not found in [directory], Permission denied (publickey),** or **Authentication failed, permission denied**, while connecting to your instance using SSH, then check the appropriate username and private key file were used for the instance.

Unprotected private key file:

Other users must not access your private key file for read and write operations, and it should be protected by you. You can fix this error by changing the chmod permission to 0400 for your private key file.

Server refused our key or No supported authentication methods available:

If you get an error message such as **Error: Server refused our key** or **Error: No supported authentication methods available**, while connecting to your instance using PuTTY, then check the appropriate username for the AMI and private key file has been converted correctly into the required format used by PuTTY (.ppk).

Error using MindTerm on Safari Browser:

If you get an error message such as **Error connecting to instance_ip, reason: -> Key exchange failed: Host authentication failed**, while connecting to your instance using MindTerm on the Safari browser, the browser's security settings must allow the AWS Management Console to run the Java plugin in unsafe mode.

Error using macOS RDP client:

If you get an error message such as **Remote Desktop Connection cannot verify the identity of the computer that you want to connect to**, while connecting to your instance using the **Remote Desktop Connection client from the Microsoft website**, then download the Remote Desktop app from the Apple store and use this application to connect to the instance.

Cannot ping instance:

The ping command is a type of ICMP traffic and if you are not able to ping the instance, then check the inbound rules. If you are not able to execute a ping command from the instance, then check the outbound rules.

Troubleshooting stopping your instance

If your EBS-backed instance stopped and is stuck in the stopping state, then it might be an issue with the underlying host computer. You can stop the instance again using the `-force` option from the command line using the `stop-instances` command. Again, if you are unable to stop it, you can create an AMI from that instance and launch another instance. If you are unable to create an AMI for the instance, then you can create a replacement instance. If you are unable to create a replacement instance, then post a request for help to the Amazon EC2 forum, including your instance ID, and listing the steps you followed.

Troubleshooting terminating (shutting down) your instance

It you terminate your instance, it will change its state to shutting-down. But sometimes the following scenarios happen:

Instance termination delay:

- The instance is in the shutting-down state for more time than a few minutes, due to shutdown scripts run by the instance
- Problems with the underlying host machine
- Amazon EC2 will consider this instance as a stuck instance and terminate it

Terminated instance still displayed:

If the terminated instance still remains visible and has not been deleted, then you can contact the support team.

Automatically launch or terminate instances:

Following are reasons that you have used Amazon EC2 Auto Scaling or Elastic Beanstalk to scale your resources automatically based on the requirement:

- If you terminate the instance and AWS is launching a new instance
- If you launch a new instance and AWS is terminating another instance
- You stop an instance and AWS is launching a new instance

Troubleshooting instance recovery failures

Here are scenarios where your instance failed because of automatic recovery:

- Insufficient temporary capacity of replacement hardware
- The storage instance has unsupported configuration for automatic instance recovery
- A Service Health Dashboard event prevents the recovery process from executing it successfully
- The instance has already reached its maximum daily allowance of recovery attempts

Troubleshooting instances with failed status checks

Sometimes an instance status check fails due to the instance not running as expected. In a Linux-based instance, we might solve the issue by restarting.

If you see the error after rebooting the instance, then try to retrieve system logs. Here are some of the common system log errors and general actions to fix them:

- **Out of memory: Kill the process**:

```
[115981.261711] Out of memory: kill process 20243 (httpd) score 1289779
or a child
[115981.269791] Killed process 1021 (php-cgi) vsz:4645684kB, anon-
rss:101186kB, file-rss:204kB
```

- **VFS: Unable to mount root fs on unknown-block** (Root filesystem mismatch):

```
Kernel command line:  root=/dev/sda1 ro 4
...
Registering block device major 8
...
Kernel panic - not syncing: VFS: Unable to mount root fs on unknown-block(8,1)
```

- **XENBUS: Timeout connecting to devices** (Xenbus timeout):

```
XENBUS: Timeout connecting to devices!
...
Kernel panic - not syncing: No init found.  Try passing init= option to kernel.
```

General actions to fix the preceding errors:

Instance type	Suggestion
Amazon EBS-backed	Do any action: • Stop the instance. Modify with different and suitable instance type. Start the instance. • Reboot the instance. Problem might fix if you will change the instance type.
Instance store-backed	Do any action: • Terminate the instance. Launch a new instance with different and suitable instance type. • Reboot the instance. Problem might fix if you will change the instance type.

Here are some errors and suggestions for solving them:

- **I/O Error** (Block Device Failure):

```
[9912662.053217] end_request: I/O error, dev sde, sector 52428288
[9912664.191262] end_request: I/O error, dev sde, sector 52428168
[9912664.191285] Buffer I/O error on device md0, logical block 209713020
[9912664.191297] Buffer I/O error on device md0, logical block 209713021
```

- **I/O ERROR: neither local nor remote disk** (Broken distributed block device):

```
...
block drbd1: Local IO failed in request_timer_fn. Detaching...
Aborting journal on device drbd1-8.
block drbd1: IO ERROR: neither local nor remote disk
Buffer I/O error on device drbd1, logical block 557056
lost page write due to I/O error on drbd1
JBD2: I/O error detected when updating journal superblock for drbd1-8.
```

General actions to fix the preceding errors:

Instancetype	Suggestion
Amazon EBS-backed	• Stop the instance than detach the volume. Try to recover the volume. • Re-attach volume to the instance and start the instance. Note: It is good practice that you take the snapshot of your Amazon EBS volume often. It will decrease the data loss risk.
Instance store-backed	Terminate the instance. Launch a new instance. Note: It is good practice that you use Amazon S3 or Amazon EBS to store backup. Instance store volumes are tied with single host and single disk failure.

Here are some errors and suggestions to solve them:

- **request_module: runaway loop modprobe** (Looping legacy kernel modprobe on older Linux versions):

```
BIOS-provided physical RAM map:
 Xen: 0000000000000000 - 0000000026700000 (usable)
0MB HIGHMEM available.
...
request_module: runaway loop modprobe binfmt-464c
```

- **FATAL: kernel too old and fsck: No such file or directory while trying to open /dev** (Kernel and AMI mismatch):

```
...
FATAL: kernel too old
Kernel panic - not syncing: Attempted to kill init!
```

- **FATAL: Could not load /lib/modules or BusyBox** (Missing kernel modules):

```
FATAL: Could not load /lib/modules/2.6.34-4-virtual/modules.dep: No such file or
directory
ALERT! /dev/sda1 does not exist. Dropping to a shell!

BusyBox v1.13.3 (Ubuntu 1:1.13.3-1ubuntu5) built-in shell (ash)
Enter 'help' for a list of built-in commands.
```

- **ERROR Invalid kernel** (EC2 incompatible kernel):

```
ERROR Invalid kernel: elf_xen_note_check: ERROR: Will only load images
built for the generic loader or Linux images
xc_dom_parse_image returned -1
```

- **fsck: No such file or directory while trying to open...** (File system not found):

```
[/sbin/fsck.ext3 (1) -- /mnt/dbbackups] fsck.ext3 -a /dev/sdh
fsck.ext3: No such file or directory while trying to open /dev/sdh

/dev/sdh:
The superblock could not be read or does not describe a correct ext2 filesystem.  If
the device is valid and it really contains an ext2 filesystem (and not swap or ufs or
something else), then the superblock is corrupt, and you might try running e2fsck
with an alternate superblock: e2fsck -b 8193 <device>

[FAILED]

*** An error occurred during the file system check.
*** Dropping you to a shell; the system will reboot
*** when you leave the shell.
Give root password for maintenance
(or type Control-D to continue):
```

- **fsck died with exit status...** (Missing device):

```
Checking file systems...fsck from util-linux-ng 2.16.2
/sbin/fsck.xfs: /dev/sdh does not exist
fsck died with exit status 8
```

General actions to fix the preceding errors:

Instancetype	Suggestion
Amazon EBS-backed	Stop the instance. Modify ramdisk and kernel attributes to use new kernel and start the instance.
Instance store-backed	Terminate the instance. Start new instance with kernel and ramdisk as parameters.

Here are some errors and suggestions to solve them:

- **General error mounting filesystems** (Failed mount):

```
init: mountall main process (221) terminated with status 1

General error mounting filesystems.
A maintenance shell will now be started.
CONTROL-D will terminate this shell and re-try.
Press enter for maintenance
(or type Control-D to continue):
```

- **Error: Unable to determine major/minor number of root device...** (Root file system/device mismatch):

```
Root device '/dev/xvda1' doesn't exist. Attempting to create it.
ERROR: Unable to determine major/minor number of root device '/dev/xvda1'.
You are being dropped to a recovery shell
    Type 'exit' to try and continue booting
sh: can't access tty; job control turned off
```

- **XENBUS: Device with no driver**:

```
XENBUS: Device with no driver: device/vbd/2048
drivers/rtc/hctosys.c: unable to open rtc device (rtc0)
Initalizing network drop monitor service
Freeing unused kernel memory: 508k freed
```

- **Bringing up interface eth0: Device eth0 has different MAC address than expected, ignoring.** (Hard-coded MAC address):

```
...
Bringing up loopback interface:  [  OK  ]

Bringing up interface eth0:  Device eth0 has different MAC address than expected,
ignoring.
[FAILED]

Starting auditd: [  OK  ]
```

- **Unable to load SELinux Policy. Machine is in enforcing mode. Halting now**. (SELinux misconfiguration):

```
audit(1314445302.626:2): enforcing=1 old_enforcing=0 auid=4294947295
Unable to load SELinux Policy. Machine is in enforcing mode. Halting now.
Kernel panic - not syncing: Attempted to kill init!
```

General actions to fix preceding errors:

Instance type	Suggestion
Amazon EBS-backed	1. Stop the instance and detach the root volume. 2. Attach this volume to a working instance, run filesystem check and fix any errors. 3. Detach the volume from the working instance and attach it to the stopped instance. 4. Start the instance and check the instance status.
Instance store-backed	Start a new instance. Or contact support center for technical assistance.

Troubleshooting instance capacity

You will get the following error for instance capacity:

- **Error: InsufficientInstanceCapacity**

    When AWS doesn't have enough capacity to serve your request, you will get this error while launching or starting an EC2 instance.

    You can try the following ways to fix this:

    - Wait for a few minutes and try to submit the request again
    - Reduce the number of instances and submit a new request
    - Submit a new request without specifying Availability Zone and/or different instance type
    - Try to purchase Reserved Instances for long-term capacity reservation

- **Error: InstanceLimitExceeded**

  When you reach the concurrent running instance limit, you will get this error. In that case, you can send a request to the Amazon support team to increase the EC2 Instance limit.

Getting console output and rebooting instances

You can use the console output to diagnose the problems. It is useful for troubleshooting service configuration issues and kernel problems that cause instances to terminate or become unreachable. You can reboot the instance when it is unreachable.

My instance is booting from the wrong volume

Sometimes volumes other than the attached volume become the root volume of the instance. You can solve this by using the same e2label command to change the label. In some cases, UUID also resolves this issue.

Troubleshooting Windows instances

Here are some tips to help you troubleshoot Amazon EC2 Windows instance problems:

- **High CPU usage shortly after Windows starts**:

  If you have set **Check for updates but let me choose whether to download and install them** for Windows updates, then it will consume 50-99% of the CPU on the instance. It will cause a problem for your application and you can manually change it.

- **No console output**:

  In a Windows instance, the EC2Config service, which provides the console output, is disabled by default. To get the output on the console, you need to enable it.

- **Instance terminates immediately**:

  It is always best practice to check the status after you launch an instance and it should be in running state after the pending state and not the terminated state.

  From the Amazon EC2 console, AWS CLI, or API, you can get the reason for instance termination.

  For that, log on to the Amazon EC2 console, navigate to the **Instances**, and select your instance. Under the **Description** tab, check **State transition reason** and **State transition reason message**.

  Or you can execute this command on AWS CLI: `awsec2 describe-instances --instance-id instance_id` passing with your instance ID. It will return a JSON response. Check the code and message under the **StateReason** tag.

- **Remote Desktop can't connect to the remote computer**:

  Try the following to resolve issues related to connecting to your instance:

  - Verify the public DNS hostname.
  - If the instance doesn't have a public IP address, then you can associate an Elastic IP address with it.
  - Check the security group rule to allow traffic from public IP addresses on the proper port.
  - If you are getting an error, your credentials did not work, try typing the password manually when prompted.
  - Verify your instance has passed status checks.
  - Check the password has not expired. You can reset it if it has.
  - If you are getting an error, **The user cannot connect to the server due to insufficient access privileges**, verify you have given permission to the user to log on locally.
  - If you are getting an error, Your Remote Desktop Services session has ended. Another user connected to the remote computer, and your connection was lost, it means you are trying to connect with more than the maximum allowed concurrent RDP sessions.

- **RDP displays a black screen instead of the desktop**:

Try the following to resolve this issue:

- Verify the console output for more information by getting the system logs from the Amazon EC2 console
- Make sure that you have the latest version of RDP Client
- It might happen that the server is over utilized and stops responding. You can monitor the instance and if need be, change to a larger size

- **Instance loses network connectivity or scheduled tasks don't run when expected**:

Sometimes when you restart you instance, it will lose network connectivity and it might be possible that the wrong time has been set for the instances. It might also give you an error such as scheduled task not running as expected. To fix this error and set the timezone other than UTC for the instance persistently you must set the `RealTimeIsUniversal` registry key.

- **Insufficient instance capacity**:

We have covered this topic in the *Troubleshooting instance capacity* section.

- **EBS volumes don't initialize on Windows Server 2016 AMIs**:

The `EC2Config` service has been deprecated on Windows Server 2016 AMIs and replaced by `EC2Launch`. `EC2Launch` is a bundle of Windows PowerShell scripts that perform many of the tasks performed by the `EC2Config` service. By default, EC2Launch does not initialize secondary volumes. You can configure `EC2Launch` to initialize disks automatically by either scheduling the script to run, or by calling `EC2Launch` in user data.

- **Common messages**:

This section includes tips to help you troubleshoot issues based on common messages:

- **Password is not available**:

  To solve this issue, you can use the account and password from the original instance from which AMI was created, or retrieve an autogenerated password for an Administrator account. You can also reset the password if password generation is disabled.

- **Password not available yet**:

  If you retrieve the autogenerated password and get this error, and if it takes more than 4 minutes, then it might be possible that EC2Config is disabled. Also, verify that the ec2:GetPasswordData action is allowed in IAM for that user.

- **Cannot retrieve Windows password**:

  When you launch the instance and don't specify the key-value pair, you will get this message. You can terminate the instance and launch a new instance with a specified key to fix this issue.

- **Waiting for the metadata service**:

  By default, the WaitForMetaDataAvailable setting ensures that the EC2Config service will wait for the instance metadata to be accessible before continuing the boot process.

  You can try the following if you are unable to connect to the metadata server:

  - Verify that you have the latest version of the EC2Config service downloaded and installed
  - If using a Windows instance running RedHat PV drivers then you need to update the Citrix PV drivers
  - Ensure that IPSec, firewall, and proxy are not blocking the outgoing traffic for the metadata service or KMS service
  - Make sure that you have a route to the metadata service and also make sure there are no network issues that affect the Availability Zone for the instance

- **Unable to activate Windows**:

    You will get this error when Windows try to activate. The error code is 0xC004F074, when your Windows instance is unable to reach the Windows KMS activation. This Windows KMS activation must be within 180 days. EC2Config will connect to the KMS Server before the activation period expires and will ensure that the Windows instance will remain activated.

    Here are some of the points to verify for Windows activation issues:

    - You have routes for KMS Servers and KMS Client key is set properly.
    - Make sure that the system has the correct time and time zone. You can temporarily disable Windows Firewall if it is enabled.

- **Windows is not genuine (0x80070005)**:

    Windows KMS activation is used by a Windows instance. If a Windows instance fails to complete the activation process it gives an error that Windows is not genuine.

- **No Terminal Server License Servers available to provide a license**:

    By default, two simultaneous users can connect to the Remote Desktop for Windows Server. You have to purchase a Remote Desktop Service **Client Access License (CAL)** if you want to provide access for more than two simultaneous users. Then, you have to install the Remote Desktop Session Host and Remote Desktop Licensing Server roles.

In the next section, we will learn about Elastic Load Balancing, Auto Scaling, and Fault tolerance.

Elastic Load Balancing, auto scaling, and fault tolerant

Elastic Load Balancing (ELB) is a service from AWS to balance the load automatically. It helps to distribute incoming traffic and scale resources automatically to meet demands. Users enable it within a single or multiple availability zones to maintain application performance.

Features of ELB

ELB provides these features:

- **Highly available**: In ELB, incoming traffic will be distributed automatically between multiple targets such as Amazon EC2 instances, IP addresses, and containers in a single or multiple Availability Zones.
- **Health checks**: In ELB, it will detect unhealthy instances or targets. It will not send traffic to them. This traffic will be sent to healthy instances or targets.
- **Security Features**: You can create security groups in **Virtual Private Cloud** (**VPC**) and manage them. These security groups are associated with ELB and provide additional networking and security. You can create non-internet-facing or internal load balancers.
- **TLS termination**: ELB provides SSL decryption and integrated certificate management. It provides you the facility to centrally manage SSL settings for the load balancer and offload the CPU intensive work for the application.
- **Layer 4 or Layer 7 Load Balancing**: Provides you with the load balance from the connection layer (Layer 4) for applications that rely on the TCP protocol. It also provides you with the load balance from the application layer (Layer 7) for applications that rely on the HTTP/HTTPS protocol.
- **Operational Monitoring**: You can get real-time performance monitoring and request tracing for your application by integrating ELB with Amazon CloudWatch.

ELB supports three types of load balancer – **Application Load Balancer** (**ALB**) for flexible applications, **Network Load Balancer** (**NLB**) for extreme performance, and static IP, and **Classic Load Balancer** (**CLB**) for existing applications built on the EC2-classic network. Now let's look at some of the key features of all these load balancers.

Benefits of Application Load Balancer

Following are the benefits of **Application Load Balancer** (**ALB**):

- ALB operates at Layer-7 specific features. It is used to load balance for HTTP/HTTPS applications.
- It supports HTTPS termination between the load balancer and clients.
- **Server Name Indication** (**SNI**) is an extension of the TLS protocol. It indicates that it should connect for the TLS handshake. ALB supports a smart certificate algorithm with SNI to determine the best certificate to be used.

- Host-based routing uses the Host field of the HTTP header to route client requests.
- Path-based routing uses the URL path of the HTTP header to route client requests.
- ALB supports HTTP/2, which is a newer version of **HyperText Transfer Protocol** (**HTTP**) that allows single and multiplexed connections.
- ALB supports WebSockets. WebSockets are the protocol for real-time exchange of messages without requests from end users.
- On ALB, you can enable delete protection. It will prevent from accidental deletion.
- ALB supports sticky sessions. A Sticky session is a mechanism where the same target will receive the request from the same client. ALB uses cookies generated by the load balancer to achieve this. You can define this stickiness at the target group level.
- ALB can integrate with Amazon CloudWatch to get metrics reports such as error counts, error types, request counts, and request latency.

Benefits of Network Load Balancer

Following are the benefits of **Network Load Balancer** (**NLB**):

- NLB can handle millions of requests per second, maintaining ultra-low latencies.
- It can handle volatile and sudden traffic patterns using a static single IP address per Availability Zone.
- NLB is connection-based load balancing. You can route connections to different targets such as Amazon EC2 instances, containers, microservices, and IP addresses.
- NLB is highly available and it distributes incoming traffic across targets from clients within the same Availability Zones. It only routes traffic to healthy targets.
- NLB preserves source IP address, supports static IP addresses, and provides the option to allow Elastic IP addresses.
- If NLB itself is unhealthy in a specific zone, then Amazon Route 53 will redirect traffic to NLB in a different Availability Zone.
- NLB can integrate with other AWS services such as Amazon Route 53, Auto Scaling, AWS CodeDeploy, AWS CloudFormation, Amazon EC2 Container Service, and AWS Config.
- NLB supports the same API as ALB and it provides support for long-lived TCP connections.

- NLB can integrate with Amazon CloudWatch to get metrics reports such as New Flow Count, Active Flow Count, Healthy Host Count, and Processed Bytes. It is also integrated with AWS CloudTrail to tracks API calls.

Benefits of Classic Load Balancer

Following are the benefits of **Classic Load Balancer** (**CLB**):

- CLB operates at both the request and connection level, and provides basic load balancing
- CLB is highly available and distributes incoming traffic to single or multiple Availability Zones
- CLB supports SSL termination, which includes SSL decryption offloading, centrally managed SSL certification, and backend instance encryption
- CLB supports sticky user sessions using cookies
- CLB supports IPv4 and IPv6 for EC2-classic networks
- CLB uses both Layer 4 and Layer 7 for load balancing, which support the TCP and HTTP/HTTPS protocols, respectively
- CLB can integrate with Amazon CloudWatch to get metrics reports, such as request latency and request count

Here are the differences between these three load balancers:

Features	ALB	NLB	CLB
Protocols	HTTP, HTTPS	TCP	HTTP, HTTPS, TCP, SSL
Platforms	VPC	VPC	EC2-Classic, VPC
Health checks, CloudWatch metrics, Logging, Zonal fail-over, Connection draining (deregistration delay)	Yes	Yes	Yes
Load Balancing to multiple ports on the same instance, WebSockets, IP addresses as targets, Load balancer deletion protection	Yes	Yes	No
Path-Based Routing, Host-Based Routing, Native HTTP/2, Server Name Indication (SNI)	Yes	No	No
Configurable idle connection timeout, Cross-zone load balancing, SSL offloading, Sticky sessions, Back-end server encryption	Yes	No	Yes
Static IP, Elastic IP address, Preserve Source IP address	No	Yes	No

Auto scaling and fault tolerance

AWS Auto Scaling monitors the application and ensures that the correct number of EC2 instances are available; if not, then it will automatically adjust and scale the capacity to maintain predictable and steady performance at the lowest cost. AWS Auto Scaling provides a powerful and simple console to set up the application scaling easily for multiple services and multiple resources.

For Amazon EC2 Auto Scaling, collections of EC2 instances are created and known as **Auto Scaling Groups** (**ASGs**). In an Auto Scaling Group, you can define the minimum and maximum number of instances, so an Auto Scaling Group will not go below or above these sizes, respectively.

Now, let's understand Auto Scaling capabilities on AWS:

- When AMIs are invalid or removed, ASGs are unable to launch new EC2 instances and fail to handle the load. This will directly have a serious impact on application performance.
    - Make sure that ASG's launch configuration is using active Amazon Machine Images.
- When ELBs are inactive or deleted, ASGs are unable to launch new backend instances and fail to add compute power to the instances. This will directly have a significant impact on application performance.
    - Make sure that ASGs are using active Elastic Load Balancers to keep the auto-scaling process healthy and evenly distribute application loads.
- When Security Groups are inactive or deleted, ASGs are unable to add compute resources. It will have a negative impact on application performance.
    - Make sure that ASGs' launch configurations use active Security Groups to keep the auto-scaling process healthy.
- Sometimes, newly launched EC2 instances will take some time to boot, configure the software, and take the workload, so for that, ASGs need to implement a cool-down period to suspend any scaling activities temporarily.
    - Ensure that ASGs properly configure the cool-down period and provide some time to newly launched EC2 instances to start up and handle the application traffic.

- You are getting high network latency by using different Availability Zones for your load balancers and ASGs.
    - Make sure that the ASG is using the same Availability Zone for its associated load balancers to increase performance and reduce latency.
- ASG can increase the availability and reliability of the application. It can use the notifications to auto scale the environment by mitigating any scaling issues and act fast.
    - Make sure that you have configured notifications properly for ASG to scale any event to launch or terminate the instances.
- If the health check is not properly configured for ASGs, then it might decrease the availability and/or reliability of applications.
    - Make sure that you have properly configured the health check feature of ASGs. This feature will enable health check for ELB and register healthy EC2 instances.
- You have set up your AWS ASGs in a multi-AZ environment, but if one AZ is not available or unhealthy, then ASG should launch new instances in healthy and unaffected AZs to provide reliability and availability.
    - Make sure that ASG will set up on multi-AZ environment within AWS an region.
- ASGs should be monitored for suspended processes. It also resumes promptly, maintaining the ASGs reliability.
    - Make sure that there are no suspended processes in the ASG that disrupt the auto scaling workflow.
- It is a best practice to identify unused or empty Auto Scaling Launch configuration templates and delete them from the account for better management of Auto Scaling components.
- It is best practice to identify unused or empty Auto Scaling Groups and delete them for better management and cost optimization of Auto Scaling components.

Fault tolerance in AWS for Amazon EC2

Following are a few of the points regarding Fault tolerance on an Amazon EC2 instance:

- You can increase the fault tolerance in your application by taking advantage of health checks of instances, auto scaling, multi-AZ environments, and backups.

- Snapshots of **Amazon Elastic Block Store** (**Amazon EBS**) volumes either in use or available and you can verify EBS volume by its age. Failures can occur even though the EBS volumes are replicated. For durable storage, persist your snapshots to **Amazon Simple Storage Service** (**Amazon S3**).
- You can protect your application from single point of failure by launching the instances in the same region but in multiple Availability Zones.
- Verify the configuration of the load balancer. It is recommended to use an equal number of instances within the same region across multiple AZs when using Elastic Load Balancer for your Amazon EC2, to increase fault tolerance levels. Proper configuration of the load balancer also helps in cost optimization.
- Verify the available resources that are associated with Auto Scaling Group and launch configurations. Auto Scaling Groups will launch only healthy instances. This helps to handle spikes by automatically launching and terminating the resources.
- Check whether ELB connection draining is enabled or not. If connection draining is enabled, then the load balancer will not send any new requests to the deregister instance, but will keep serving to the active request. If connection draining is not enabled, then the load balancer will remove the Amazon EC2 instance, and not send any requests to this connection and close it.
- Verify that cross-zone load balancing is not enabled for the load balancer. Regardless of the Availability Zone of the instance, cross-zone load balancing will help to distribute requests evenly. It will also reduce the uneven distribution of traffic and make it easier to manage and deploy the application.
- Verify your EC2 Config service for Amazon EC2 Windows instances. It will alert you if the EC2 Config agent is not configured properly or is out of date. It is always recommended to use the latest EC2 Config version.

In the next section, we will look at monitoring and optimizing the cost of your EC2 infrastructure.

Monitoring and optimizing the cost of the EC2 infrastructure

In traditional on-premises applications, optimization of cost is really very challenging because you have to predict future business needs and capacity.

The following best practices will help you to build a cost-optimized architecture:

- Make sure that your demands and costs move in line with each other
- Analyze the cost
- Ensure that costs will reduce with time
- Use appropriate AWS resources to minimize the costs

Optimization of cost is a continuous process in the improvement and refinement of your system over its complete life cycle. Your system should utilize all the resources fully and meet its functional requirements while minimizing costs.

You can use the following design principles to optimize costs in the cloud:

- **Adopt a model for consumption**: You should adopt a model that will help you to identify the consumption of computing resources, and it should increase or decrease through auto scaling as per the business requirements. It should not be based on forecasting. Let's say your typical environment is used for eight hours on weekdays and you can manage it by stopping the resources when it is not used. This will save you 75% of your costs, or you can say it saves 128 hours of charges.
- **Measure efficiency**: You should measure the cost associated with business output systems. You should understand by increasing or decreasing the output by reducing its cost.
- **Cost savings on data center operations**: AWS provides all kinds of IT infrastructure as per your business needs, to save on data center operations and concentrate on client needs to make your business successful.
- **Analyze your cost**: It is always good to optimize resources and analyze the cost of the systems accurately to get the maximum ROI.
- **Reduction of cost by using managed services**: Managed services removes the burden at the operational level and scale in the cloud to provide lower cost service or its transactions.

As we have discussed design principles, let's see some best practices for cost optimization:

- Cost efficient resources
- Supply-demand matching
- Know your expenses
- Optimization over time

Cost efficient resources

You should use the appropriate resources, instances, and managed services to save on costs.

AWS provides a vast variety of cost-efficient and flexible pricing options to use EC2 instances as per your requirements:

EC2 instances	Description
On-demand instances	Pay per hour; no minimum commitments
Reserved instances	Reserved capacity; 1- or 3-year commitments; save up to 75% off then on-demand instance
Spot instances	Can bid for unused Amazon EC2 instances; on-demand instances at a discounted price; no minimum commitments; Useful for spot block, fleet, big data

You can regularly review AWS usage by monitoring the resource utilization and adjusting the deployments by using AWS Trusted Advisor. You can also use the AWS Cost Explorer tool to see the pattern of your AWS resources over time, track trends to understand their usage, and identify key areas for improvement.

You should consider the cost when you are selecting AWS resources such as Amazon EC2, Amazon S3, or Amazon EBS, known as building blocks, or Amazon DynamoDB and Amazon RDS, known as managed services. By using these services, you can optimize the cost of your architecture. Using managed services will remove the administration and operation overhead.

Analyze and identify the service that will reduce cost by optimizing the license, using container-based or serverless architecture, and using suitable storage, database, and application-level services.

You should select the right type, size, provisioned throughput, and storage of resources to optimize costs.

To meet cost targets, you should select the appropriate pricing model as per your workload. You should also consider the region cost while selecting any resources.

Supply-demand matching

To reduce the cost of a system, you can match supply with demand, and that supply should be sufficient supply either it is provisioning the resources or individual failure of resources. When the demand is varied or fixed, then automation helps to ensure that it will not affect the cost significantly. In that case, you can use managed services.

In AWS, you can automatically match demand by provisioning resources for Auto Scaling, and using the buffer and time-based approaches to allow new resources or remove the existing resources.

To match supply and demand, you should consider your usage patterns and the time required to provision new resources. You must ensure that whatever you pay is used and avoid under utilizing instances.

You can also consider the following approach:

- **Demand-based**: To respond and handle variable demand, you can use Auto Scaling. Auto Scaling will help to add or remove new resources without overspending.
- **Buffer-based**: Buffer work until you have enough capacity to process it.
- **Time-based**: Follow a time-based scheduling approach, such as monthly, quarterly, or annually. Instance can be turned off over weekend.

Know your expenses

You should encourage innovation for faster development and deployment, and over time eliminate manual processes associated with hardware specification, negotiating quotations, provisioning on-premises infrastructure, managing orders, and deploying resources. You should understand which products are profitable and where to allocate the budget.

In AWS, allocation tags are used to categorize and track AWS costs. These tags are used to generate a cost allocation report with cost and usage, to organize the costs across multiple services.

You can use the AWS Simple Monthly Calculator to calculate your monthly data transfer costs and set billing alerts to notify of predicted overspending.

You can set Amazon CloudWatch alarms and **Amazon Simple Notification Service (Amazon SNS)** to send notifications to warn you if the forecasted amount will go over your budgeted amount.

You should consider the data transfer charges in your architectural decisions to save some of the costs. For example, a content provider company can save costs by serving content using Amazon CloudFront **Content Delivery Network (CDN)** instead of serving from an Amazon S3 bucket.

You can optimize data transfer by using proper application design, multiple AZs, region selection, CDN, or AWS Direct Connect.

You should monitor your usage by defining policies and procedures to control costs. You should consider who is using which services, at what cost, by using AWS-provided tools to get a proper understanding of the business needs.

You can tag all the resources in your infrastructure, load and interpret the billing reports, and notify the team if spending moves outside the limits to make them aware about expenditure.

You should also consider the following points:

- Decommission resources that are non-critical or not required
- Temporarily stop the resource if it is not needed
- Handle the resource gracefully for termination
- Identify and decommission orphaned resources

You should also govern AWS usage by establishing groups/roles and tracking the project life cycle to avoid using unnecessary resources.

Optimization over time

It is always good practice to be aware of the new services/features available from AWS and review your existing architecture to make sure that it is the most cost effective. When requirements change or new requirements are added, be sure to decommission resources, entire services, or systems that are not required. AWS managed services help to optimize your solution significantly.

You can visit the *What's New* section on the AWS website and the AWS Blog to be informed about newly launched service or features. AWS Trusted Advisor also inspects on your behalf to find idle resources or eliminate unused resources.

In the next section, we will understand how to configure Elastic Load Balancer and Auto Scaling, and implement it in a CI and CD workflow.

Continuous Integration and Continuous Deployment workflow

In this section, we will understand two things to configure, Load Balancing and Auto Scaling. We will continue with the same example we discussed in Chapter 5, *CI/CD in AWS Part 2 – CodeDeploy, CodePipeline, and CodeStar* and update the example with Auto Scaling Group. We will stop the instance and see the behavior in the EC2 console, and Auto Scaling Group should automatically launch the instances with a predefined script.

Now, let's see how to create and configure Load Balancing. Load Balancing is divided into two parts – Load Balancers and Target Groups.

As we already discussed, Load Balancers come in three types. You can choose whichever Load Balancer you need:

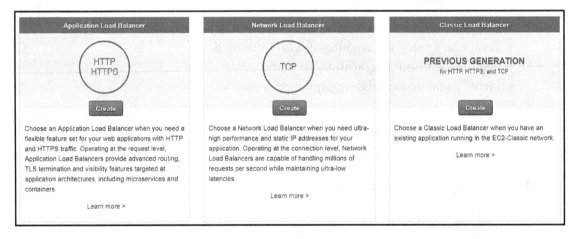

In this example, if you select **Application Load Balancer**, then it will navigate to the **Configure Load Balancer screen**. You can add the required fields, such as **Name**, and select the specific **Availability Zone**. You can also add **Listeners** such as **HTTPS**:

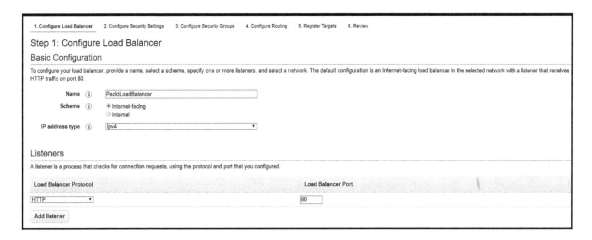

You will see the following screen if you have added the **HTTPS Listener** in the previous screen. Here, you have to select the value for **Certificate type**, **Certificate name**, and **Security Policy**. In the next step, you can configure your security groups:

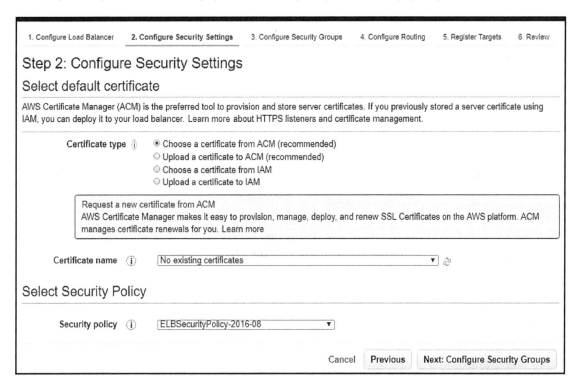

As per the following image, in step 4 you can select the routing configurations and health check settings. The name of the target group is mandatory:

| 1. Configure Load Balancer | 2. Configure Security Settings | 3. Configure Security Groups | 4. Configure Routing | 5. Register Targets | 6. Review |

Step 4: Configure Routing

Your load balancer routes requests to the targets in this target group using the protocol and port that you specify, and performs health checks on the targets using these health check settings. Note that each target group can be associated with only one load balancer.

Target group

Target group ⓘ	New target group ▼	
Name ⓘ		
Protocol ⓘ	HTTP ▼	
Port ⓘ	80	
Target type ⓘ	instance ▼	

Health checks

Protocol ⓘ	HTTP ▼	
Path ⓘ	/	

▸ Advanced health check settings

Cancel   Previous   Next: Register Targets

On the next screen, you can register targets and select instances. Then you can move to the **Review** page. Once you review configuration information, you can create the **Launch Configuration**. This configuration will also create the target group, which we have configured in *Step 4*. We can attach this load balancer to the Auto Scaling Group.

Now, let's understand how to create and configure Auto Scaling. Auto Scaling is divided into two parts. One is Launch Configuration, and the other is Auto Scaling Group.

Launch Configuration in Auto Scaling Group is a template used to launch an EC2 instance. You should specify the launch information for the instance, such as the **Amazon Machine Image** (**AMI**) ID, instance type, one or more security groups, key pair, and block device mappings. You can use the same information if you already launched the EC2 instance before.

You can create Auto Scaling Group by specifying the launch template, EC2 instance, or launch configuration. It is recommended to use launch templates instead of launch configurations.

You can specify one launch configuration at a time for an Auto Scaling Group. You cannot change the launch configuration once you have created it. You must create a new launch configuration and update the Auto scaling Group with the new launch configuration.

The Auto Scaling Group contains a collection of EC2 instances with similar characteristics and is treated as a logical group to scale and manage the instance. It will automatically scale the instance based on the criteria or maintain a fixed number of instances. The Amazon EC2 Auto Scaling service has core functionality to automatically scale and maintain the number of instances in Auto Scaling Group.

When you select Launch Configurations or Auto Scaling Groups, you will be redirected to the following screen if you don't have any Launch Configurations or Auto Scaling Groups created:

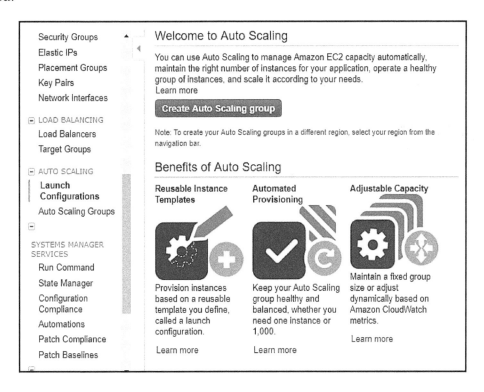

Now, click on **Create Auto Scaling Group**.

This will navigate to the quick start screen, where you can select AMIs, such as Amazon Linux AMI, Red Hat Enterprise Linux 7.2, Ubuntu Server 14.04 LTS, or Microsoft Windows Server 2012 R2 Base, then **Select** it.

On the next page, select the instance type and select **next: Configure details**.

On the **Configure details** page, enter the name for the launch configurations and select the **IAM role**. Expand **Advanced Details** and add the value for the user data field.

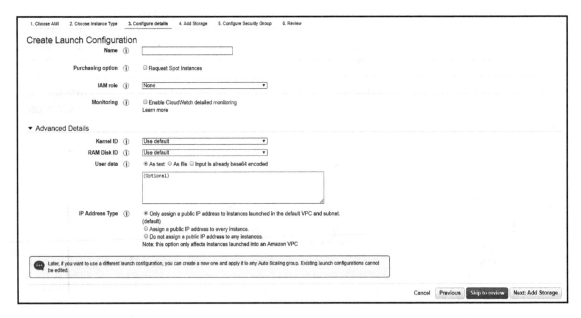

In this example, we are integrating Auto Scaling with AWS CodeDeploy. So, add the following code into the user data field as per the selected instance. Also make sure to change the bucket name, because this is the name of the Amazon S3 bucket that contains the required AWS CodeDeploy Resource Kit files for your region. If you are in the N.Virginia region then you can replace `aws-codedeploy-us-east-1` with bucket-name in following code:

Instance type	Value for User data
Amazon Linux & RHEL Amazon EC2 instances	#!/bin/bash yum -y update yum install -y ruby cd /home/ec2-user curl -O https://bucket-name.s3.amazonaws.com/latest/install chmod +x ./install ./install auto
Ubuntu Server Amazon EC2 instances	#!/bin/bash apt-get -y update apt-get -y install ruby apt-get -y install wget cd /home/ubuntu wget https://bucket-name.s3.amazonaws.com/latest/install chmod +x ./install ./install auto
Windows Server Amazon EC2 instances	\<powershell\> New-Item -Path c:\temp -ItemType "directory" -Force powershell.exe -Command Read-S3Object -BucketName bucket-name/latest -Key codedeploy-agent.msi -File c:\temp\codedeploy-agent.msi Start-Process -Wait -FilePath c:\temp\codedeploy-agent.msi -WindowStyle Hidden \</powershell\>

After that, leave the rest of the fields at their defaults and choose **Skip** to review.

On the **Review** page, select **Create Launch Configuration**.

Once the launch configuration has been created, then you will navigate to the **Create Auto Scaling Group** screen. Add the value for **Group name** and select the subnet as per your network. On the **Advanced Details** screen, you can select **Target Groups**, which we created in an earlier section. Click on **Next: Configure scaling policies**:

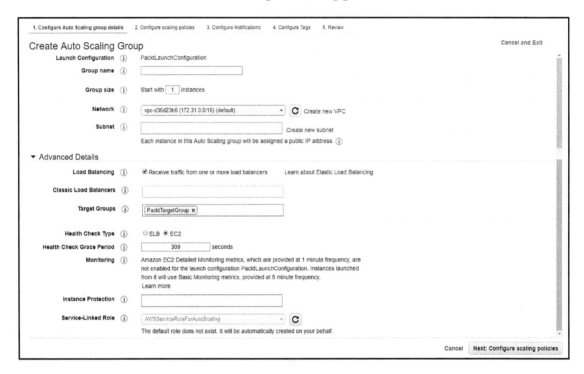

In the next section, you can add scaling policies, or you can skip that section with the default value **Keep this group at its initial size** and click **Next: Configure Notifications**. In the next section, you can add notifications, or you can skip that section and click on **Review**. Now, select the **Create Auto Scaling group** and then select **Close**. In the **Auto Scaling Console**, select the newly created instance tab. Wait until you see **InService** in the **Lifecycle** column, and **Healthy** in the **Health Status** column:

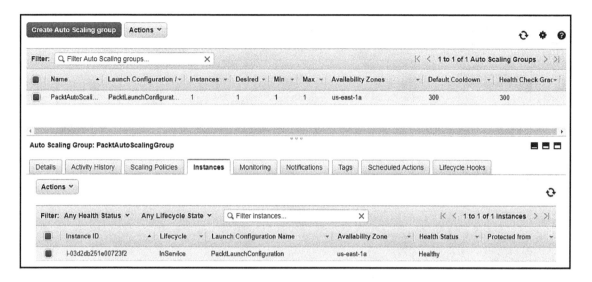

Now we have configured the Load Balancer and Auto Scaling Group, we will verify the changes by stopping the existing resources. This will automatically start a new instance and copy the required resources into the new instance. In the following screenshot, the instance ID ending in **2fb** has been terminated, while **21c** is initializing:

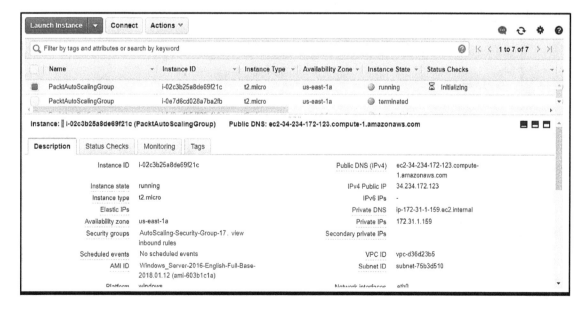

You can verify from the Auto Scaling Group that the instance ID ending in **2fb** is in the **Unhealthy Status** and **21c** is in the **Healthy Status**:

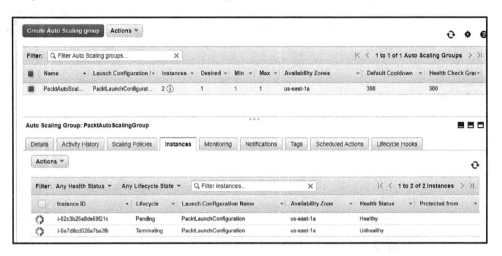

As we already discussed in `Chapter 5`, *CodeDeploy, CodePipeline, and CodeStar*, we can configure an Amazon EC2 instance as follows:

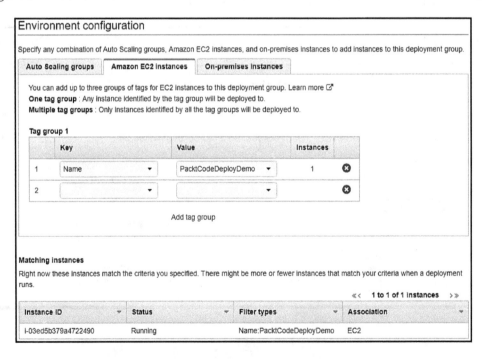

Now you can change this configuration from Amazon EC2 instances to Auto Scaling Groups. An Auto Scaling Group will be populated with all the available groups, and also display the instances. You can see the instances ending with the **21c** instance ID. You can enable the load balancer by selecting the **Enable load balancing** checkbox and choosing the appropriate load balancer from the dropdown:

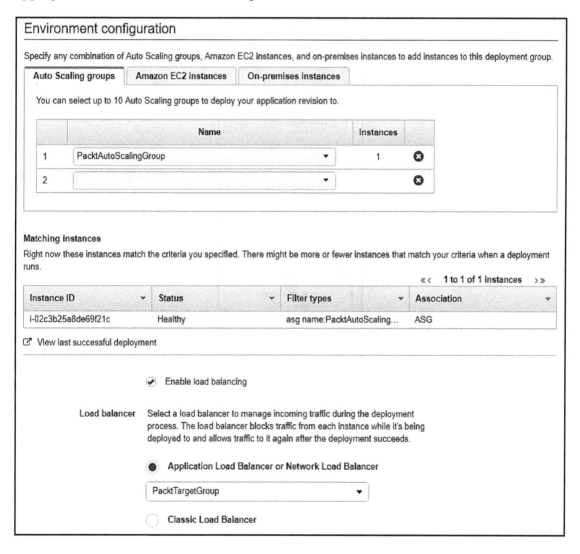

After making these changes, verify your AWS CodePipeline. It should execute the whole process successfully:

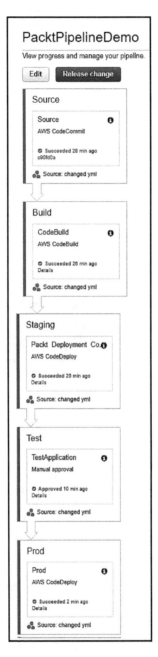

You can verify your application once it has been deployed successfully, by executing the public DNS. You will see the following output:

We have completed this section by implementing a CI and CD environment.

Summary

So far, we have learned Amazon EC2 best practices and troubleshooting, and understood Elastic Load Balancing, Auto Scaling, and fault tolerance. We have also learned about the optimization of cost and implemented Auto Scaling and Load Balancing in a CI and CD environment.

In the next chapter, we will implement CI and CD on an Amazon EC2 Container Service.

Amazon EC2 Container Service

9

In the previous chapter, we discussed Amazon EC2's best practices and troubleshooting capabilities. We also learned about Elastic Load Balancing, Auto Scaling, fault tolerance, and monitoring and optimizing the infrastructure cost. We also modified AWS CodeDeploy for CI/CD applications with Auto Scaling.

In this chapter, we will look at Docker, container instances, clusters, scheduling tasks, and Windows containers. Finally, we will deploy an example of a CI/CD application with Amazon EC2 Container Services.

In this chapter, we will cover the following topics:

- Docker, container instances, clusters
- Scheduling tasks
- Windows containers (beta)
- Monitoring and optimizing the cost of the infrastructure
- Continuous Integration (CI) and Continuous Deployment (CD) workflow

Now let's start with our first topic, Docker:

Docker

As we've already learned in Chapter 7, *Evaluating the Best Architecture*, Docker is a Linux-based container technology. It allows your distributed applications to build, run, test and deploy. The Amazon EC2 Container Service provides container-based services that use Docker images in their task definitions and start containers on an EC2 instance.

Let's look at an example of Docker. You will install Docker, create a Docker image, and verify a simple web page.

Docker is currently available for different operating systems, such as Linux distributions, Windows, and macOS. You can launch an EC2 Linux instance, if you have any, and install Docker. You can use Docker without a local machine.

The following are the steps to install a Docker image on the instance of an Amazon Linux-based AMI:

1. Launch an Amazon Linux AMI instance and connect to it.
2. Execute the following command to update the installed package. It will also cache on the instance:

   ```
   sudo yum update -y
   ```

3. Now, execute the following command to install the package for the Docker Community Edition on your instance:

   ```
   sudo yum install -y docker
   ```

4. Execute the following command to start the Docker service:

   ```
   sudo service docker start
   ```

5. To execute the Docker command on your instance without `sudo`, you can add –user to the Docker group. In this case, the user is `ec2-user`:

   ```
   sudo usermod -a -G docker ec2-user
   ```

To get new group permissions for Docker, you must log out and log in to the instance. You can close your existing terminal window to log out and reconnect it with a new session. You will get the correct Docker group permissions in your new SSH session. To make sure you can execute the following command, it should be executed without a `sudo` command:

```
docker info
```

Note that in some cases you will get the following error:

Cannot connect to the Docker daemon. Is the docker daemon running on this host?

This means you have to reboot your instance to give permission for the `ec2-user` to access the Docker commands.

Once Docker has installed successfully, you can create a Docker image of a simple web application, and test it on a browser. Once it works successfully, then you can push this image to Amazon ECR or Docker Hub, to use it as an Amazon ECS task definition.

Now, let's create the manifest file called a Dockerfile. It will describe the base image that you will use for the Docker image, and other information such as what software packages you want to install and run:

```
touch Dockerfile
```

Add the following content in this Dockerfile. It will execute the FROM command to access the Ubuntu image. It will execute the RUN command to update the software package cache and install the Apache web server. It will create the index.html and write the content in this file. You can expose port 80 with the EXPOSE command on the container and the CMD command to start the web server:

```
FROM ubuntu:12.04
# Update the docker and Install dependency like apache
RUN apt-get update -y
RUN apt-get install -y apache2

# Create web page with Hi from Packt message
RUN echo "Hi from Packt!!!" > /var/www/index.html

# Configure the apache
RUN a2enmod rewrite
RUN chown -R www-data:www-data /var/www
ENV APACHE_RUN_USER www-data
ENV APACHE_RUN_GROUP www-data
ENV APACHE_LOG_DIR /var/log/apache2
# Mention the port number
EXPOSE 80

# Command to start apache web server
CMD ["/usr/sbin/apache2", "-D", "FOREGROUND"]
```

With this created Dockerfile, you can execute the following command to build the Docker image:

```
docker build -t packt-demo .
```

```
ec2-user@ip-172-31-28-90:~
[ec2-user@ip-172-31-28-90 ~]$ docker build -t packt-demo .
Sending build context to Docker daemon   7.168kB
Step 1/11 : FROM ubuntu:12.04
 ---> 5b117edd0b76
Step 2/11 : RUN apt-get update -y
 ---> Using cache
 ---> 95ec3f37fcb2
Step 3/11 : RUN apt-get install -y apache2
 ---> Using cache
 ---> 229f11e07a37
Step 4/11 : RUN echo "Hi from Packt!!!" > /var/www/index.html
 ---> Using cache
 ---> a8a422c8532f
Step 5/11 : RUN a2enmod rewrite
 ---> Using cache
 ---> ddda1a15d5f9
Step 6/11 : RUN chown -R www-data:www-data /var/www
 ---> Using cache
 ---> a2a9e944f269
Step 7/11 : ENV APACHE_RUN_USER www-data
 ---> Using cache
 ---> 28e5809785b2
Step 8/11 : ENV APACHE_RUN_GROUP www-data
 ---> Using cache
 ---> 2c7076f7fced
Step 9/11 : ENV APACHE_LOG_DIR /var/log/apache2
 ---> Using cache
 ---> 22b37714a710
Step 10/11 : EXPOSE 80
 ---> Using cache
 ---> 0453834d9ee1
Step 11/11 : CMD /usr/sbin/apache2 -D FOREGROUND
 ---> Using cache
 ---> 49e2d92ef214
Successfully built 49e2d92ef214
Successfully tagged packt-demo:latest
[ec2-user@ip-172-31-28-90 ~]$ 
```

In some Docker versions, you need to specify the full path to your Dockerfile, instead of a relative path.

You can execute the `docker images` command to verify that the image has been created successfully. You can also add a filter attribute to get a particular image:

```
docker images --filter reference=packt-demo
```

Now, execute `docker run` with the `-p 80:80` option which will expose port `80` with container port `80`.

 You can ignore the warning message for Apache web server in the terminal window – **Could not reliably determine the server's fully qualified domain name.**

You can test the application by pointing to the server that is hosting the container and running Docker in the following ways:

- You can point to `http://localhost/` if you are running it locally.
- You can connect with the public DNS value if you are running the EC2 instances. This is the same address from which you were connected to the instance with SSH. Ensure that you are allowing inbound traffic on port `80` in the security group.
- You can use the `docker-machine ip` command to find out the IP address of the virtual box, if you are using Windows or a Mac machine. You can replace your `machine-name` with a Docker machine:

```
docker-machine ip machine-name
```

You can see the web page with **Hi from Packt!!!** by entering the localhost or public DNS or IP address:

Once you verify the application, you can stop the Docker container with *Ctrl + C*.

Amazon Elastic Container Registry (**Amazon ECR**) is a managed Docker registry service from AWS where users can push, pull, and manage images from Docker CLI.

 You need AWS CLI for this section. You can download it from the AWS website, if you don't have it.

You can execute `create-repository` to store your `packt-demo` image in the Amazon ECR repository and save the `repositoryUri` from the output:

```
aws ecr create-repository --repository-name packt-demo
```

The output is as follows:

```
{
    "repository": {
        "registryId": "aws_account_id",
        "repositoryName": " packt-demo",
        "repositoryArn": "arn:aws:ecr:us-
east-1:aws_account_id:repository/packt-demo",
        "createdAt": 1519231176.0,
        "repositoryUri": "aws_account_id.dkr.ecr.us-
east-1.amazonaws.com/packt-demo"
    }
}
```

Tag the `packt-demo` image with the `repositoryUri` value from the output of the previous step:

```
docker tag packt-demo aws_account_id.dkr.ecr.us-east-1.amazonaws.com/packt-
demo
```

To get the `docker login` authentication command, you need to execute the `aws ecr get-login --no-include-email` command, given here, to get the string for your registry.

It is recommended you use AWS CLI, starting with version 1.11.91 or later for the latest versions of Docker (17.06 or later). You can check your AWS CLI version by executing the `aws --version` command. If your Docker version is 17.06 or later, you can include the `--no-include-email` option after `get-login`. Install a recent version of AWS CLI, if you are getting an error, such as unknown options: `--no-include-email`.

```
aws ecr get-login --no-include-email
```

You will get the `docker login` command with an authorization token, as the output of the previous `get-login` command. The validity of an authorization token is 12 hours.

In the preceding steps, the `docker login` command provides you with a command string that might be visible by others on your system. There is a risk that other users might see your authentication credentials and use them to push and pull access to the repositories. You can omit them by providing the –p password option and then entering the password when it prompts.

With the `repositoryUri` value from the previous steps, you can push the image to Amazon ECR:

```
docker push aws_account_id.dkr.ecr.us-east-1.amazonaws.com/packt-demo
```

```
[ec2-user@ip-172-31-28-90 ~]$ docker push 499651321398.dkr.ecr.us-east-1.amazonaws.com/packt-demo
The push refers to a repository [499651321398.dkr.ecr.us-east-1.amazonaws.com/packt-demo]
c9e4e57de9eb: Pushed
5ab47bccc841: Pushed
24f39b42024f: Pushed
71ec0451e27d: Pushed
f56e38d36b79: Pushed
3efd1f7c01f6: Pushed
73b4683e66e8: Pushed
ee60293db08f: Pushed
9dc188d975fd: Pushed
58bcc73dcf40: Pushed
latest: digest: sha256:f4823d9113ee841e8bfc4f65be589383a976993e14f68f450079a9407ae9f240 size: 2404
[ec2-user@ip-172-31-28-90 ~]$
```

Once the image has been pushed, you can use this image in the Amazon ECS task definition to run the task.

You can register the task definition with the image file. To do this, create the JSON file (`packt-demo-task-def.json`) with the following information and specify the image field value as `repositoryUri` from the previous section:

```
{
  "family": "packt-demo",
  "containerDefinitions": [
      {
          "name": "packt-demo",
          "image": "aws_account_id.dkr.ecr.us-east-1.amazonaws.com/packt-
demo",
          "cpu": 10,
          "memory": 500,
          "portMappings": [
                  {"containerPort": 80, "hostPort": 80}
          ],
          "entryPoint": [
              "/usr/sbin/apache2", "-D", "FOREGROUND"
          ],
          "essential": true
      }
  ]
}
```

You can execute `register-task-definition` to register the task definition with the JSON file, (`packt-demo-task-def.json`):

```
aws ecs register-task-definition --cli-input-json file://packt-demo-task-
def.json
```

```
ec2-user@ip-172-31-28-90:~
[ec2-user@ip-172-31-28-90 ~]$ aws ecs register-task-definition --cli-input-json file://packt-demo-task-def.json
{
    "taskDefinition": {
        "status": "ACTIVE",
        "family": "packt-demo",
        "placementConstraints": [],
        "requiresAttributes": [
            {
                "name": "com.amazonaws.ecs.capability.ecr-auth"
            }
        ],
        "compatibilities": [
            "EC2"
        ],
        "volumes": [],
        "taskDefinitionArn": "arn:aws:ecs:us-east-1:499651321398:task-definition/packt-demo:1",
        "containerDefinitions": [
            {
                "environment": [],
                "name": "packt-demo",
                "mountPoints": [],
                "image": "499651321398.dkr.ecr.us-east-1.amazonaws.com/packt-demo",
                "cpu": 10,
                "portMappings": [
                    {
                        "protocol": "tcp",
                        "containerPort": 80,
                        "hostPort": 80
                    }
                ],
                "entryPoint": [
                    "/usr/sbin/apache2",
                    "-D",
                    "FOREGROUND"
                ],
                "memory": 500,
                "essential": true,
                "volumesFrom": []
            }
        ],
        "revision": 1
    }
}
```

You need to launch the container instance into the cluster before you run tasks in Amazon ECS.

Execute the following command to run the task with the task definition:

```
aws ecs run-task --task-definition packt-demo
```
So far, we have completed Docker and its installation. Now let's look at container instances.

Container instances

We will divide container instances into the following different topics, and discuss them:

- Basic concepts of a container instance
- Life cycle of a container instance
- Checking an instance role for an account
- AMIs for container instances
- Update notification subscribing to Amazon ECS–optimized AMI
- Launching an Amazon ECS container instance
- Bootstrapping container instances with Amazon EC2 user data
- Connecting your container instance
- Container instances with CloudWatch Logs
- Container instance draining
- Remotely managing your container instances
- Deregistering your container instance

Basic concepts of a container instance

- A container instance must run the Amazon ECS container agent to register the clusters. If your AMI is Amazon ECS-optimized then the agent is already installed. For different operating systems, you must install the agent.
- The Amazon ECS container agent makes calls to the Amazon ECS on your behalf. Your container instance must be launched with a proper IAM role to authenticate the account and provide the appropriate resource permission.
- If you need any external connectivity from the containers to your associated task, you can map network ports to the ports on the host Amazon ECS container instance, so that it is reachable from the internet. In this case, you must provide inbound access to the ports that you want to expose in the security group.
- It is recommended you launch the container instance inside the VPC to get more control on the network and more extensive configuration capabilities.
- External network access requires your container instances to communicate with Amazon ECS service endpoints. If the container instance doesn't have a public IP address, then it must use the **Network Address Translation** (**NAT**) to provide the access.

- Your EC2 instance, selected for container service, determines the available resource in the cluster. Amazon EC2 provides a variety of instance types, with different CPUs, storage, memory, and networking capacity to run your tasks.
- Each container instance stores unique state information locally and within Amazon ECS:
    - You can't change the instance type and stop the container instance. It is recommended you terminate the current container instance and launch a new container instance with the required instance size and the latest Amazon ECS-optimized AMI in the cluster.
    - Your instance cannot deregister in one cluster and reregister in another cluster. For this kind of relocate container instance scenario, it is recommended you terminate the existing container instance from the cluster and launch a new container instance with latest Amazon ECS-optimized AMIs in the required cluster.

Life cycle of a container instance

If an Amazon ECS container agent registers an instance in a cluster, then the agent connection will report its status as **TRUE** and the container instance will report its status as **ACTIVE**. This container instance will accept run task requests.

When you stop the Amazon ECS container instance, its status will remain as **ACTIVE** but the agent connection's status will change to **FALSE**, within a few minutes. Again, when you start the Amazon ECS container instance, this container agent reconnects with the Amazon ECS service and makes the instance available to run the tasks.

When you stop, start, or reboot the container instance, then an older Amazon ECS container agent will register a new instance, without deregistering the old or original container instance ID. In this scenario, you will see more Amazon ECS in the container instance list. You can verify the duplicate container instance ID and deregister it if its agent connection status is **FALSE**. This issue has been fixed in the latest version of the Amazon ECS container agent. The container instance will change its status immediately to **INACTIVE** if you deregister or terminate it. When you list the container instance, it will no longer be reported, but you can describe it for the next hour after termination. After one hour the description is also not available.

A new task will not be placed in the container if you change the status to **DRAINING**. Any service tasks that are in a running state will be removed, so that you can perform system updates.

Checking the instance role for the account

The Amazon ECS instance role will be created automatically when you run the application for the first time. The role will be created with the name `ecsInstanceRole` and you can verify it in the IAM console. If it doesn't exist, then you need to create it.

AMIs for a container instance

The Amazon **Elastic Container Service** (**ECS**) instance should contain the following:

- The latest Linux distribution
- The Amazon ECS container agent
- The latest Docker daemon with runtime dependencies

Update notification subscribing to Amazon ECS–optimized AMI

You can get regular updates for agent change, Docker versions, or Linux security updates for Amazon ECS optimized AMI. You can subscribe to the Amazon SNS topic to receive notifications such as when a new Amazon ECS-optimized AMI is available. You will get the notifications in all the available formats that Amazon SNS supports. You can subscribe to AMI update notifications from AWS Management Console or AWS CLI.

Your user must have IAM permissions, such as `sns::subscribe`, to subscribe to an SNS topic. Also, you can subscribe to the Amazon SQS queue for notification topics. You can trigger AWS Lambda functions when any notifications are received.

Launching an Amazon ECS container instance

You can launch an Amazon ECS container instance from AWS Management Console, and most of the steps are the same as when you are creating an Amazon EC2 instance. You should change a few things or modify them to make your instance an Amazon ECS container instance.

Once you launch this instance you can successfully run the tasks.

From the AWS Management Console, you can select **Launch Instance**. On the **Quick Start** page you can select **Community AMIs** and search for the `amazon-ecs-optimized` AMI. It will provide you with more than 100 instances. You can select the `amzn-ami-2017.09.i-amazon-ecs-optimized` latest AMI.

On the **Configure Instance Details** page, you can set the **Number of instances** field depending on the instances you want to add into the cluster. You can select **ecsInstanceRole** as the **IAM** role. You should provide the correct IAM permissions to connect the Amazon ECS agent with your cluster.

You can configure your Amazon ECS container with user data. The Amazon EC2 user data script will execute once the instance launches. This container instance launches into the default cluster, but you can launch it in a non-default cluster, by adding the script in **User Data** under **Advanced Details** section:

```
#!/bin/bash
echo ECS_CLUSTER=non_default_cluster_name >> /etc/ecs/ecs.config
```

If you have created an `ecs.config` file, then you can also specify that file from the **As file** option in the **User data** field.

If your Amazon ECS-optimized AMI instance is from before the 2015.09.d version, then it has a single volume, and that volume is shared by Docker and the operating system.

If your Amazon ECS-optimized AMI instance is after the 2015.09.d version, then it has two configured volumes. The first volume is the **Root** volume that is used for the operating system's use, and the other volume is the **Amazon EBS** volume and it will be used by Docker.

You can view the instance status from the **Instances** screen. It will get a public DNS name once the status is in the **RUNNING** state.

Bootstrapping container instances with Amazon EC2 user data

You can pass user data when you launch an Amazon ECS container instance. This data will perform some automated configuration or run the scripts, when the instance boots. The most common use case to add a user data configuration is to pass the Docker daemon and Amazon ECS container agent information. You can also add the cloud boot hooks, cloud-init directives, and shell scripts.

You can write a single agent configuration variable by using echo to copy the variable in the `ecs.config` file. If you want to write multiple agent configuration variables, then you can use the heredoc format by adding the lines between cat and end of the `ecs.config` file.

Docker daemon configuration can be specified with Amazon EC2 user data. You must write this configuration before the Docker daemon starts.

The `cloud-init` package provides you with the `cloud-init-per` utility to create `boothook` commands to run the instance at a specified frequency.

The syntax of `cloud-init-per` is as follows:

```
cloud-init-per frequency name cmd [ arg1 [ arg2 [ ... ] ]
```

Here, `frequency` states how often you run the `boothook`. It has options such as `once`, `instance`, or `always`. The `name` includes the semaphore file path, and `cmd` and `arg1` are the command and argument that `bookhook` should execute.

You can also combine multiple user data blocks into a single user data block called a MIME multi-part file.

Connecting your container instance

You can perform administrative tasks on instances, such as updating or installing software and accessing diagnostic logs by connecting to the instance using SSH. Your container instance must meet the following pre-requisites to connect the instance using SSH:

- To connect using SSH, your instance needs external network access
- Your instance must launch with a valid Amazon EC2 key pair
- SSH uses port 22 so you must open this port in your security group to connect the instance

Container instances with CloudWatch Logs

You can configure container instances to send CloudWatch Logs information. You can enable to it to get all the CloudWatch Logs from one location for all the container instances.

You must create an IAM policy that will allow container instances to use the CloudWatch API logs. This policy must attach to the `ecsInstanceRole`.

You can install the CloudWatch Logs agent to the container instances, after successfully attaching the policy.

CloudWatch contains a logs agent configuration file (`/ect/awslogs/awslogs.conf`), that will describe the log files to send to CloudWatch Logs. In this file, the **general** section defines the common configurations. These configurations will apply to all log streams. You can also add individual log stream sections.

The following are some common log files with their description, which are configured for the Amazon ECS-optimized AMI:

File path	Description
`/var/log/dmesg`	Linux kernel's message buffer
`/var/log/messages`	Global system messages
`/var/log/docker`	Log messages for Docker daemon
`/var/log/ecs/ecs-init.log`	Amazon ECS container initialize job log message
`/var/log/ecs/ecs-agent.log`	Amazon ECS container agent log message
`/var/log/ecs/audit.log`	Audit log messages from IAM roles for task

After providing the correct IAM permissions, configuration and starting the container agent you can view and search logs from within the AWS Management Console.

A new instance launch will take a few minutes to send CloudWatch Logs data.

Container instance draining

To perform activities, such as system/Docker daemon updates or scaling down the cluster, you might need to remove an instance from the cluster.

By enabling container instance draining, you can remove the instance from the cluster without impacting the existing task. Amazon ECS prevents a new task being scheduled for placement in the container instance, when you set the instance as **DRAINING**.

For available resources, a replacement service task will start on other container instances. For **PENDING** state resources on the container, the instance will stop immediately. For **RUNNING** state resources on the container, the instance will stop and replace, as per the parameters in deployment configuration. The container instance will complete the draining when there are no resources in the **RUNNING** state.

The Amazon ECS scheduler will schedule the task on the instance again, when the container status changes from **DRAINING** to **ACTIVE**.

Remotely managing your container instance

You can remotely and securely manage the Amazon ECS container instance configuration. Without logging in to the instance locally, you can use the Run command to perform common administrative tasks. Across the cluster, you can simultaneously execute commands on multiple instances to manage configuration changes. You can get status and results of each command by executing the Run command reports.

You can perform tasks with the Run command, such as installing/uninstalling packages, performing security updates, cleaning up Docker images, starting/stopping service, viewing system resources/ loging files, and performing file operations.

You must attach the IAM policy that will allow the access for the Amazon EC2 System Manager (SSM) API to ecsInstanceRole before it execute the send command with Run commands on container instance. You have to install the SSM agent to process the Run command's request, and configure the instance that is specified in the request. Once this SSM agent is installed in your instance, you can use Run commands to send commands to your container instance.

Deregistering your container instance

You can deregister your container once you finish with it. Once you deregister it, then you are no longer able to accept the tasks. Running tasks under deregistered container will remain running or stopping. So this task becomes orphaned and no longer monitored by Amazon ECS.

If it might be possible that an orphaned task is still part of the Amazon ECS service, then the service scheduler will start another copy of the same task on a different instance. Orphaned tasks that are registered with the Application Load Balancer or Classic Load Balancer target group are deregistered.

After deregistering the container instance, it will remove the instance from the cluster but it will not terminate the EC2 instance. You should terminate the Amazon EC2 manually.

When you terminate a running instance from the Amazon ECS container agent, then the agent will deregister the instance automatically. Instances with disconnected agents or stopped container instances will not deregister automatically when terminated.

So far we have looked at container instances. Now let's look at Amazon ECS clusters.

Amazon ECS clusters

An Amazon ECS cluster is a logical group that contains tasks or services. If your task or service uses the EC2 launch type then the cluster is a grouping of container instances. The first time, Amazon ECS will create a default cluster for you. To keep your resources separate, you can create multiple clusters.

We will look at the following in relation to Amazon ECS clusters:

- Cluster concepts
- Creating a cluster
- Scaling a cluster
- Deleting a cluster

Cluster concepts

- Clusters are region-specific and contain tasks using Fargate or EC2 launch types
- IAM policies are used to allow or restrict users from accessing your clusters
- With EC2 launch type, your cluster can contain different container instance types; this container instance type will be part of one cluster at a time

Creating a cluster

You can create the cluster using AWS Management Console by performing the following steps. If you use the EC2 launch type to launch the task, you should register your container instance with the cluster, after creating it.

 This wizard will help you to create a cluster in a simple way, with the resources required by an Amazon ECS cluster. It will allow you to customize common configuration options for the cluster.

To create a cluster:

1. Log in to the AWS and navigate to the Amazon ECS console at `https://console.aws.amazon.com/ecs/`.
2. Select **Cluster** from the left-hand side of the navigation page and choose **Create Cluster**.
3. For **cluster compatibility**, you can select any template from the following and then select **Next step**. All the templates are allowed to run the containerized application:

Cluster Templates	Description
Networking only	Launch cluster with Fargate launch type No need to provision/backend infrastructure
EC2 Linux + Networking	Launch EC2 launch type cluster using Linux containers
EC2 Windows + Networking	Launch EC2 launch type cluster using Windows containers

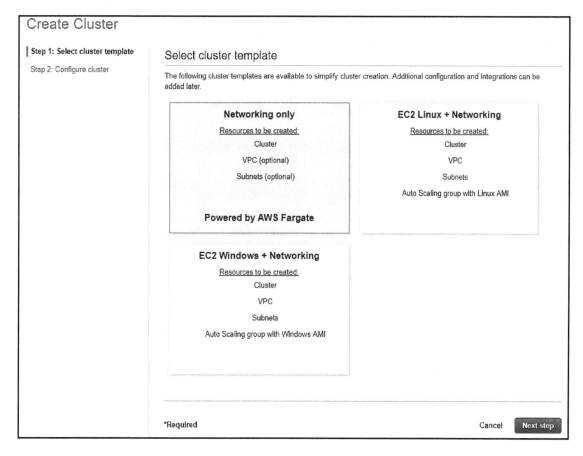

Perform the following steps for the **Networking only cluster** template:

1. Add **Cluster name** on the **Configure cluster** page.
2. You can configure VPC for your cluster in the **Networking** section. It has two options: you can create a cluster with default settings, or by creating a new VPC. If you have selected to create a new VPC, then you have to add the value for the CIDR Block and subnets.
3. Select **Create**.

Follow these steps for **EC2 Linux + Networking** or **EC2 Windows + Networking** templates:

1. Add **Cluster name** on the **Configure cluster** page.
2. You can select **create an empty cluster** if you want to create a cluster without any resources. Select **Create**.

3. Select any one option for the **Provisioning model**.
    - **On-Demand Instance**: You can pay per hour for compute capacity without any upfront payment or long-term commitment.
    - **Spot**: You will bid for available Amazon EC2 instances and get them up to 90% cheaper than the On-Demand price.
      Note: You should avoid Spot instances for the applications that can't interrupt.
      If you have selected Spot instances then it will provide you with these two options.
        - **Spot Instance allocation strategy**: Select a strategy from Diversified or Lowest Price as per your needs.
        - **Maximum bid price (per instance/hour)**: Mention the bid price. Your selected instance type will launch if your bid price is higher than the Spot price.

4. For EC2 instance types, select the appropriate EC2 instance type for container instances.

5. For number of instances, enter the value for number of EC2 instances you want to launch into your cluster.

6. For EBS storage (GiB), select the size of the Amazon EBS volume that will use to store the data in your container instances. Amazon ECS-optimized AMI launches with an 8 GB root volume and a 22 GB data volume, by default.

7. For a key pair, select an Amazon EC2 key pair to connect with your container instances for SSH access. If you do not specify any key pair then you will not be able to connect the container instance with SSH.

8. In the **Networking** section, you can configure the VPC to launch container instances. By default, this wizard will create a new VPC with two subnets in different **Availability Zones** (**AZ**), and a security group open to the internet on port 80. It is a basic setup and it works well for an HTTP service. However, you can modify existing settings in the following way. For VPC, select an existing VPC or create a new one:
    - (Optional) If you create a new VPC, then for a CIDR block you can modify the CIDR block value or you can keep as it is.
    - For subnets, select the subnets to use for your VPC. If you chose to create a new VPC, you can keep the default settings, or you can modify them to meet your needs. If you chose to use an existing VPC, select one or more subnets in that VPC to use for your cluster.
    - For **Security group**, select the security group that you want to attach to the container instances. If you have selected to create a new security group, you can specify the CIDR block with port range and protocol.

- In the **Container instance IAM role** section, select the appropriate IAM role to use the container instances. If an account has an **ecsInstanceRole** that was created for you from the console first-run wizard, then it is selected by default. You can select to create the role, if you don't do that, you can specify another IAM role with container instances.

 The Amazon ECS Agent will not connect to the cluster without the correct IAM permissions.

9. If you have selected **Spot Instance** under **Provisioning Model** earlier, then the **Spot Fleet IAM role** section indicates that an IAM role **ecsSpotFleetRole** will be created.
10. Select **Create**.

Scaling a cluster

In your cluster, you can scale a number of Amazon EC2 instances.

 Clusters with Fargate tasks can scale using Auto Scaling.

If the cluster was created after November 24th, 2015 with console first-run experience, then the Auto Scaling group can scale the cluster, to add or remove the container instances.

If the cluster was created after November 24th, 2015 without console first-run experience, then you cannot scale your cluster from Amazon ECS console.

You can follow these steps to scale the cluster:

1. Log in to the AWS and navigate to the Amazon ECS console at `https://console.aws.amazon.com/ecs/`.
2. Select **Cluster** from the left-hand side of the navigation page and select **cluster to scale**.

3. On the **Cluster: name** page, select **ECS Instances**:

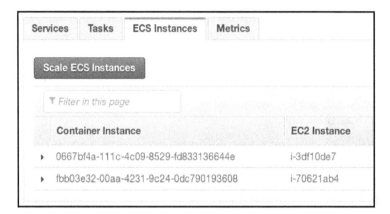

If the button with **Scale ECS Instances** appears, then you can scale it in the next step. If not, then you must have manually adjusted the **Auto Scaling group** to scale the instances, or manually launched or terminated the instances in the Amazon EC2 console.

4. Select **Scale ECS Instances.**
5. For **Desired number of instances**, enter the number of instances to scale your cluster and select **Scale.**

 If you reduce the number of container instances, then it will randomly select the container instances to terminate until the desired count is achieve, and any tasks running on terminated instances are stopped.

Deleting a cluster

You can delete the cluster once you have finished using it. In the Amazon ECS console, when you delete the cluster, then associated resources will be deleted, and it also depends on how the cluster was created.

If the cluster was created after November 24th, 2015 with console first-run experience, then the AWS CloudFormation stack, which was created with the cluster, will also be deleted when you delete the cluster.

If the cluster was created before November 24th, 2015, then you must terminate any container instance associated with the cluster before you delete the cluster. After the cluster is deleted, you can delete any AWS CloudFormation resource or Auto Scaling groups, associated with the cluster.

You can follow these steps to delete a cluster:

1. Log in to the AWS and navigate to the Amazon ECS console at `https://console.aws.amazon.com/ecs/`.
2. Select **Cluster** from the left-hand side of the navigation page and select the cluster to delete.

 You must deregister or terminate the registered container instance in the cluster.

3. Select **Delete Cluster**. You will see either of these confirmation prompts when you delete:
   - **Deleting the cluster also deletes the CloudFormation stack EC2ContainerService-name_of_cluster**: Deleting this cluster will clean up the associated resources that were created with the cluster, such as Auto Scaling groups, load balancers, or VPCs.
   - **Deleting the cluster does not affect CloudFormation resources...**: Deleting this cluster will not clean up any resources that are associated with the cluster that includes Auto Scaling groups, load balancers, or VPCs. Also, you must deregister or terminate any container instances that are registered with this cluster.

So far, we have looked at Amazon ECS clusters. Now let's look at how you can schedule tasks on Amazon ECS.

Scheduling tasks

The Amazon ECS is an optimistic concurrency system in a shared state with elastic scheduling capabilities for containers and tasks. Amazon ECS uses Amazon ECS API's same state information for clusters to make appropriate decisions for placement. Amazon ECS has the ability to manually run tasks (for single run task or batch jobs) or service schedulers (for long-running tasks), where it places the task on the cluster for you. It allows you to define constraints and a task placement strategy, to run the task in the configuration you have selected, such as spread out in Availability Zones. You can also integrate with third-party or custom schedulers.

We can divide this section into the following topics:

- Service scheduler
- Manually running tasks
- Running tasks on a cron-like schedule
- Custom schedulers
- Task life cycle
- Task retirement

Service scheduler

The service scheduler is best suited for applications and long running services that are stateless. It will ensure that the stated numbers of tasks are running constantly, and when any task fails it will reschedule it. Service scheduler optionally ensures that the tasks are registered against Amazon **Elastic Load Balancer** (**ELB**). You can update the service that the service scheduler is maintaining, such as deploying a new task definition or changing the number of running tasks.

By default, tasks are spread across different AZs to the service scheduler, but you can customize these task placement decisions by configuring the task placement strategies and constraints.

Manually running tasks

The **RunTask** action is best suited for batch job processes that will perform the work and then stop. As an example, if you have a **RunTask** process, when the work comes into the queue then the task pulls the work from queue, performs the desired work, and exits.

You can randomly distribute tasks across the cluster by allowing the task placement strategy using **RunTask**. In that case, a single instance will get the appropriate number of tasks. You can customize the task placement strategy and constraints to use **RunTask**.

Manually running the task is ideal in some situations. Let's say you have developed a task but you don't want to deploy this task with the service scheduler. If your task is a periodic batch job or one-time job, then it is pointless to keep it running or restart it when finished. You can use the Amazon ECS service scheduler to state the number of running tasks or place it behind the load balancer.

Follow these steps to run the task using the Fargate launch type:

1. Log in to the AWS and navigate to the Amazon ECS console at `https://console.aws.amazon.com/ecs/`.

2. Select **Task Definitions** from the left-hand side of the navigation pane and choose **Task Definition** to run:
   - You can select the checkbox next to the task definition to run the latest version
   - You can select task definition to view earlier active revisions and select the required revision to run

3. Select **Actions**, and **Run Task**:

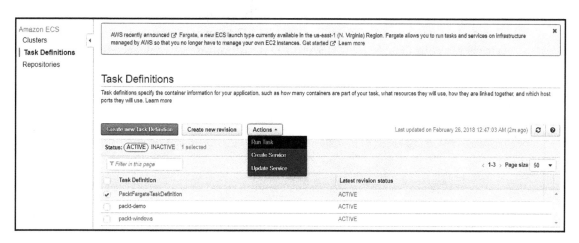

4. Select **FARGATE** for **Launch type** and select **LATEST** for **Platform version**.

5. Select **Cluster** to **default**. Add value for **Number of tasks** to launch. Add a name for **Task Group**.

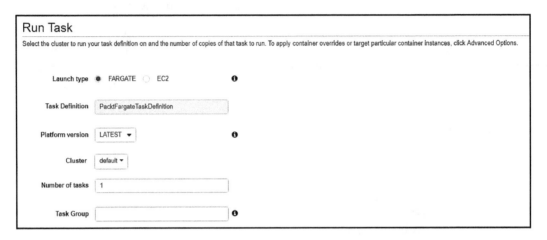

6. For **Cluster VPC**, select the VPC for tasks to use.
7. For **Subnets**, select available subnets.
8. For **Security groups**, a newly created security group allows HTTP traffic from the internet (0.0.0.0/0). By selecting Edit, you can edit the name or the rules of the security group, or select an existing security group.
9. For **Auto-assign public IP**, select **ENABLED** to provide outbound network access for your task. Select **DISABLED** if outbound network access is not required:

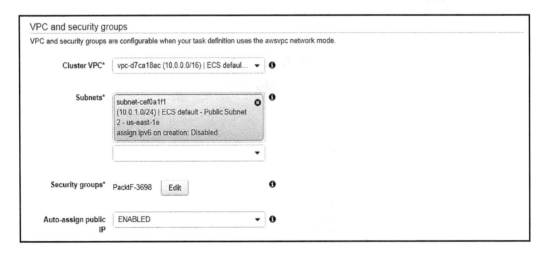

10. (Optional) select **Advanced Options** to configure the command or environment variable override and complete the following steps:
    1. For **Task Role Override**, select IAM roles to provide permission to make AWS API calls:
       - Roles with an **Amazon EC2 Container Service Task Role** trust relationship will be shown here.
    2. For **Task Execution Role Override**, select IAM roles to provide permission to make AWS API calls:
       - Roles with an **Amazon EC2 Container Service Task Execution Role** trust relationship will be shown here.
    3. For **Container Overrides**, select a container to send command or environment variable overrides:
       - For **Command override**: Type the `override` command to send.
       - For **Environment variable overrides**: For **Add Environment Variable** you can add an environment variable called **Key**, and type a string value as an environment value for the **Value** field:

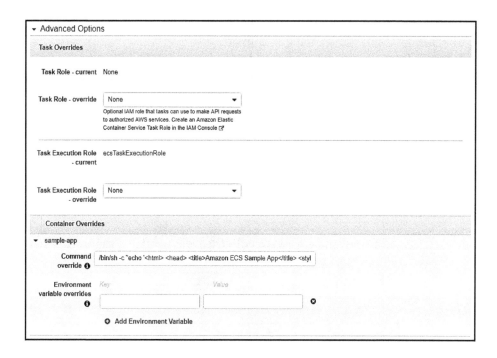

Review the task information and select **Run Task**.

The task moves from **PENDING** to **STOPPED**, if it disappears from the **PENDING** status then there is some error in your task.

Follow these steps to run the task using the EC2 launch type:

1. Log in to the AWS and navigate to the Amazon ECS console at `https://console.`
   `aws.amazon.com/ecs/`.
2. Select **Task Definitions** from the left-hand side of the navigation pane and
   choose **Task Definition** to run:
     - You can select the checkbox next to the task definition to run the latest
       version
     - You can select task definition to view earlier active revisions and select
       the required revision to run

3. Select **Actions, Run Task**.
4. Select **EC2 for Launch Type**.
5. Select **Cluster** to user. Add a value for **Number of tasks** to launch. Add a name
   for **Task Group**.
6. For **Cluster VPC**, select a VPC for the tasks to use.
7. For **Subnets**, select the available subnets.
8. For **Security groups**, a newly created security group allows HTTP traffic from the
   internet (**0.0.0.0/0**). By selecting **Edit**, you can edit the name or the rules of the
   security group, or select an existing security group.

(Optional) For **Task Placement**, you can select placement strategies and constraints for your task. You have the following options to choose from:

Placement strategy	Description
AZ Balanced Spread	Distribute your task across Availability Zones and container instances
AZ Balanced BinPack	Distribute your task with the least available memory across Availability Zones and container instances
BinPack	Task distribution on the least available amount of CPU or memory
One Task Per Host	At least place one task on each container instance
Custom	State the strategy for your own task placement

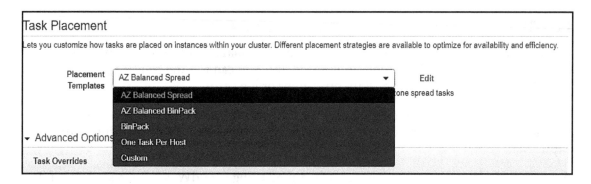

(Optional) Select **Advanced Options** to send command or environment variables and complete the following steps:

1. For **Task Role Override**, select IAM roles to provide permission to make AWS API calls:
   - Roles with an **Amazon EC2 Container Service Task Role** trust relationship will be shown here.
2. For **Task Execution Role Override**, select IAM roles to provide permission to make AWS API calls:
   - Roles with an **Amazon EC2 Container Service Task Execution Role** trust relationship will be shown here.
3. For **Container Overrides**, select a container to send command or environment variable override:
   - For **Command override**: Type the `override` command to send.
   - For **Environment variable overrides**: For **Add Environment Variable** you can add an environment variable called **Key**, and type a string value as an environment value for the **Value** field.

Review the task information and select **Run Task.**

> The task moves from **PENDING** to **STOPPED**, if it disappears from the **PENDING** status then there is some error in your task.

Running tasks on a cron-like schedule

You can create the CloudWatch events rule from the Amazon ECS console. This will run one or more tasks at specified times in your cluster. You can run the task at a specific time by setting the intervals to take backup operations or log scans.

You can set a schedule event rule at a specific interval such as a task that runs at every N minutes, hours, or days. You can set a complicated schedule event rule by using a cron expression.

Amazon ECS tasks can be run like cron scheduling using CloudWatch Events targets and rules.

 Scheduled tasks are not supported by task definitions that use awsvpc network mode.

Follow these steps to create a scheduled task:

1. Log in to the AWS and navigate to the Amazon ECS console at `https://console.aws.amazon.com/ecs/`.
2. Select the **Cluster** in which you want to create the scheduled task.
3. On the **Cluster: cluster-name** page, select **Scheduled Tasks**, **Create**.
4. For **Schedule rule name**, enter a unique name.
5. (Optional) For **Schedule rule description**, state the description for the rule.
6. For **Schedule rule type**, select the rule type such as **Run at fixed interval** or **cron expression**:
   - For **Run at fixed interval**, enter a value in the interval and select a unit such as minutes, hours, days for the schedule.
   - For **Cron expression**, enter a value for the cron expression for the task schedule. It contains six required fields such as **Minutes, Hours, Day-of-month**, **Month, Day-of-week, Year**. All these are separated by whitespace:

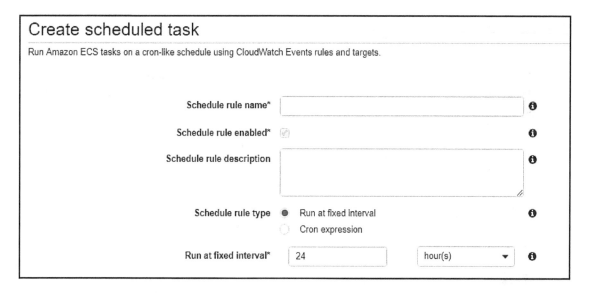

Create scheduled task

Run Amazon ECS tasks on a cron-like schedule using CloudWatch Events rules and targets.

Schedule rule name*	[_____] ❶
Schedule rule enabled*	☑ ❶
Schedule rule description	[_____] ❶
Schedule rule type	● Run at fixed interval ❶ ○ Cron expression
Run at fixed interval*	[24] [hour(s) ▼] ❶

7. Create one or more targets to run the Amazon ECS task when the schedule rule triggers.
    1. For **Target ID**, enter a unique name for target:
        - For **Task** definition, select **family:revision** from the dropdown.
        - For **Number of tasks**, enter the number of task definitions to run on the cluster when the rule executes.
    2. (Optional) For **Task role override**, select the IAM role to use for the task. Roles with an **Amazon EC2 Container Service Task Role** trust relationship will show in the dropdown:
        - For **CloudWatch Events IAM role for this target**, select an existing CloudWatch events service role or select **Create new role** to create the required IAM role.
        - (Optional) In the **Container overrides** section, you can expand a single container and override the command and environment variable.
        - (Optional) select **Add targets** to add an additional target and repeat the steps.
    3. Select **Create**.

Custom schedulers

To meet the business requirements or to leverage third-party schedulers, you can create your own custom schedulers in Amazon ECS. Blox is an open source project to get more control over your containerized applications that run on Amazon ECS. With Amazon ECS, it will enable you to build and integrate third-party schedulers and leverage Amazon ECS to fully manage and scale the clusters.

The custom scheduler uses **StartTask** API for the operation to place the task within the cluster for specific container instances.

 Custom schedulers are compatible with the tasks that use the EC2 launch type. The StartTask API does not work for Fargate launch types for the tasks.

- **Task Placement**: The **RunTask** and **CreateService** actions will enable you to specify constraints and strategies for your task placements, to customize how Amazon ECS places the task.

Task life cycle

When a task starts, either manually or as part of a service, it passes from several states before it finishes or stops.

Some tasks are run as batch jobs and progress from **PENDING** status to **RUNNING** status to **STOPPED** status. Some tasks run indefinitely and can scale up and down.

The Amazon ECS container agent tracks the status of the task, such as the last known status and desired status of the task.

The following is a flow chart that explains the different paths and status change, based on the action:

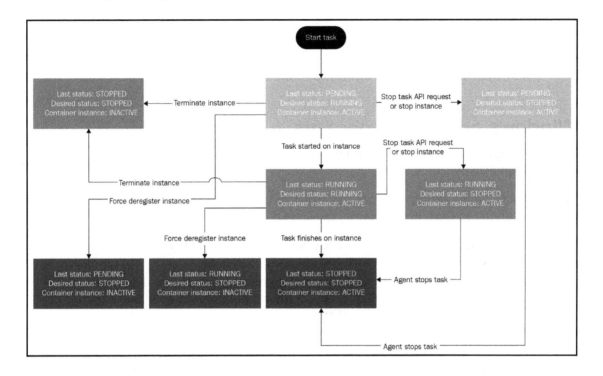

Task retirement

When AWS detects an irreparable failure of the hardware hosting the scheduled task, then the task is to be retired. Or when the task reaches the schedules retirement date, then it stops or is terminated by AWS. The task will automatically stop and the service schedule will start a new task to replace it, if the task is part of service. You will receive a task retirement notification email, if you are using a standalone task.

So far, we have looked at scheduling tasks. Now, let's look at Windows containers on Amazon ECS.

Windows containers (beta)

Amazon ECS also supports Windows containers instances to launch with Amazon ECS-optimized Windows AMI. The Amazon ECS container agent on Amazon ECS-optimized Windows AMI runs as a service on the host, and not inside the container, because it is using the host registry.

Let's discuss the following topics in this section:

- Windows container concepts
- A web application with Windows containers

Windows container concepts

The following are some important things you should be aware of with Windows containers and Amazon ECS.

Windows and Linux container instances cannot run on each other's container instances. You should ensure that Windows and Linux tasks are placed inside separate containers.

- Windows containers are currently NOT supported for Fargate launch types and support only the EC2 launch type.
- A Windows container and its instances can't support all task definition parameters that are available for a Linux container and its instances. Some parameters are not supported at all, or if you use them, they might behave differently on Windows than Linux.
- A Windows Server Docker image size is large, around 9 GiB, so you need more storage space for your container instance than a Linux container instance
- You should provide the IAM role for the task feature when you configure Windows container instances. It will allow your containers to run the PowerShell code. This task feature will use a credential proxy (occupies port 80) to provide credentials for the container.

A web application with Windows containers

Let's walk through a web application using Windows containers that runs on Amazon ECS. In this example, you will create a Windows container instance cluster, launch the container instance into the cluster, register a task definition, to use a Windows container image, create a service which will use the task definition and view the created web page when the container runs.

You can follow these steps to create a web application on a Windows instance:

1. Create a Windows cluster
2. Launch a Windows container instance into the cluster
3. Register a task definition for Windows
4. Create a service with the task definition
5. View the service

Create a Windows cluster

You can create a new cluster in a Windows container. In this application you will create a `PacktWindowsCluster` cluster for a Windows container.

The following are the steps on AWS Management Console.

1. Log in to the AWS and navigate to the Amazon ECS console at `https://console.aws.amazon.com/ecs/`.
2. Select **Cluster** from the left-hand side of the navigation page and choose **Create Cluster**.
3. Select **EC2 Windows + Networking** and click **Next step**.
4. Add **Cluster name** for your cluster (in this example, `PacktWindowsCluster` is the **Cluster name**).
5. Select **Create an empty cluster** and then click **Create**:

From AWS CLI, you can execute the `create-cluster` command to create a cluster:

```
aws ecs create-cluster --cluster-name PacktWindowsCluster
```

Launch a Windows container instance into the cluster

Follow these steps to launch a Windows container instance:

1. Log in to the AWS and navigate to the Amazon EC2 console at `https://console.aws.amazon.com/ec2/`.
2. Select **Launch Instance** from the console dashboard.
3. In **Choose an Amazon Machine Image (AMI)** page, select **Community AMIs**.
4. Type `ECS_Optimized` in the **Search community AMIs** and press the *Enter* key. Now **Select** the **Windows_Server-2016-English-Full-ECS_Optimized-2018.01.10** AMI:

5. On the **Choose an Instance Type** page, select the hardware configuration of your instance. By default, the selected instance type is **t2.micro**.
6. Select **Next: Configure Instance Details**.
7. On the **Configure Instance Details** page, select **Enable for Auto-assign Public IP** to make it accessible from the public internet. If this is selected as **Disable**, then your instance will not be accessible from the internet.
8. Select an **ecsInstanceRole IAM role** value to create the container instance.

If you don't have the correct IAM permissions to launch the container instance, then Amazon ECS agent will be unable to connect to the cluster.

9. Expand the **Advanced Details** section and add the PowerShell script, as mentioned in the following screenshot, into the **User Data** field. If you want to change the cluster, from `PacktWindowsCluster`, you can change the name. To enable IAM roles, you need to add `−EnableTaskIAMRole` for tasks:

10. Select **Next: Add Storage**.
11. On the **Add Storage** page, configure the storage for the container instance. It has a 50 GiB default volume size for Amazon ECS-optimized Windows AMI because an approximate 9 GiB size is for the Windows Server core base layers. You can use more containers and images by using a large root volume size up to 200 GiB.
12. Select **Review and Launch**.
13. On the **Review Instance Launch** page, under **Security Groups**, you can see that the wizard has created and selected a security group.
14. By default, it will come with port `3389` for RDP connectivity. You can open other ports as well by editing the security group.
15. On the **Review Instance Launch** page, select **Launch**.
16. In the **Select an existing key pair or create a new key pair** dialog box, select the options and when you are ready you can select the acknowledgement field and click on **Launch Instances**.
17. You can view the instance status from the **Instances** screen. It will get the public DNS name once the status is in a **RUNNING** state.

It will take approximately 15 minutes for your Windows container instance to register with the cluster.

Register a task definition for Windows

You must register a task definition before you run Windows containers in an Amazon ECS cluster. The following example will display a web page on port 8080 for the container instance with the *microsoft/iis* container image.

Follow these steps to register a task definition with the AWS Management Console.

1. Log in to the AWS and navigate to the Amazon ECS console at https://console. aws.amazon.com/ecs/.
2. On the **Task Definitions** page, select **Create new Task Definition**.
3. Scroll to the bottom and select **Configure via JSON**.
4. Replace the pre-populate JSON code with the following task definition JSON code in the text area and select **Save**:

```
{
  "family": "packt-windows",
  "containerDefinitions": [
    {
      "name": "packt_simple_app",
      "image": "microsoft/iis",
      "cpu": 100,
      "entryPoint":["powershell", "-Command"],
      "command":["New-Item -Path
C:\\inetpub\\wwwroot\\index.html -Type file -Value '<html> <head>
<title>Welcome to Packt!!!</title> </head><body> <div style=text-
align:center> <h1>Welcome to Packt!!!</h1><p>You have successfully
created application in Amazon ECS Container.</p></body></html>';
C:\\ServiceMonitor.exe w3svc"],
      "portMappings": [
        {
          "protocol": "tcp",
          "containerPort": 80,
          "hostPort": 8080
        }
      ],
      "memory": 500,
      "essential": true
    }
```

```
        ]
    }
```

5. Verify the information and click **Create**.

Follow these steps to register the task definition with the AWS CLI.

1. Create a `packt-windows.json` file.
2. Open the file in a text editor and add the JSON code stated previously in the file and save it.
3. Using the AWS CLI, run the `register-task-definition` command to register the task definition with Amazon ECS.

Ensure that the AWS CLI and Windows clusters are using the same region or add the `--region cluster_region` option in to the command, `aws ecs register-task-definition --cli-input-json file://packt-windows.json`.

Create a service with the task definition

Once the task definition has been registered, you can place the task in the cluster. You can create a service with the task definition and place one task in the cluster:

- **Using AWS Management Console**:
    1. On the **Task Definition: packt-windows** registration confirmation page, select **Actions**, **Create Service**.
    2. On the **Create Service** page, enter the following information and then choose **Create service**:
        - **Cluster**: `PacktWindowsCluster`
        - **Number of tasks**: `1`
        - **Service name**: `PacktWindowsService`

- **Using the AWS CLI**:

    Run the following command to create your service:

    ```
    aws ecs create-service --cluster PacktWindowsCluster --task-
    definition packt-windows --desired-count 1 --service-name
    PacktWindowsService
    ```

View the service

Once the service launchs a task into the cluster, you can view the service and open the web application in the browser.

> It will take upto 15 minutes for your instance to download and extract the Windows container base layers.

Follow these steps to view the service:

1. Log in to the AWS and navigate to the Amazon ECS console at `https://console.aws.amazon.com/ecs/`.
2. Select **Cluster** from the left-side navigation page and select **PacktWindowsCluster**.
3. In the **Services** tab, select the **PacktWindowsService** service.
4. On the **Service: PacktWindowsService** page, select the task ID for the task in the service.
5. On the **Task** page, expand the container to view its information.
6. In the **Network bindings** of the container, select the **External Link** with the IP address and port and open it. It will show you the web application:

So far, we have looked at Windows containers. Now, let's look at how to monitor and optimize the cost of the infrastructure on Amazon ECS.

Monitoring and optimizing the cost of the infrastructure

The following are some of the benefits of using ECS:

- Lower AWS bills by switching from EC2 to ECS:
    - **Better resource utilization**: Docker allows you to improve resource utilization on EC2 by running instance on more than a single service. You can use two or multiple services on a single instance type.
    - **Spot by default**: If you use the Spot fleets in your cluster, then it has a lower risk and lower cost of instance turnover. Docker allows you to take advantage of diversity because containers don't care about the machine size on which they run. Containers are fast to start and stop which allows you to save costs on a spot price.
    - **Centralized EC2 cost management**: Running the ECS service with the correct reservations on the cluster helps to make EC2 cost-optimized. Also, centralizing control of EC2 makes it much easier to manage.
- Better security and credentials management:
    - You have to manage logging, security infrastructure, and metrics on every single EC2 instance. With ECS, you can provision the cluster and all the systems are consolidated, so if any logging credentials are compromised, you will rotate the credentials at a single place.

- Consistency across teams and services:

    - With ECS and Docker, you don't need to know different things about server instance to work on. It means you can work effectively and share knowledge across other resources in a team for better application.

- Less environment confusion:

  - To understand the EC2 environment is a bit confusing, if the developers don't know where to look. Use of Docker for developers is more explicit for the runtime environment and least dependent on another system. In Docker, your code will run locally but much closer to production. It will help you to find issues easily without spending time on different stages of the process or iterations.

So far, we have looked at monitoring and optimizing the cost of infrastructure on Amazon ECS. Now, let's understand Continuous Integration and Continuous Deployment Workflow using Amazon ECS.

Continuous Integration (CI) and Continuous Deployment (CD) Workflow

In this tutorial, we will create an end-to-end Continuous Integration (CI) and Continuous Deployment (CD) pipeline, using AWS CodePipeline and Amazon ECS.

Before you start this tutorial, you must have a few resources available to create the CD pipeline. We have mostly covered all the resources in the previous sections.

 You should create all the required resources within the same AWS Region.

The prerequisites are as follows:

- **A source control repository**: AWS CodeCommit is used with Dockerfile and an application source in this tutorial
- **A Docker image repository**: Amazon ECR is used containing an image that will be built from Dockerfile and an application source
- **An Amazon ECS task definition**: To refer the Docker image that is hosted in image repository
- **An Amazon ECS cluster**: To run a task definition service

Once you have finished with the prerequisites, then proceed with the tutorial to create the AWS CodePipeline.

Step 1 – addding required files source repository

AWS CodeBuild will build a Docker image and push it to the Amazon ECR. Create `buildspec.yml` and add this file to the repository that tells AWS CodeBuild about how to build.

Build specification files contain the following stages:

- Pre-build stage:
  - Log in to Amazon ECR.
  - Set repository URI for Amazon ECR image. Add image tag with the first seven characters of Git commit ID.
- Build stage:
  - Build Docker image. Tag image as the latest and with the Git commit ID.
- Post-build stage:
  - You can push the image to the Amazon ECR repository with both the tags.
  - Create a file `PacktECS.json` that contains the Amazon ECS container name and its image and tag. In the deployment stage, the CD pipeline will use this information to create the task definition's new revision and then update the service to use it for the new task definition. AWS CodeDeploy ECS job worker requires this `PacktECS.json` file:

```
version: 0.2

phases:
 pre_build:
 commands:
    - echo Logging in to Amazon ECR...
    - aws --version
    - $(aws ecr get-login --region $AWS_DEFAULT_REGION --no-
include-email)
    - REPOSITORY_URI=012345654321.dkr.ecr.us-
east-1.amazonaws.com/packt-demo
    - IMAGE_TAG=$(echo $CODEBUILD_RESOLVED_SOURCE_VERSION | cut
-c 1-7)
 build:
    commands:
      - echo Build started on `date`
      - echo Building the Docker image...
      - docker build -t $REPOSITORY_URI:latest .
```

```
                        - docker tag $REPOSITORY_URI:latest
        $REPOSITORY_URI:$IMAGE_TAG
         post_build:
           commands:
             - echo Build completed on `date`
             - echo Pushing the Docker images...
             - docker push $REPOSITORY_URI:latest
             - docker push $REPOSITORY_URI:$IMAGE_TAG
             - echo Writing image definitions file...
             - printf '[{"name":"packt-demo","imageUri":"%s"}]'
        $REPOSITORY_URI:$IMAGE_TAG > PacktECS.json
        artifacts:
             files: PacktECS.json
```

The build specification was written for the following task definition, used by the Amazon ECS service for this tutorial. The REPOSITORY_URI value corresponds to the image repository (without any image tag), and the packt-demo value near the end of the file corresponds to the container name in the service's task definition:

```
{
    "taskDefinition": {
      "family": "packt-demo",
      "containerDefinitions": [
        {
          "name": "packt-demo",
          "image": "012345654321.dkr.ecr.us-east-1.amazonaws.com/packt-
demo",
          "cpu": 100,
          "portMappings": [
            {
              "protocol": "tcp",
              "containerPort": 80,
              "hostPort": 80
            }
          ],
          "memory": 128,
          "essential": true
        }
      ]
    }
}
```

Follow these steps to add the `buildspec.yml` file to the source repository.

1. Write the preceding build specification code into the new file.
2. Change the value for **REPOSITORY_URI (012345654321.dkr.ecr.us-east-1.amazonaws.com/packt-demo)** with your Amazon ECR repository URI for the Docker image.
3. Change the value for `packt-demo` to your container name.
4. Add, commit, and push the `buildspec.yml` file to the source repository.
   1. Add files to the repository:

      git add .

   2. Commit the change with specific comments.

      git commit -m "Add comment here."

   3. Push the code that was committed.

Step 2 – creating a Continuous Deployment pipeline

Using AWS CodePipeline wizard, you can create different stages for pipelines and connect with a source code repository for your Amazon ECS service:

Follow these steps to create your pipeline:

1. Log in to the AWS and navigate to the AWS CodePipeline console at `https://console.aws.amazon.com/codepipeline/`.
2. Select **Create pipeline** on **Welcome**.
3. On the **Step 1: Name** page, enter **Pipeline name**, for the pipeline and select **Next step**.
4. On the **Step 2: Source** page, for **Source provider**, select **AWS CodeCommit**:
   1. For **Repository name**, select the AWS CodeCommit repository where your source is located for the pipeline.
   2. For **Branch name**, select the branch to use and click **Next step**.

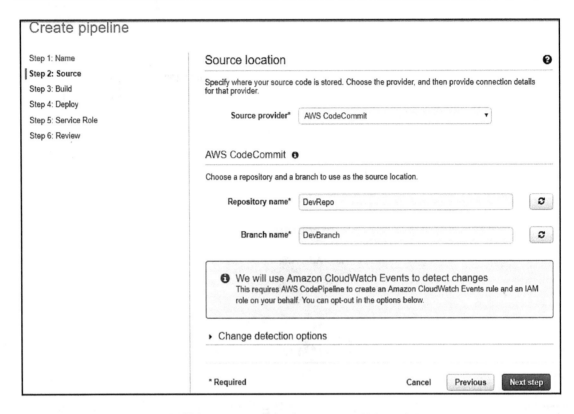

5. On the **Step 3: Build** page, select **AWS CodeBuild**, and then select **Create a new build project**.

6. For **Project name**, enter a unique name for build project.

7. For **Operating system**, select **Ubuntu**.

8. For **Runtime**, select **Docker**.

9. For **Version**, select **aws/codebuild/docker:17.09.0**.

10. Select **Save build project**.

11. Select **Next step**.

 The wizard will create the service role for an AWS CodeBuild, called `code-build-project-name-service-role`. You need to update this service role to add Amazon ECR permissions.

Configure your project

○ Select an existing build project
● Create a new build project

Project name* | PacktECSCodeBuild | ℹ

Description   ⊕ Add description

Environment: How to build

Environment image*   ● Use an image managed by AWS CodeBuild
○ Specify a Docker image

Operating system* | Ubuntu ▾ |

Runtime* | Docker ▾ |

Version* | aws/codebuild/docker:17.09.0 ▾ |

Build specification   ● Use the buildspec.yml in the source code root directory
○ Insert build commands

12. On the **Step 4: Deploy p**age, select Amazon ECS as **Deployment provider**.
     1. For **Cluster name**, select the Amazon ECS cluster where your service is running.
     2. For **Service name**, select your existing service.

3. For **Image filename**, specify your JSON filename and then select **Next step**:

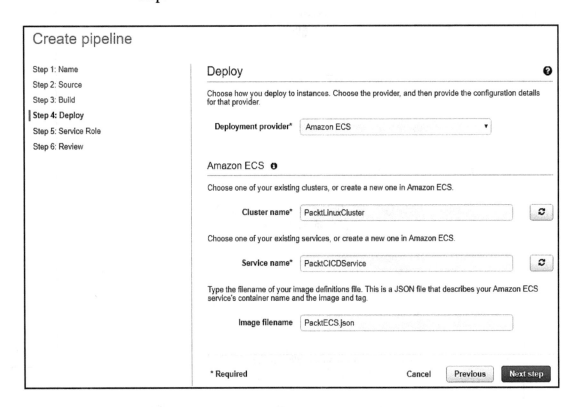

13. On the **Step 5: Service Role** page, select from the existing role or **Create role** and select **Next step**.

14. On the **Step 6: Review** page, review the pipeline configuration and select **Create pipeline**.

 Once the pipeline has been created, then it will pass through different stages. The IAM role for AWS CodeBuild doesn't have permission to execute some commands mentioned in buildspec.yml, so the build will fail. In the next section, you will add the required permissions for Amazon ECR.

Step 3 – adding Amazon ECR permissions to the AWS CodeBuild role

Now in the previous section, you have created the CodePipeline using the AWS CodePipeline wizard including the IAM role for the AWS CodeBuild project such as `code-build-project-name-service-role`. But the build failed because the `buildspec.yml` file is going to call the Amazon ECR API and it doesn't have permission to make these calls. So, you must attach the appropriate permissions to AWS CodeBuild. In this case, you have to attach the `AmazonEC2ContainerRegistryPowerUser` policy to your `code-build-project-name-service-role`.

Step 4 – testing your pipeline

Now your pipeline is ready to run end-to-end native AWS Continuous Integration and Continuous Deployment. You can test the functionality by pushing the code change into the repository.

The following screenshot shows AWS CodeCommit, AWS CodeBuild, and Amazon ECS operations:

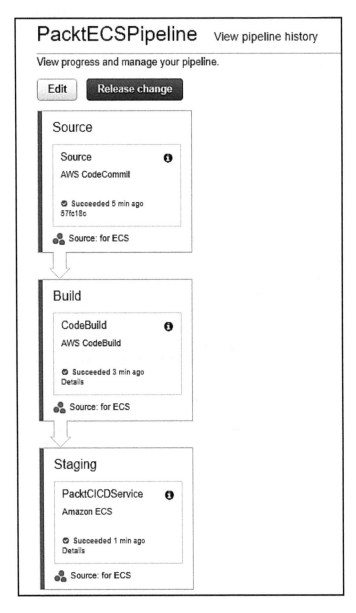

Summary

So far, we have looked at Docker, container instances, clusters, scheduling tasks, and Windows containers. Finally, we deployed an example of a CI/CD application with Amazon EC2 Container Services.

In the next chapter, we will discuss the Microservices Architecture, Lambda and Lambda@Edge advanced topics, the **Serverless Application Model** (**SAM**) and the Serverless Application Framework.

Amazon Lambda – AWS Serverless Architecture

10

Bingo! You have reached the last chapter. I hope you have enjoyed what has been mentioned about AWS and thought that it was quite an interesting journey to complete all the previous chapters. But still, the excitement is not over yet. In the previous chapter, we discussed Docker, container instances, clusters, scheduling tasks, and Windows containers. We also learned about **Elastic Load Balancing** (**ELB**), Auto Scaling, fault tolerance, and monitoring and optimizing infrastructure costs. We also modified AWS CodeDeploy for CI/CD applications with Auto Scaling.

The excitement starts here, because we will learn about the Serverless Framework, as many companies are interested to see how it affects their existing system or how they can integrate serverless architecture with their existing applications to get the benefit of it.

In this chapter, we will discuss more about microservices, the Serverless Framework, how you can achieve serverless on the AWS platform using AWS Lambda, and how you can deploy the applications with the AWS **Serverless Application Model** (**SAM**). We will also learn how to use CI and CD on the Serverless Framework.

In this chapter, we will cover the following topics:

- Microservices architecture, Lambda, and Lambda@Edge advanced topics and best practices
- Deploying with AWS SAM and AWS CloudFormation
- Introducing the Serverless Application Framework
- Monitoring and optimizing the cost of the infrastructure
- CI and CD workflow

Now, let's start with our first topic, microservices architecture, followed by the Lambda and Lambda@Edge advanced topics, and the best practices.

Microservices architecture

A microservice is a method used to develop a scalable software system that will support any kind of device. It is an easily and independently deployable modular service that will run a unique process, and communicates through a lightweight mechanism to fulfill business requirements.

To understand microservices architecture, you need to understand what a monolithic architecture style is and why we need microservices. In a monolithic architecture, an application is created with tightly coupled modules as single units and is deployed on the web or an application. If you want to modify or scale the application, then you need to build and deploy an entire application or scale the whole application, instead of specific components. In this case, microservices can help you.

The following diagram shows the difference between monolithic and microservices architecture:

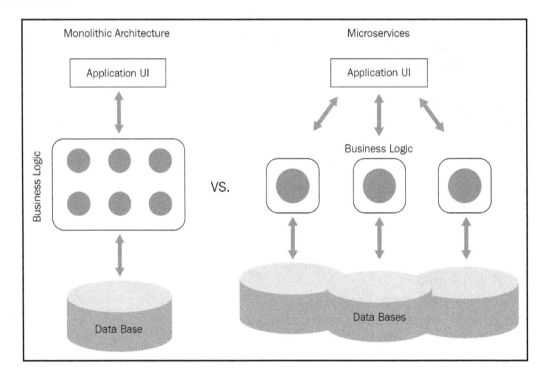

Microservice characteristics

The following are the characteristics of microservices:

- A microservice can break down your software into multiple service components, and all these services can be easily deployed, modified, and redeployed independently, without affecting application integrity. In this case, you will deploy only the necessary services and not the whole application.
- A microservice is organized around business priorities and capabilities, and utilizes cross-functional teams. Every team is responsible for developing one or more services for specific products, based on requirements. If any changes are required, then a specific product team is responsible for making these changes.
- A microservice has smart endpoints, which help to process information, apply business logic, and pass it to the flows. This means it receive requests, processes them, and then generates the response accordingly.
- A microservice involves different kinds of platforms and technologies. It is favored for decentralized governance since developers can use existing code libraries or use different technologies to develop the application. It is also favored to do decentralized data management by assigning a unique database to each service.
- A microservice is designed to cover failures. Different services communicate with each other, and a service could fail at any stage for any reason. In this case, its neighboring service will take over for that service, and the failed service will stop in a graceful manner if possible.

It depends on your business requirements whether you use microservices in your project. Look at the following pros and cons.

The pros of microservices are as follows:

- Microservices can be developed by a small team.
- Developers have the freedom to develop and deploy services independently.
- Different services can be written in different programming languages.
- They can be integrated easily and deployed automatically by using open source tools.
- Developers develop the code as per business requirements and can use the latest technologies if they wish.
- Developers can easily understand and modify the services, which helps newcomers become productive quickly.

- Deployment is much faster because web containers can start quickly.
- There is no need to modify the whole application and redeploy it. If changes are required in certain services, you can modify that service and deploy it.
- If one service fails, the other service will continue to work, so it will not impact on the entire system.
- You can integrate it with other third-party services and scale it easily.
- There is no long-term commitment for the technology stack.

The cons of microservices are as follows:

- Testing is tedious and complicated because of distributed deployment
- Developers have to mitigate network latency, fault tolerance, load balancing, and different message formats, adding more complexity
- There might be some duplication effort since it is a distributed system
- Management and integration become complicated as whole products when services are increasing
- Developers need to put in extra effort when implementing the mechanism for communication between services
- There are a number of information barriers when the number of services is increasing

So far, we have completed microservices architecture. Now, let's understand advanced topics and best practices concerning AWS Lambda and AWS Lambda@Edge.

Lambda and Lambda@Edge advanced topics and best practices

In Chapter 7, *Evaluating the Best Architecture*, we learnt about AWS Lambda basics. Here, we will discuss advanced topics and best practices about AWS Lambda and AWS Lambda@Edge.

The following sections provide advanced features to build Lambda applications:

- **Environment variables**
- **Dead letter queues (DLQ)**

Environment variables

Environment variables are key-value pairs. You can create and modify them from function configuration using the AWS Lambda Management Console, AWS Lambda CLI, or AWS Lambda SDK. For key-value pairs, AWS Lambda makes these available from the Lambda function code, which is using standard APIs. These APIs can support any language, such as Node.js functions, which is using `process.env`.

Lambda functions enable environment variables to pass settings dynamically to the libraries and function code without any code being changed. Libraries can use environment variables to know which directory to install files to, where to store connection and outputs, logging settings, and much more. You can separate application logic from these settings. It also helps to change the function behavior for different settings without updating the function code.

Setting up

If you want, your Lambda function can have different configurations or settings when it moves from different life cycle states like from development to test to production. For example, development, test, and production environments, which contain databases and functions needed to connect to the database. All of these have different environments and so they have different connection information. In this case, you can create the environment variables, reference it for the database name, DB connection information, and in which stage like development, test, and production that function is executing in without any code change. Using AWS console, you can modify and configure environment variables.

- Here, you are configuring the variable for the development stage function:

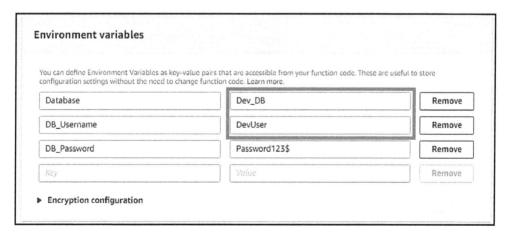

- In the following screenshot, you are configuring the variable for the test stage function:

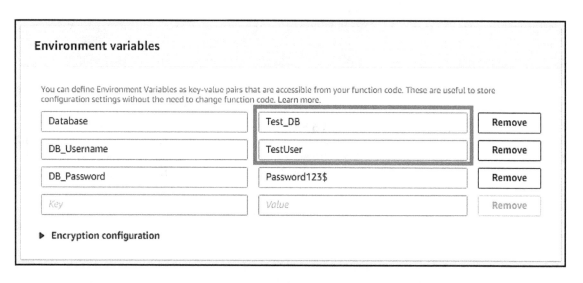

- Here, you are configuring the variable for the production stage function:

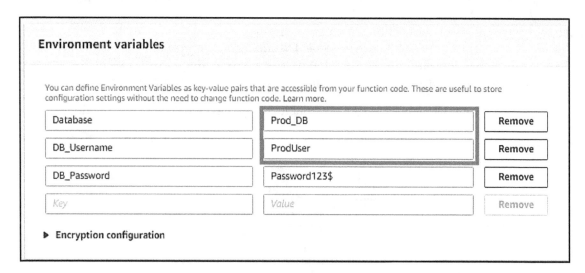

Using the AWS CLI, you can create a Lambda function with an environment variable. Using AWS CloudFormation, you can create and update a function with environment variables. It can also be used when you configure settings that are language-specific or where your function will include the library.

For example, you can set PATH for the directory where all executables will be stored, which includes runtime-specific variables such as NODE_PATH for Node.js or PYTHONPATH for Python.

In the following example, we will create a Lambda function, HiPacktFunction, and set the LIBRARY_PATH environment variable, which will specify the directory where it will load shared libraries at runtime. You have provided the path for the shared library, which is the /usr/bin/packtFunction/lib64 directory. The runtime parameter is using python3.6:

```
aws lambda create-function --region us-east-1 --function-name
HiPacktFunction --zip-file fileb://hi_packt.zip --role
arn:aws:iam::499651321398:role/service-role/LambdaRole --environment
Variables="{LIBRARY_PATH=/usr/bin/packtFunction/lib64}" --handler
hi_packt.my_handler --runtime python3.6 --timeout 15 --memory-size 512
```

The output of running the preceding code can be shown as follows:

```
Command Prompt                                                  —   □   ×

D:\AWS Lambda>aws lambda create-function --region us-east-1 --function-name HiPacktFun
ction --zip-file fileb://hi_packt.zip --role arn:aws:iam::499651321398:role/service-ro
le/LambdaRole --environment Variables="{LIBRARY_PATH=/usr/bin/packtFunction/lib64}" --
handler hi_packt.my_handler --runtime python3.6 --timeout 15 --memory-size 512
{
    "FunctionName": "HiPacktFunction",
    "LastModified": "2018-03-03T14:18:58.471+0000",
    "RevisionId": "e9fdbc61-4145-40f1-ba0e-229f3d182ed1",
    "MemorySize": 512,
    "Environment": {
        "Variables": {
            "LIBRARY_PATH": "/usr/bin/packtFunction/lib64"
        }
    },
    "Version": "$LATEST",
    "Role": "arn:aws:iam::499651321398:role/service-role/LambdaRole",
    "Timeout": 15,
    "Runtime": "python3.6",
    "TracingConfig": {
        "Mode": "PassThrough"
    },
    "CodeSha256": "fINyhgYQoEdbWxw6prLc0UMRSx7jLD2wbUJPcGqA8SQ=",
    "Description": "",
    "CodeSize": 280,
    "FunctionArn": "arn:aws:lambda:us-east-1:499651321398:function:HiPacktFunction",
    "Handler": "hi_packt.my_handler"
}
```

You can verify the created function in the AWS console, and see the generated function with the environment variable:

Naming convention rules for environment variables

You can create a number of environment variables, and the total size of the set can be no more than 4 KB. The name must start with any letters from [a-zA-Z], and can contain alphanumeric characters and underscores, such as [a-zA-Z0-9_].

In addition to that, AWS Lambda reserves some specific sets of keys. You will receive an error message if you try to set values for any of the reserved keys.

Environment variables and function versioning

In AWS Lambda, you can enable version provisioning for your functions to manage and publish different versions for different stages such as development to test to production. For each version of Lambda functions, you have different environment variables for different stages, and these environment variables are also saved as snapshots of that version; they cannot changed.

If requirements change, then you can create a new version of the Lambda function. Updating environment variables is done to create new versions to meet requirements. Then, you can publish the new version. The function's current version should be marked as $LATEST:

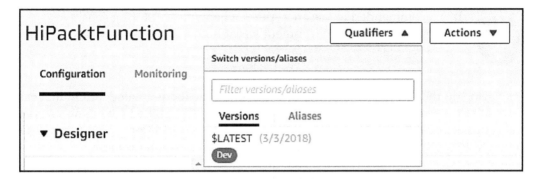

You can also contain aliases to point to a particular version in your function. Aliases provide the advantage to roll back to a previous version of your function, and you will point out the aliases for that version. They also contain the same environment variables required for that version:

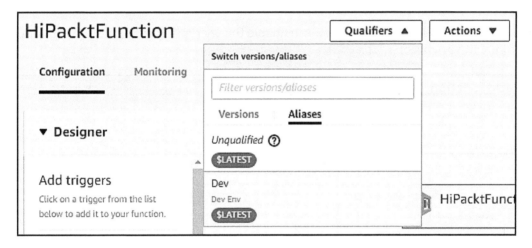

Environment variable encryption

AWS Lambda uses AWS **Key Management Service** (**KMS**) to encrypt the environment variables. When you invoke the Lambda function, these values will be decrypted and available in the Lambda code. When you create or update your first Lambda function in a region that uses environment variables, then it will create the default service key automatically within AWS KMS. This key will encrypt the environment variables.

It is recommended to use encryption when you are storing sensitive information in your environment variable.

You can also add the AWS KMS key after the Lambda function is created, but in that case you cannot select the default key. If this is the case, you will get billed when you use your own key, but not billed if you use the default service key. No additional IAM permissions are required to use the default KMS service key for Lambda. You have to add kms:Decryptto in your role to use the custom KMS key. Also, users must require permission to create and update the Lambda function in order to use the KMS key.

 On the client side, you cannot encrypt sensitive information using the default Lambda service key.

As shown in the following image, you can enable the encryption configuration for your environment variables:

Error scenarios

There are a few error scenarios that can occur when you use environment variables, which are as follows:

- You get a configuration error for the create or update operation when the function configuration exceeds 4 KB, or when you use a reserved key as an environment variable key provided by AWS Lambda.
- It might be possible that the encryption or decryption of an environment variable fails during execution.
- Due to AWS KMS service exceptions, AWS Lambda is unable to decrypt environment variables. In this case, AWS KMS will return an error message with the error conditions. It will log in to log-stream in Amazon CloudWatch.
- You get the following error message when you access the environment variables using a disabled AWS KMS key:

```
Lambda was unable to configure access to your environment variables
because the KMS key used is disabled.
Please check your KMS key settings.
```

Dead letter queues (DLQ)

A failed Lambda function invokes asynchronously by default. It is retired twice. Then, the Lambda function event is discarded. AWS Lambda gets an indication to use DLQ for the unprocessed events. These unprocessed events send you to an Amazon SNS topic or an Amazon SQS queue where you will take further action.

You can configure DLQ by mentioning a target **Amazon Resource Name** (**ARN**) in the `DeadLetterConfig` parameter in the Lambda function for the Amazon SQS queue or Amazon SNS topic where the event payload will be delivered. Functions without any association with DLQ discard those events after exhausting their retries.

To access your DLQ resources, you need to provide explicitly receive and/or delete and/or sendMessage roles as part of the execution role for the Lambda function. The payload written to the DLQ target ARN is the original payload without any modifications to the message body.

Attributes of the message contain the following information so that you can understand why the event wasn't process:

Name	Type	Value
RequestID	String	Unique request identifier
ErrorCode	Number	HTTP error code in a three-digit format
ErrorMessage	String	Error message truncated to 1 KB

If the event payload consistently fails for some reason, for example, to reach the target ARN, then Lambda will call `DeadLetterErrors` to increment the CloudWatch metric and delete that event payload.

Best practices for working with AWS Lambda functions

The following are the recommended best practices for using AWS Lambda:

Function code

The following are the best practices for function code:

- You can separate your entry point or Lambda handler logic into core logic to create more unit-testable functions.
- You can improve the performance of your function code by taking advantage of externalized configurations or dependencies for the code, so that you can retrieve the referenced code and store it locally after its initial execution. You can limit the re-initialization of objects and/or variables on every invocation. Reuse the existing connections and keep the previous connections alive, which were established during previous invocations.
- To pass operational parameters, you can use environment variables for your functions. Let's say you want to use the Amazon S3 bucket name in your function. You can pass this value as an environment variable instead of hard-coding the bucket name.

- You can control the dependencies in a function's deployment package. If you are using libraries in your function, and if these libraries are updated with some set of latest features and security updates, it is recommended to package all your dependencies within the same deployment package.
- You can reduce the time it takes to download the deployment package and unpack it before invocation. Avoid uploading the entire AWS SDK functions that have been written in .NET core or Java. Instead, you can select the dependent modules that your SDK needs.
- You can reduce the time it takes to unpack the deployment package. For example, you can put your dependency .jar file in a separate lib directory for Java functions instead of putting all your code in a single .jar file with all the required .class files.
- For your dependencies, you can minimize complexity by using simple frameworks so that they load quickly.
- You should avoid using recursive code.

Function configuration

The following are the best practices for function configuration:

- You should do performance testing for Lambda functions by picking the optimum memory size configurations. A memory size increase will trigger an equivalent CPU increase in your function. You can determine the memory usage by viewing the AWS CloudWatch logs. In the logs, you can analyze the maximum memory used and determine if it has been over-provisioned or it needs more memory.
- You should do load testing to determine the optimum timeout value. It will help you analyze how long the function will run to determine the dependency service. It is also important that your Lambda function makes network calls to the resources that might not handle Lambda scaling.
- You can set the IAM policies for restrictive permissions.
- You should be familiar with all the required AWS Lambda limits.
- You should delete the Lambda functions that are no longer needed or unused, so unnecessarily increase the deployment package size.

Alarming and metrics

The following are the best practices for Alarming and Metrics:

- You can use Amazon CloudWatch alarms and AWS Lambda metrics instead of using the alarms and metrics in Lambda function code. You can catch the issues in the early stage of the development process. You can set up and configure an alarm based on your expected time to run a Lambda function execution.
- You can leverage AWS Lambda metrics and dimensions, as well as the logging directory, to catch any app errors.

Stream event invokes

The following are the best practices for stream event invocations:

- For the stream processing function, you can test your code with different sizes of batches and records so that you get to know how quickly your function will complete a specific task. If there are not enough records, then the stream processing function will process a lesser number of records instead of waiting.
- By adding extra shards, you can increase your Kinesis stream processing throughputs. In Kinesis, if you have 100 active shards, then you have to invoke at least 100 Lambda functions to increase the processing throughput.
- To know whether your Kinesis stream is processed or not, you can use Amazon CloudWatch on IteratorAge. You can configure Amazon CloudWatch alarm settings by a maximum of 30 seconds.

Async invokes

To address the async functions errors, you can create and use a **Dead Letter Queue** (DLQ).

Lambda VPC

The following are the best practices for Lambda VPC:

- From the following diagram, you can decide whether to use the **Virtual Private Cloud** (**VPC**) or not:

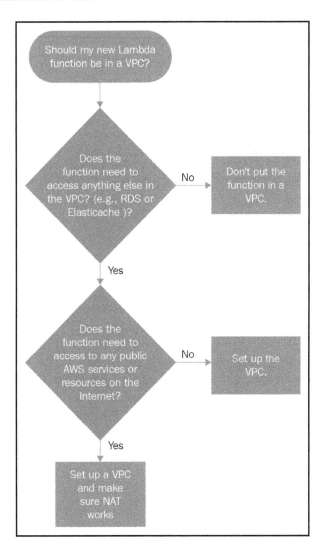

- Lambda will create an **Elastic Network Interface** (**ENI**) in the VPC to access the internal resources.
- You can request to increase the ENI capacity if you don't have enough capacity. You can request to create a large subnet if you don't have enough IP addresses.
- In your VPC, you can create dedicated Lambda subnets. You can create a custom route table for NAT gateway traffic without changing your existing subnets. It will create a dedicated address space for Lambda and it will not share the resources with others.

Lambda@Edge

AWS Lambda@Edge allows you to easily run code across different AWS locations globally. It will provide low latency to the end user. Your AWS Lambda function can be triggered by Amazon CloudFront events, such as content requested to or from origin servers and viewers. AWS Lambda will take care of all the necessary actions such as replication, routing, and scaling the code with high availability at different AWS locations close to the end user when you upload the code to AWS Lambda.

There is no charge when the code is ideal, and you will pay for the compute time your function consumes.

Lambda@Edge benefits

The benefits of Lambda@Edge are as follows:

- Lambda@Edge runs the function code at different AWS locations close to the end user to provide low latency with rich and more personalized contents.
- Lambda@Edge scales the applications automatically by running code in response to each Amazon CloudFront event trigger. Your function code processes each trigger individually, runs in parallel, and scales precisely with the workload.
- Lambda@Edge runs code automatically without provisioning or managing servers for different AWS locations. You will write the code, upload to AWS Lambda, and then the code will run close to the end user's locations.
- Lambda@Edge charges you every 50 ms for executing the code, but this also depends on the number of times it is triggered. You will pay nothing when your code is ideal.

So far, we have completed advanced topics and best practices for AWS Lambda and AWS Lambda@Edge. In the next section, we will discuss AWS **Serverless Application Model (SAM)**. You will also deploy applications using AWS SAM and AWS CloudFormation.

AWS Serverless Application Model (SAM)

Serverless applications can be defined by AWS SAM. Previously, it was known as **project flourish**. Natively, AWS SAM is supported by AWS CloudFormation. It expresses resources for serverless applications with simple syntax. AWS SAM with AWS CloudFormation can define AWS Lambda functions, APIs, and Amazon DynamoDB tables, which are needed by a serverless application in a simple way. With CloudFormation templates, you can define serverless resources with a few lines of code. Two new commands have also been introduced to AWS CloudFormation CLI that will simplify packaging serverless applications and deploying with AWS CloudFormation.

To deploy the application, you need to specify the resources, along with the permission policy in the AWS CloudFormation template file, which is written in YAML or JSON, a package that deploys artifacts, and finally, deploys the templates. A SAM file or template is referred by the AWS SAM model as an AWS CloudFormation template with serverless resources.

The following is an example that defines how you can leverage AWS SAM to declare components for serverless applications:

```
AWSTemplateFormatVersion: '2010-09-09'
Transform: AWS::Serverless-2016-10-31
Resources:

    Your_Function_Name:
        Type: AWS::Serverless::Function
        Properties:
            Handler: index.handler
            Runtime: runtime
            CodeUri: s3://your_s3_bucket_name/your_packaged_code.zip
```

- `Handler:` When the Lambda function is invoked, it will execute the code.
- `index:` The name of the file in the handler that is containing the code. You can mention as many function you want in your serverless application.

You can also mention the environment variables that we have discussed in previous sections.

 You can add the resources into the AWS CloudFormation template, but this is not supported by the current SAM model.

Deploying with AWS SAM and AWS CloudFormation

In this section, we will create a simple serverless application, which consists of a single function. It will return Amazon S3 bucket name that is specified as an environment variable.

Create the `index.js` file with the following code:

```
var AWS = require('aws-sdk');

exports.handler = function(event, context, callback) {
  var bucketName = process.env.S3_BUCKET;
  callback(null, bucketName);
}
```

Create the `packt.yaml` file with the following code:

```
AWSTemplateFormatVersion: '2010-09-09'
Transform: AWS::Serverless-2016-10-31
Resources:
  PacktFunction:
    Type: AWS::Serverless::Function
    Properties:
      Handler: index.handler
      Runtime: nodejs6.10
      Environment:
        Variables:
          S3_BUCKET: packtdemo
```

Create the `packt_app` folder and add the `index.js` and `packt.yaml` files into that folder. Now, you can package the `packt_app` folder for the serverless application.

Packaging and deployment

Once you create the `index.js` file, which is a package handler, and the `packt.yaml` file, you need to package and deploy them. You can use the AWS CLI for the packaging and deployment of this serverless application.

Packaging

You can use your existing Amazon S3 bucket or create a new bucket to package the application. Execute the `package` command to upload the deployment package to S3.

Execute the following command to create an Amazon S3 bucket in your specified region:

```
aws s3 mb s3://bucket-name --region region
```

You can execute the following command on the command prompt to create the packaged artifacts. It will return the command for deployment once it is successfully packaged:

```
aws cloudformation package --template-file packt.yaml --output-template-
file serverless-output.yaml --s3-bucket packtdemo
```

The output of running the preceding command is as follows:

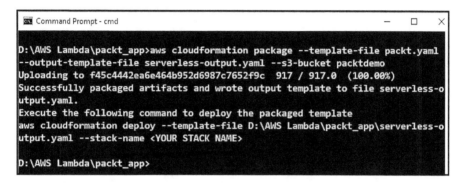

It will create the package under the specified Amazon S3 bucket and provide the command for deployment:

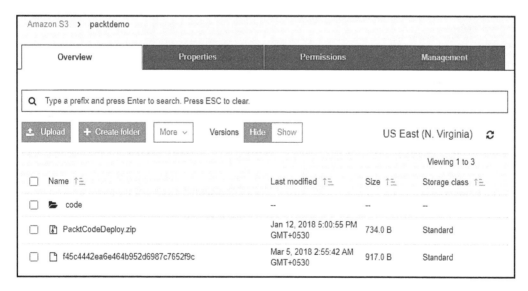

This command will generate a template file for AWS SAM. This package command will generate an AWS SAM template file. We have specified the `serverless-output.yaml` file in the previous command with the `output-template-file` attributes. This template file also contains `CodeUri`. `CodeUri` specifies the path where the deployment file is stored in the S3 bucket.

This template file is a serverless application. It is now ready for deployment:

Deployment

The application will be deployed by executing the following command:

```
aws cloudformation deploy --template-file serverless-output.yaml --stack-
name PacktFunction --capabilities CAPABILITY_IAM
```

The screenshot of running the preceding command is shown as follows:

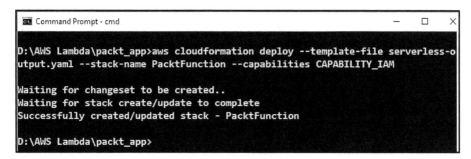

You can specify the `--capabilities` parameter with your deployment command to create a role for AWS CloudFormation. In the template file, the type is created with the `AWS::Serverless::Function` resource. It will create the role that is used to execute the Lambda function. You can execute the `aws cloudformation` command to create a ChangeSet for AWS CloudFormation. It contains a change list in the AWS CloudFormation stack and deploys it later.

You can verify your newly created stack by opening the AWS CloudFormation console:

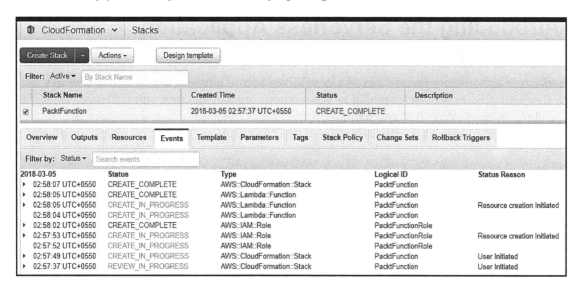

You can verify your Lambda function by opening the AWS Lambda console:

So far, we have talked about SAM and deployed the application using AWS SAM and AWS CloudFormation. In the next section, we will learn about the Serverless Application Framework.

Introducing the Serverless Application Framework

Serverless architecture means that as a developer, you will focus on the code and won't bother with the servers. Servers will be somewhere. As a developer, you will focus on building an application that can handle production ready traffic. You don't have to provision and manage the servers and scale your application. You will not pay for unused resources.

This technology is still in its early stages, although many developers have already implemented it and launch their applications rapidly with lesser costs.

What makes an application serverless?

The serverless movement was started with the release of AWS Lambda. AWS Lambda is a **Function-as-a-Service (FaaS)** compute service, but serverless is far more than FaaS. Serverless focuses on your efforts to provide value to users. This means using the managed service for databases, including the search index, queue, email delivery, and SMS messaging. You can tie these services using stateless and ephemeral computes.

If you upgrade your Linux server or manage the RabbitMQ server, it will not provide any value to the user, but if you add some new features for your shipping products, this will provide value to users. The Serverless Framework suggests that you can focus on your business logic and everything else will be taken care by them.

Serverless applications benefits

You should know about the core benefits offered by serverless applications:

- **No administration**: You will deploy your code without any provisioning or managing. You don't need to worry about the concepts of fleet, instance, or the operating system. There is also no need for the Ops department.
- **Auto-scale**: As a developer, you need to fire alerts or write scripts to scale the servers up and down. The serverless service provider manages this scaling activity.
- **Pay-per-use**: You will pay for what you used for FaaS compute and not for the pre-provisioned capacity. You will not pay for a single penny for the idle time, any resource that you haven't used, and if you haven't completed resource utilization. It will cut down the cost by 90%.
- **Increased velocity**: You can reduce the time from idea, to implementation, to deployment to production, since you have less provisions upfront, which are managed after deployment. In this case, a small team can deliver more features.

The Serverless Framework

The serverless application is in cloud native development and it requires automation. Since you have multiple managed services and functions, you cannot rely on a manual process. You should be able to create applications with a command. This is the reason that the Serverless Framework comes into the picture. You can build and deploy an application on any cloud provider with a consistent experience using the Serverless Framework CLI.

Based on the language you have used in your application and the cloud provider you have used for deployment, this Serverless Framework will automatically identify cloud vendor settings for you. Previously, we have discussed serverless application benefits. Now, we will discuss Serverless Framework benefits.

Serverless Framework benefits

You should know about the core benefits offered by the Serverless Framework:

- **Development speed increased**: With the Serverless Framework CLI, developers can build, test, and deploy the application in the same environment. Developers will write their functions using YAML, and the deployment of a service can be done using a single command. Practically, your code will be deployed to multiple providers with different deployment versions, and can be rolled back if necessary.
- **Avoid cloud vendor lock-in**: Different cloud providers use different deployment methods and different formats. This framework helps put the application into a single package, and this package can be deployed to any cloud providers.
- **Infrastructure as Code (IaC)**: Across multiple clouds, you can configure the infrastructure. The Serverless Framework will integrate with every compute service to provide you with a standardized infrastructure as code.
- **Existing ecosystem**: These Serverless Framework is pluggable, so you can used it with any existing system. There are many community contributed plugins available on GitHub. This framework is widely adopted so you can participate in active discussion on forums. There is a wide range of available tutorials that can help you get started.

Many developers are moving to serverless to decrease monotony and increase velocity for the application.

Now, we will discuss some serverless use cases to encourage you to think beyond it. Serverless is extensible, flexible, and used to address a wide range of application problems:

- **Auto-scaling websites and APIs**: In serverless, you can develop websites and applications without setting up any infrastructure. You can launch a fully functional sites in days. Your serverless backend scales automatically on demand.
- **Event streaming**: Serverless compute will trigger from event logs and pub/sub topics to give you a scalable and elastic pipeline without maintaining the complicated clusters. With an event streaming pipeline, you can power the analytics system, modify the cache, update the secondary data stores, or feed the monitoring system.

- **Image and video manipulation**: Serverless allows you to build a performance-enhancing image and video service for an application. You can call the serverless service to dynamically resize an image and change the trans coding of the video for different languages. The application will use image recognition to improve a user's experience, such as an ecommerce website that allows customers to upload their credit card photograph instead of typing the credit card number in manually. You can also user Amazon Rekognition to recognize images and faces for profile photos. You can also reformat or automatically process the uploaded images or resize them into thumbnails in specific dimensions.

- **Hybrid-cloud applications**: Every cloud provider has some limitations, and they will not meet each and every business requirement on their own. Teams need to utilize the best feature from cloud vendors and acquire them to deploy services for multiple providers within a single application. But this is not easy for cloud providers. Serverless helps to achieve this by tweaking the functions to fit cloud vendors' unique formats. You can easily deploy to any vendor you choose to maximize application efficiency and utilize the best part from each cloud vendor.

- **Multi-language applications**: With the Serverless Framework, your application can be multi-lingual. When building an application, the first discussion is usually about which language to use. The language chosen isn't always about what suits the project best, but rather which resources are already on-hand. This encourages multilingual teams and enables seamless integration of services in applications written by a specific team. It prevents a team to use the specific language, and the new language can used for new services. These new services can talk to legacy services as necessary.

- **CI/CD**: The ability to quickly revise software is far more important nowadays. With Continuous Integration and Continuous Deployment, you can ship your code in small iterations to fix bugs and other updates on a daily basis. Serverless can automate these processes. As an example, checking code in to the repository will trigger for website builds, and if the builds is successful, it will redeploy it automatically. With Serverless, you can automate processes and cut down manual tasks.

So far, we have talked about the serverless application framework. In the next section, we will understand monitoring and optimizing the cost of the infrastructure.

Monitoring and optimizing the cost of the infrastructure

In the early stages, if you do not estimate and optimize Lambda costs, then your Lambda functions can cost thousands of dollars unnecessarily. You can save this money with pre-planning and cost optimizations.

The cost of AWS Lambda is cheaper when you have a low volume, but when you start executing it on a production scale, then you can't ignore it.

How does Lambda pricing work?

AWS Lambda is a pay-as-you-go service in cloud computing. You can upload the function, execute it, and pay for the execution time. If you don't execute the function or it is idle, then you don't pay anything.

The following factors can determine the cost of AWS Lambda:

- You will pay for the number of times the Lambda function executes.
- It depends on the duration of each Lambda function execution. You will pay more if your function takes a long time to execute. This will encourage you to write efficient application code. The maximum timeout for a Lambda function is 5 minutes, and you will be charged in 100 ms increments.
- You have to configure the required memory for the successful execution of the Lambda function. You should avoid under-allocation or over-allocation of memory.
- You will pay standard EC2 rates for data transfer.

How do you keep AWS Lambda costs down?

Uses and configurations are combinations that can be problematic for some budgets. The following are some ways to keep your AWS Lambda costs down:

- **Your functions should be executed at the right frequency**: You have to identify which factor can affect how frequently your Lambda functions need to trigger. Let's say you are using Kinesis as a Lambda function trigger; you can simply adjust the batch size. If the batch size is higher, then your Lambda function will execute less frequently. You have to check your triggers and see if you can reduce the number of executions.

- **Write efficient code that executes fast**: If your function completes the execution in half of the time, then it will save you half of your money. Execution time is directly proportional to how much you will pay. You could check the CloudWatch logs for duration metrics. If the function is taking more time to execute, then you should optimize it.

- **Provision the right amount of memory**: If the function is configured with 512 MB and it is using 15 MB for execution, then it is wasting around 97% of its capacity. If the function is executed 100 times per second, then it will cost you approximately $1,780 USD monthly. But if you reduce the memory size from 512 MB to 128 MB, then it will not affect your execution time. You will see approximately $480 USD in your monthly bill. This means that you will save around $1,300 USD every month and $15,600 USD at the end of the year. Higher memory allocation results in more CPU capacity allocation, which could result in faster execution with a lower cost. It is recommended that you test the function at scale with different memory allocation, check the execution time, and calculate the cost.

- **Keep an eye on data transfer**: When you execute a Lambda function, it will charge you at standard EC2 data transfer rates. You can do the following things when it concerns data transfer:

  - You can verify the AWS cost and usage report. Filter it by your Lambda function and find the values in the `transferType` column; you will get the usage amount.
  - You can log the data transfer operation size in Lambda code and configure it for the CloudWatch Metric filter.

So far, we have talked about monitoring and optimizing the cost of the infrastructure. In the next section, we will understand the CI/CD workflow using AWS CloudFormation.

CI and CD workflow

In this section, we will create an end-to-end CI and CD pipeline using AWS CodePipeline and AWS CloudFormation.

Before you start,you must have a few resources available to create a CD pipeline. We have covered most of these resources in the previous chapters.

 You should create all the required resources within the same AWS region.

The prerequisites are as follows:

- **AWS CodeBuild**: You can use AWS CodeBuild to build, test, and package your serverless application
- **AWS CloudFormation**: You can use AWS CloudFormation to deploy your serverless application
- **AWS CodeDeploy**: You can use AWS CodeDeploy to deploy updates on your serverless application
- **AWS CodePipeline**: You can use AWS CodePipeline to model, visualize, and automate the steps required for the serverless application

The following section will describe how to integrate all these tools from AWS CodePipeline to automate the deployment of serverless applications. You have to create an AWS CloudFormation role and attach the AWSLambdaExecute policy:

1. Log in to AWS and open the IAM console from: `https://console.aws.amazon.com/iam/`.
2. Create an IAM role for the AWS CloudFormation service.

3. Proceed with the following steps to create a role:

    1. In **Select Role Type**, select the **AWS Service Roles** option, and then select **CloudFormation**. Select **Next: Permissions**.

    2. In **attach permissions policies**, in the search bar, find and select **AWSLambdaExecute**. Select **Next: Review**.

    3. In the role name, uses unique name and then select **Create role**.

    4. Open the created role and select **Add inline policy** under the **Permissions** tab.

    5. In **Create Policy**, select the **JSON** tab and add the following code:

Replace the ID and region with your corresponding account ID and region.

```
{
  "Statement": [
    {
      "Action": [
        "s3:GetObject",
        "s3:GetObjectVersion",
        "s3:GetBucketVersioning"
      ],
      "Resource": "*",
      "Effect": "Allow"
    },
    {
      "Action": [
        "s3:PutObject"
      ],
      "Resource": [
        "arn:aws:s3:::codepipeline*"
      ],
      "Effect": "Allow"
    },
    {
      "Action": [
        "lambda:*"
      ],
      "Resource": [
        "arn:aws:lambda:region:id:function:*"
      ],
      "Effect": "Allow"
    },
```

```
    {
      "Action": [
        "apigateway:*"
      ],
      "Resource": [
        "arn:aws:apigateway:region::*"
      ],
      "Effect": "Allow"
    },
    {
      "Action": [
        "iam:GetRole",
        "iam:CreateRole",
        "iam:DeleteRole",
        "iam:PutRolePolicy"
      ],
      "Resource": [
        "arn:aws:iam::id:role/*"
      ],
      "Effect": "Allow"
    },
    {
      "Action": [
        "iam:AttachRolePolicy",
        "iam:DeleteRolePolicy",
        "iam:DetachRolePolicy"
      ],
      "Resource": [
        "arn:aws:iam::id:role/*"
      ],
      "Effect": "Allow"
    },
    {
      "Action": [
        "iam:PassRole"
      ],
      "Resource": [
        "*"
      ],
      "Effect": "Allow"
    },
    {
      "Action": [
        "cloudformation:CreateChangeSet"
      ],
      "Resource": [
"arn:aws:cloudformation:region:aws:transform/Serverless-2016-10-31"
      ],
```

```
      "Effect": "Allow"
    },
    {
      "Action": [
        "codedeploy:CreateApplication",
        "codedeploy:DeleteApplication",
        "codedeploy:RegisterApplicationRevision"
      ],
      "Resource": [
        "arn:aws:codedeploy:region:id:application:*"
      ],
      "Effect": "Allow"
    },
    {
      "Action": [
        "codedeploy:CreateDeploymentGroup",
        "codedeploy:CreateDeployment",
        "codedeploy:GetDeployment"
      ],
      "Resource": [
        "arn:aws:codedeploy:region:id:deploymentgroup:*"
      ],
      "Effect": "Allow"
    },
    {
      "Action": [
        "codedeploy:GetDeploymentConfig"
      ],
      "Resource": [
        "arn:aws:codedeploy:region:id:deploymentconfig:*"
      ],
      "Effect": "Allow"
    }
  ],
  "Version": "2012-10-17"
}
```

6. Select **Validate Policy** and then select **Apply Policy**.

Step 1 – setting up the repository

In the following example, we will use Node.js to create a few files. To set up your repository, do the following:

1. Create the `index.js` file with the following code:

```
var time = require('time');
exports.handler = (event, context, callback) => {
    var currentTime = new time.Date();
    currentTime.setTimezone("America/New_York");
    callback(null, {
        statusCode: '200',
        body: 'Time in New York : ' + currentTime.toString(),
    });
};
```

2. Create the `packt.yaml` file with the following code. This is a SAM template file to define the resources. It will define a Lambda function which will be triggered by the API gateway:

```
AWSTemplateFormatVersion: '2010-09-09'
Transform: AWS::Serverless-2016-10-31
Description: Outputs the time
Resources:
  PacktStack:
    Type: AWS::Serverless::Function
    Properties:
      Handler: index.handler
      Runtime: nodejs6.10
      CodeUri: s3://codepipeline-us-east-1-514478780013/.
      Events:
        PacktCICDApi:
          Type: Api
          Properties:
            Path: /PacktCICDResource
            Method: GET
```

3. Create the `buildspec.yml` file with the following code. This file is in YAML format, and it contains the build commands and related settings. AWS CodeBuild will use this file to run the build.

4. In the following example:

   - It will install npm with the time package
   - Execute the `package` command for the deployment package

- It will also change the `--s3-bucket` parameter value with your Amazon S3 bucket:

```
version: 0.1
phases:
  install:
    commands:
      - npm install time
      - aws cloudformation package --template-file packt.yaml
--s3-bucket codepipeline-us-east-1-514478780013 --output-
template-file OutputPackt.yaml
      - aws cloudformation deploy --template-file
OutputPackt.yaml --stack-name PacktStack --capabilities
CAPABILITY_IAM

artifacts:
  type: zip
  files:
    - packt.yaml
```

Step 2 – creating the pipeline

Proceed with the following steps to create the AWS CodePipeline:

1. Log in to AWS and navigate to the AWS CodePipeline console at: `https://console.aws.amazon.com/codepipeline/`.

2. Click on the **Create pipeline** button, add the pipeline name for your pipeline, and click on the **Next step** button:

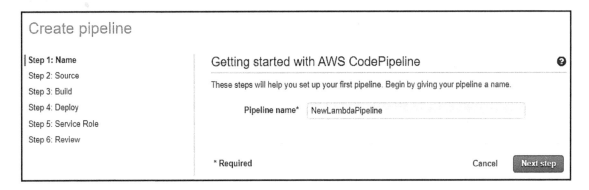

3. In the **Source provider** dropdown, select the **AWS CodeCommit** option.

4. Select the repository name and branch name to connect to every push to the branch you selected. Click on the **Next step** button:

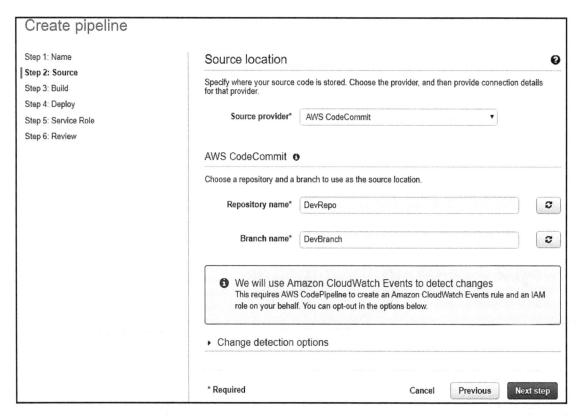

5. Select the **AWS CodeBuild** option as the build provider.

6. Click on the **Create a new build project** option and enter the project name.

7. Select **Ubuntu** as the operating system and **Node.js** as the runtime.

8. In the **Version** option, select **aws/codebuild/nodejs:** version.

9. In the **Build specification**, select the **Use the buildspec.yml in the source code root directory** option.

10. Select **Save build project**.

 It will automatically create a service role for AWS CodeBuild.

11. Select the **Next step** button:

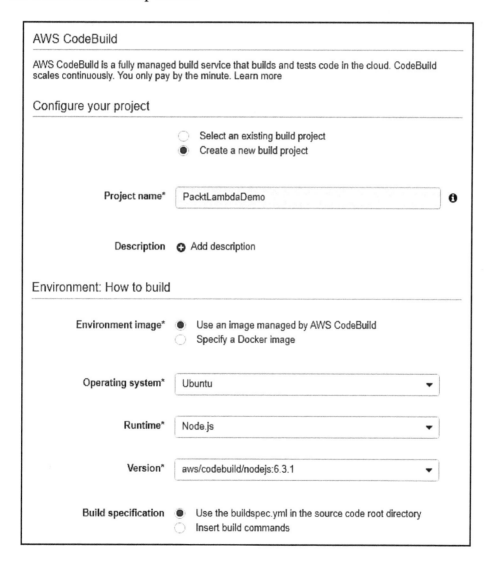

12. In the **Deployment provider** dropdown, select the **AWS CloudFormation** option. AWS CloudFormation commands will deploy the SAM template.

13. In the **Action mode** dropdown, select the **Create or replace a change set** option.

14. In **Stack name**, add `PacktStack`.

15. In **Change set name**, add `PacktStackChanged`.

16. In the **Template file**, add `packt.yaml`.

17. In **Capabilities**, select **CAPABILITY_IAM**.

18. In **Role name**, select the role for AWS CloudFormation that you created at the beginning of this section, and then click on the **Next step** button:

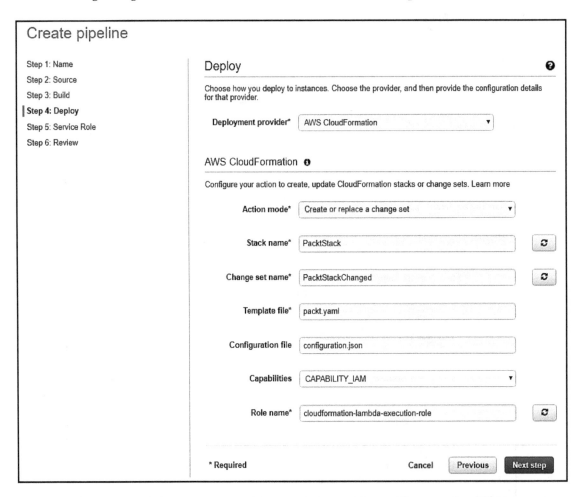

19. Select **create role**. Select **Next** and then select **Allow**. Click on the **Next step** button.

20. Review the pipeline and select **Create pipeline**.

Step 3 – modifying the generated policy

Proceed with the following steps to allow CodeBuild to upload build artifacts to your Amazon S3 bucket:

1. Log in to AWS and open IAM console from `https://console.aws.amazon.com/iam/`.

2. Select **Roles** and open the role that was generated for that project. Typically, it should look like `code-build-project-name-service-role`.

3. Under the **Permissions** tab, select **Add inline policy**.

4. In **service**, select **Choose a service**.

5. In **Select a service**, choose **S3**.

6. In **Actions**, select **actions**.

7. Under **Access level groups**, expand **write**, and then select **PutObject**.

8. Select **Resources** and select any checkbox.

9. Select **Review policy**.

10. Add the name and then select **Create policy**.

Step 4 – completing your deployment stage

Proceed with the following steps to complete the stage:

1. Select the **Edit** button and select the edit icon next to `PacktStack`.

2. In the action category, select **Deploy** if not selected.

3. In **Deployment provider**, select **AWS CloudFormation** if not selected.

4. In **Action mode**, select **Execute a change set**.

5. In **Stack name**, add or select `PacktStack`.

6. In **Change set name**, add `PacktStackChange`.

7. Select **Add action** and then select **Save pipeline changes**.

8. Select **Save and continue**.

Now, your pipeline is ready. Any code commits or pushes to the branch you connected to this pipeline will trigger a deployment. You can test your pipeline and deploy the application for the first time, then do any of the following:

1. Perform a code commit to your Git branch connected to the pipeline
2. Go to the AWS CodePipeline console and select the name of the pipeline you created, and then click on the **Release change** button:

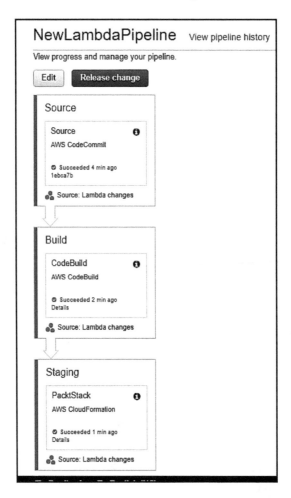

Summary

We have looked at microservices architecture, AWS Lambda, SAM, the serverless application framework, continuous integration, and continuous workflow.

I hope you have enjoyed this, and gained much more knowledge than expected after reading this book. All the best and happy coding!

Other Books You May Enjoy

If you enjoyed this book, you may be interested in these other books by Packt:

Mastering AWS Security
Albert Anthony

ISBN: 978-1-78829-372-3

- Learn about AWS Identity Management and Access control
- Gain knowledge to create and secure your private network in AWS
- Understand and secure your infrastructure in AWS
- Understand monitoring, logging and auditing in AWS
- Ensure Data Security in AWS
- Learn to secure your applications in AWS
- Explore AWS Security best practices

Learning AWS - Second Edition
Aurobindo Sarkar, Amit Shah

ISBN: 978-1-78728-106-6

- Set up your AWS account and get started with the basic concepts of AWS
- Learn about AWS terminology and identity access management
- Acquaint yourself with important elements of the cloud with features such as computing, ELB, and VPC
- Back up your database and ensure high availability by having an understanding of database-related services in the AWS cloud
- Integrate AWS services with your application to meet and exceed non-functional requirements
- Create and automate infrastructure to design cost-effective, highly available applications

Leave a review - let other readers know what you think

Please share your thoughts on this book with others by leaving a review on the site that you bought it from. If you purchased the book from Amazon, please leave us an honest review on this book's Amazon page. This is vital so that other potential readers can see and use your unbiased opinion to make purchasing decisions, we can understand what our customers think about our products, and our authors can see your feedback on the title that they have worked with Packt to create. It will only take a few minutes of your time, but is valuable to other potential customers, our authors, and Packt. Thank you!

Index

T

tasks
  custom schedulers 322
  executing, on cron-like schedule 320
  life cycle 322
  manual execution 314, 318
  retirement 323
  scheduling 314
  service scheduler, using 314
  Windows containers (beta) 323
Test Automation
  about 99
  Cucumber 99
  JUnit 99
  Selenium 99
Test-Driven Development (TDD) 99
traditional web hosting
  about 219
  challenges 219, 220
  versus web hosting, on cloud AWS used 218

V

Virtual Infrastructure 102
Virtual Private Cloud (VPC) 239, 254, 268, 356

W

Web Application Firewall (WAF) 244
web hosting
  versus traditional web hosting, on cloud using
    AWS 218
What You Pay is What You Use (WYPWYU) 106,
  121
Windows container
  concepts 324
  instance, launching into cluster 326
  service, creating with task definition 329
  service, viewing 330
  task definition, registering 328
  web application, using with 324
  Windows cluster, creating 325

www.ingramcontent.com/pod-product-compliance
Lightning Source LLC
Chambersburg PA
CBHW060651060326
40690CB00020B/4597